TWAYNE'S WORLD LEADERS SERIES

EDITOR OF THIS VOLUME

Hans L. Trefousse

Brooklyn College

The City University of New York

Cato the Censor

TWLS 49

Cato the Censor

By NELS W. FORDE

University of Nebraska, Lincoln

TWAYNE PUBLISHERS
A DIVISION OF G. K. HALL & CO., BOSTON

Library of Congress Cataloging in Publication Data

Forde, Nels W
  Cato the censor.

  (Twayne's world leaders series)
  Bibliography: pp. 277–80.
  Includes Index.
  1. Cato, Marcus Porcius, Censorius. 2. Rome — History —
Republic, 265–30 B. C. I. Title
DG253.C3F67   937'.04'0924 [B]   74-28128
ISBN 0-8057-3017-6

Contents

About the Author

Nels W. Forde is associate professor of history at the University of Nebraska. He holds a degree in ancient history from the University of Minnesota. Before coming to Nebraska, he was chairman of the department of History at Luther College, Decorah, Iowa. His primary research interests include Sumerian cuneiform studies, the Roman Republic, and the history of Greece in the 4th Century B.C.

Mr. Forde's published works include *Nebraska Cuneiform Texts*, a precis for computerization of cuneiform tablets in *Computers and the Humanities*, and a textbook syllabus for the study of ancient history in the Nebraska extension division.

Preface

This is not, in the strict sense, a biography of Cato the Censor. Personal details are too scarce for that. It is rather a *history* of Cato the Censor, using all the facts that are available about the man, deducing private material from them, and often interpreting sketchy evidence in the ancient writers. I have not attempted to reproduce, acknowledge, or otherwise credit the many modern authors making studies of Republican Rome. Cato the Person has been lost in a flood of critical-historiographical scholarship that ignores his uniqueness by comporting with preconceived interpretations of Roman affairs based on modern tendentiousness. It has become fashionable to discount a consensus of best evidence by tracing it to conveniently "inferior annalistic sources" and then styling the most inaccurate ancient account "more reliable in this instance" because it accords with one's prior general view of Roman history. The fallacy of that approach with its "validating literary criticism" has led me to a reinterpretation not only of Cato but of every major personality with whom he was involved and of all Roman history as well. For this reason, I have confined myself rigidly to the ancient Roman sources themselves, citing secondary and tertiary works only where they illuminate the ancients, not where they impose modern views on them.

This history of Cato the Censor moralizes a good deal. My reasons for that are didactic. I believe historians are largely to blame for man's failure to progress socially, for they have attempted to teach by inspiring emulation—elevating heroic models. Unfortunately, human idols have clay feet that are exposed by objective research; these have to be explained by apologetic justifications and transparent rationalizations, making the "instructive example" one of "excusable sin." With such does our lamentable twentieth century abound! More to the point is a history that teaches by negative warning, systematically emphasizing the errors of the past and the mistakes of our fathers so that we may attempt to improve by avoiding history's blunders, not by imitating imperfect examples. Such a history is more respectable scholastically, as it places human beings in their naturally erring perspective and then expects the young to progress by heeding the dramatically delineated pitfalls. Therefore, one must objectivize relevantly, explaining such as Cato in current vernacular and contemporary ratiocination. If the Censor sounds like a late twentieth-century American statesman, it is all too deliberate; but as I have allowed him to speak only from his Latin setting, it must be a "Romanesque" statecraft.

My unending thanks are due my teacher and friend, Tom B. Jones, who has read this manuscript painstakingly and made valuable suggestions. My deepest gratitude is reserved for Janet, my long-suffering wife, who has awaited the conclusion of Cato the Censor with a gently urging patience, particularly as its slow progress barred advancement in our grim "publish or perish" scholastic environment. But above all, etched deeply upon these pages is my inner turmoil, raging derision, and shocked contempt for the events of this past year in America. It is precisely because we have experienced so much, but learned so little, that I cynically dedicate *Cato the Censor:*

To the Watergate Generation

NELS W. FORDE

University of Nebraska, Lincoln

Prooemium

Marcus Cato was a man of the soil. The thrift of nature, perseverance of the seasons, and pride of homestead were in his soul. Pleasure was tingling well water in a dusty throat; satisfaction was a full, tidy barn. Remorse came only from waste, morality was dutiful obedience, and logic a green-on-black symmetry of cultivated fields.

Kindness could be profitable, but mercy was not of nature, for in his knuckled heart Cato bore the scars of cracked summer earth. That war forged his will; ceaseless toil, his frame. Red-headed and constant as the setting sun, Cato's stolid country values were his ethic weathervane.

These were his politics: The senator thought all the world was like his Latin farm. Small wonder then, his spite of alien Greeks! Beauty, to him, was strength—as in stout oaken beams. Cato lived by the old standards, but he was born too late. War's insidious chemistry had changed Rome. His censor's call to ancient virtue was ignored. People wished to honor the old but not to live that way.

The man's clear vision of catastrophe and his zeal for reform found no response in the electorate. Admired for his own habits, the censor failed to inspire imitation and had little social influence. His strict assessments and ruinous taxes on luxury did not change consumer demand—eloquent denial that one can legislate a state of mind.

Dour Plebeian! You entered the ranks of class and wealth by work and virtue, thinking thus to remake the Rome of heroes. You found instead that the dynamo of human change drives ever on, merging past tomorrows and consolidating revolutions.

CHAPTER 1

Up from the Farm into the Ranks

I Birth and Early Training

MARCUS Porcius [Priscus] Cato was born in Tusculum, Latium, probably in 234 B.C. Mystery surrounds his birth.[1] Some maintain he was descended from Roman knights (*equites*); some, from Italian aristocracy; and some say that his was one of the first Etruscan families to settle in Tuscany.[2] Tradition has it that the Porcians were a plebeian clan, and his life-style in no way contradicted this.[3]

Whatever their station, the Porcians had a proud heritage in the Roman armies. Cato senior was a man of courage and skill. But Grandfather Cato! Many were the stories he could tell, of mighty battles and harrowing escapes, especially those in which his very horse was killed under him—five times, no less—in deeds so valorous that the national treasury furnished new mounts. Young Marcus, from the time he stood spellbound at his grandfather's knee, seems to have determined that he would follow the legions to war to win fame as his fathers had.[4]

The childhood of Marcus Cato must have been a happy one, though Romans had not yet reached the time of luxurious permissiveness toward their young or fond indulgence of all their wants. The plebeian society in which he was reared centered in the family, and there his education began.[5]

Indeed, the family circle was something of an education in itself. Sources permit only a glimpse of it, but perhaps enough to create a general impression of Cato's home life. At a very early age Cato had progressed sufficiently to plead cases in rural courts.[6] If this means that he could read, it is virtually certain he was taught at home. Doubtless his father set daily assignments in reading, writing, and doing sums. Cato's *On Agriculture* (V, IX–XVIII) demands that an estate manager be able to keep accounts, manage credit operations, set contracts, and estimate material needs of all kinds. Since Cato was probably managing his own estate before he was seventeen, presumably he was able to perform these duties and therefore could write and do sums at that time.

The plebeian families living around Tusculum seem to have been exceptionally sophisticated and active in affairs. One family was that of Tiberius Coruncanius, consul in 280 B.C., who triumphed over the Etruscans and guarded Rome against the advance of Pyrrhus. This man was the first plebeian to be chosen *pontifex maximus*, elective religious leader, and to initiate the custom of admitting the public to his discussions of the Twelve Tables of the law. He might be called Rome's first jurist.[7]

Manius Curius Dentatus, another great plebeian hero, came from a farm bordering Cato's estate in the Sabine country. This man's heritage was auspicious. One of his ancestors, Lucius Sicinius Dentatus, tribune of the plebeians in 454 B.C., left a tradition of exceptional military heroism; he was even called a Roman Achilles. Manius furthered the legacy, being elected consul three times specifically because of his military ability and appointed once (*suffectus consul*). In his first consulship Manius brought the Samnite Wars to an end, and in his third he defeated Pyrrhus, who had previously beaten the Romans in two battles. Manius had been voted three triumphs, two in one year for victories over Samnites and Sabines, and an ovation. Finally, as censor in 272 B.C., Manius commenced the *Anio Vetus*, Rome's second aqueduct.[8]

Manius and Tiberius were contemporaries of grandfather Cato, whose prowess has been mentioned, and all three were acquainted with two other illustrious plebeians, Gaius Fabricius Luscinus, mentioned just below, and Publius Decius Mus, who was famous for pledging his life in the Pyrrhic War. If one notes the histories of these families, three of which formed a kind of "circle" just east of Rome, he gains a rather extraordinary impression of plebeian activism in the national interest. Modern historians have called such combinations of plebeian families, merged with some senatorial *gentes* ("clans"—groups of families descended from a common deceased ancestor), a "new patrician-plebeian nobility."[9]

Interfamilial gatherings were rather common among these plebeian folk, if one is to believe Cicero and Plutarch (XXI.3). Cicero says (*Cato* 43, 45–6) that feasts known as *convivia* were usual in the time of Cato's forefathers, as they continued to be in his own. Ordinarily, on these occasions, a toastmaster (*arbiter bibendi* or *magister convivi*) was appointed in order that the discussion following the repast might be organized. It began at the head of the table as the wine was passed and continued down the table and into the night. This applied also to Cato's own country estate and custom there, since he remarked that even when among the Sabines he joined his neighbors in a social meal every day; he always invited congenial country neighbors and made merry with them, both young and old.

The traditions of the past and the deeds of mighty men, along with contemporary affairs, were topics of discussion on such occasions. From his elders, Cicero quotes, Cato often heard the story of Gaius Fabricius' embassy at the court of Pyrrhus. They, in turn, had heard it from old men at table. Since Fabricius was a Pyrrhic war hero with Dentatus, whose exploits were also aired at these doings, and the actions of Cato as censor, for instance, imitated the public acts of both, one realizes that these deeds of eminent plebeians, recalled at *convivia*, served as inspiration for the young as well as instruction in the past—just the sort of education known to have been customary at Rome. Cato seems versed in pithy sayings at the beginning of his career and conversant with both Greek and Roman history from an early point in life. Since he had no formal schooling, these things must have been gleaned from the "country socials" of his youth. Even Greek history entered the discussion (Plutarch III.3; Livy XXXIV.2).

The principal reasons to say that Cato was a plebeian at the beginning of his public life are these "commoners' *convivia*," which seem literally to have steeped Marcus in plebeian traditions and values. Another reason to assert plebeianism is the fact that grandfather Cato had no *praenomen* but Cato's father did have one, a fact that aligns itself also with the career of a plebeian hero—Manius Curius Dentatus—set forth at the beginning in connection with the origins of the *gens* Porcius. It is singularly interesting that Marcus inherited an estate in the Sabine country, though he himself was born in Tusculum in the district of Latium. Perhaps the former was the home of grandfather Cato, who remained a "Latin" of Sabinum and therefore had no Roman *praenomen* until Dentatus marched through Sabinum in 290 B.C. (n. 2) and finally added it to Rome with limited citizenship (*civitas sine suffragio*). Cato's father, meanwhile, probably established an estate of his own in Latium where Cato was born and raised.

Cato's life is abundant proof that he was taught thrift, even parsimony, as a way of life—but one can be thrifty and yet possess wealth. Grandfather Cato furnished his own private horse for military purposes at a time when only men of substance could do so. The state, because of his exceptional bravery, awarded him replacements for horses killed in action (Plutarch I.1; n. 4); however, the original horse was his own, not an *equus publicus*. If the guesses on the Sabine and Tusculum estates are accurate, Cato's grandfather or father had the means to purchase a second estate. Cato himself began farming on a Sabine estate. It may have been the inheritance from his grandfather, but from the first it was unusually well furnished with domestics. This implies wealth, but there was the lack of Roman knighthood and the consequent standing of plebeianism. Though Cato experienced no physical want, he was expected to succeed on his own, given the land. Hence he practised thrift and hard work as the means to that end, as he had been taught to do (Plutarch II.2, III.2).

Cato's boyhood, to summarize, was a combination of home teaching, daily lessons, hard work, thrift, and frequent, pleasurable social gatherings. If one could safely assume that Cato's treatment of his own son was an indication of the way he himself was reared—and that is usually the case with "early national" pioneers who are conservative out of necessity—one could add more detail to this general portrait.

Cato was his own son's teacher, for instance, not out of economic necessity, since he had an accomplished slave who could have tutored, but in the conviction that education was a father's business. It was not seemly that a slave, even one prepared to teach, should scold the son of his master or punish him for unprepared lessons. Further, Cato felt education too priceless a thing to be entrusted to a slave. He was his son's teacher from conviction, as his own father must have been his, perhaps from necessity (Plutarch XX.3–4).

The social situation among these Tusculum plebeians was congenial to Marcus' home education in such studies as that of the law. Conversations with the descendants of Tiberius Coruncanius and those who had attended his legal discussions at *convivia* of the sort just described must have helped Cato senior and his son with interpretations of the Twelve Tables. Certainly Marcus had such training, or he could not have pleaded the cases of others before he was seventeen (Plutarch I.4–6).

Cato senior tweaked Marcus' ears and scolded him when his lessons were not prepared but, just as valuable, gave him physical training in the essentials of military life. When the time came, Cato taught his son how to ride a horse and throw the javelin, fight in armor, box, endure cold and heat, and swim, just as his own father must have taught him the basic manual of arms. Horsemanship seems to have been traditional in the family, since grandfather Cato had been in the cavalry. Cato himself could ride, and he taught the skill to his son (Plutarch XX.4, V.6).

As might be expected, companionship bound Roman father and son closely together. There is a touching picture described by Cicero and attributed to Cato—an indication of the way father revered son. When Cato's son died, by this portrayal, Marcus comforted himself in the thought that they were not really separated, for the soul (*animus*) of his son had not deserted him but was ever looking back from eternity. Surely, Cato and his father were also very close (*Cato* 84).

All the more stark, therefore, must have been the tragedy that marred the rustic contentment of Cato's early life. Almost certainly, his father died while Cato was very young. Plutarch (I.1) and Nepos (I.1) say that Marcus, previous to his public career, lived on an estate inherited from his father. Since his military career began when he was seventeen, he must have been orphaned before that age. His estate was in the country of the Sabines and was not the place in which he was born. Cato senior is never mentioned in connection with the running of this estate. Independence and means of the type implied here would be impossible if the Latin *paterfamilias* (patriarch) were still alive. Again, Cicero pictures the solitary misery and loving sorrow of the Latin cremation funeral by making Cato say later of his son: "His body was burned by me, whereas it were more fitting that mine had been burned by him . . ."(*Cato* 84).

During those trying years after his father's death, training stood Cato in good stead. The ancient biographers speak of his working in the fields, dressed in a coarse frock or naked to the waist, sharing sparse meals of bread and sour wine with his domestics (Plutarch III.2; Cato XXIII, LVI).

Cato himself used to say that, when young, he applied himself to agriculture for profit and that he had only two ways of increasing his income: labor and thrift. Frugality served another purpose; Cato also says he was parsimonious for the sake of his country, that he might be able to endure harder services in war. It became his custom, therefore, to deride excess, and he questioned whether fat men could be of any use to their country because their bodies were all belly. This bit of puritanical jingoism, however, merely emphasizes the lack of cultural originality in Cato's conservative background, for it colorlessly parrots clichés from the early Roman tradition (Plutarch IX.4, XXV.1; Gellius VI.22.1, IV.20.11).

Though Cato did have an aptitude for the military, he had also decided from an early age to follow another road to success, that of oratory. He considered eloquence an instrument of great things, necessary for every man who does not choose to live in obscurity and inactivity. That he began training for this career at about the same time he practised the "manual of arms" seems obvious. During this period he argued cases in the local villages, solely to achieve knowledge and eloquence. There could have been no motive of pecuniary gain, for it was illegal to charge fees for that service. The country folk saw him early in the morning walking to one village or another to plead cases and then returning to work in the fields beside his slaves.[10]

Heroic as all this seems, one wonders about the boy Marcus. He was an intense lad—little indicates that he enjoyed life, as we now think of it. He lived alone, worked hard, and learned by suffering. Cato had a shrine—the tiny farmstead of Manius Curius Dentatus, thrice consul and hero of three triumphs—to which he often repaired in his early days, a kind of parental substitute. It seems to have inspired him, and it was close to his own land. Marcus would pause there, thrilling with the imagined drama of past events. Eyes alight, he would recall the story told at many an evening meal in his boyhood (Plutarch II.1–2).

There, at the fireplace now in ruins, the Samnite ambassadors found Dentatus cooking turnips for supper and attempted to bribe him. Dentatus threw the envoys out, saying that a man who could be satisfied with turnips for supper had no need of gold; even if he did, it was far more honorable to conquer those who had gold and gain it that way than merely to possess gold—and conquer them he did! Meditating on the heroism of this man, Marcus would return to his own hard work with renewed zeal.

Picture him! The orphan to whom a legend has become parent—a legend of rigorous simplicity, integrity, and endurance. Conceive the solitary, adolescent belief in righteous discipline that would endow those values with virtue! That is our young plebeian! Daily he inures himself to hardship by the assiduous practice of it. He walks instead of riding and eats slave rations so that he can subsist on almost nothing.

Cato's mode of life—the learning gained from home gatherings, home education, and local hearings in market places—attracted notice. Initially, then, it was his early maturity and native wisdom that won regard, not military prowess.

II *Valerian Patronage and Life as a Recruit*

The slaves and domestics of neighboring estates gossiped about Cato. Publius Valerius Flaccus, a patrician and senator on the next estate, heard some of this and, after questioning further, determined to invite the young lad to dinner. Plutarch says that their discourse and friendship matured after that, doubtless over leisurely *convivia* during the long fall, winter, and early spring evenings of the off-season when Cato could spare the time. His acquaintance with young Lucius Valerius Flaccus must now have matured to fast friendship, though there seems to have been some difference in their ages.[11]

Impressed by Marcus' wit and temperament, Publius probably undertook tactfully to instruct him in manners and protocol. At any rate, when Cato moved to Rome, history records no painful social blunders or costly political errors of the sort one would expect from a country plebeian on first entering public life in the capital. Later, it is certain that P. Valerius exerted influence in behalf of Cato's military advancement. The youth had originally chosen to work up from the ranks; as a matter of fact, that is where he is first to be seen.

The time was not an auspicious one. Hannibal, dominating hero of the Punic Wars between Rome and North African Carthage, seemed likely at any time to end the Second Punic War by defeating Rome. His ruinous victories at the Trebia River and Lake Trasimene had destroyed whole Roman armies. The year of Marcus Cato's first military service, 216 B.C., was Rome's darkest hour. In that year Hannibal annihilated two consular armies at the famous Battle of Cannae. Rome never suffered a worse defeat, and her allies began to fall away, one by one. Yet, indomitable spirit, she never wavered in purpose or breathed a word of peace!

That aspect, of a struggling young nation demanding material sacrifice for survival and therefore endowing physical valor with patriotic virtue, dominated Cato's thought. He was ready and believed self-sacrifice to be the most noble expression of individual patriotism. Accordingly, he wished for personal military fame, the loudest manifestation of that kind of patriotism, and for puckered scars, mute but eloquent badges of nationalistic bravery (Plutarch I.5).

While he was yet a stripling, Cato had his breast covered with honorable wounds. This statement in Plutarch's biography is followed by the pronouncement that Cato's first campaign was made when he was seventeen (I.6). Cicero says he was "adolescent" (*Cato* 10). The year was 216 B.C., because emergency levies were needed following Cannae and Livy specifically states that the dictator, Marcus Junius Pera, enlisted men from the age of seventeen for service and sent to the allied communities and the Latin confederacy for reinforcements. Twenty-five thousand men were gathered, but not until six thousand prisoners had also been freed and armed (Livy XXII.57.9).

So young Marcus Cato went off to war. There is no record of tearful leave-taking or farewell parties—friends he had; family, none. Cato marched alone. A single attendant followed, in charge of pots and pans. "Home" was a patch of ground and a cold hearth, left in the doubtful charge of a *vilicus* (overseer). "Family Spirit" was a long list of duties given the overseer so that he might maintain "the perfect farm"—much as a "wipe-your-feet" and "hang-your-coat" mother supposedly has "a perfect home." So long had the orphan's life consisted of necessity and prescribed virtues that "spirit" had now become another "thing"—to be achieved by ticking off items on a checklist (Plutarch I.7; Cato V).

Cavalrymen were a part of Pera's levy in 216, but Nepos' use (I.2) of the term "*stipendium*" and Cicero's "*miles*" (*Cato* 10) applied to Cato's first military service show that he enlisted as a private foot soldier. Further, he disdained to use horses for transport, carrying his own armor afoot (Plutarch I.7). It would have been no great burden—Cato, seventeen and inexperienced, was doubtless a light-armed soldier (*veles*), with a short Spanish sword, a plain helmet distinguished by animal skins, a small three-foot shield (*parma*) of oxhide, and light javelins (*iacula*) (Polybius VI.21.7, 22.1). It was with this armor that he acquired "honorable wounds" all over his breast. Neither heavier armor nor fighting from horseback would incur such continual exposure to wounds.

The attendant had only to see to his master's tent, cook the meals, and then supervise the loading of baggage and utensils when the camp was moved. Preparing the food was no burden, according to Plutarch, since Cato was not fastidious. He often helped with the meals and then was served by the attendant (Plutarch I.7). Each soldier received about a bushel of wheat, rations for the month, taken from his army pay — 120 *denarii* a year (3⅓ cents per day, at the old rate of ten cents per *denarius*). Also deducted from pay were the cost of required clothing and replacements for weapons. Rations for extra persons, like the attendant, had to be furnished by Cato himself. Presumably, Cato supplied his own draft animal for personal articles or else required the attendant to carry them (Polybius VI.39.12–13).

Cato must have been with the forces of the dictator Pera during the remainder of the year 216 B.C., probably growing impatient at the obvious defensive, or "Fabian," policy after Cannae. The only ray of hope for that bleak year was the plebeian *praetor* Marcus Claudius Marcellus' defense of Nola against Hannibal himself by means of unique tactics. In honor of this, Marcellus was made proconsul, as the only Roman commander to fight a successful action against Hannibal since Cannae (Livy XXIII.30.19).

Sometime in September Hannibal withdrew to winter quarters at Capua, as did Pera to Teanum (Livy XXIII.18.9, 24.5, 32.1). Hannibal broke quarters early in the spring in order to attack Casilinum. Pera, meantime, had gone to Rome to take the auspices afresh, leaving Tiberius Sempronius Gracchus, his plebeian master of horse, in charge of the army at Teanum with strict orders to take no action (Livy XXIII.19.3–5). Cato and his comrades had to stand helpless witnesses to the siege and destruction of Casilinum, for of course the first lesson of all successful war machines is that of unthinking, amoral obedience. Later action was to show Gracchus a better general than Pera, but his hands were tied on this occasion.

It is likely that Cato used such leave as he had from military duties at Teanum that winter to familiarize himself with the adjacent towns and their resources. He was not a frivolous person, as soldiers go, and did not spend his time off duty in idleness or sensual pleasure, like the Carthaginians (Livy XXIII.18.10–16). The part of Cato's later "almanac," *On Agriculture* (CXXXV.1–3), which recommends places to buy good equipment and states terms for sharecropping, is striking in that most of the places mentioned are on roads within a radius of twenty miles from Teanum or from Suessula, Cato's winter stations during the years of 216 and 215 B.C.—just the right distances for a young soldier on leave.[12]

One can almost see the earnest young farmer-soldier visiting with "folks" in different marketplaces and villages, examing their wares for quality, and chatting over comparative contract terms. Thus he spent his leave rather than sampling the fleshpots. Later, the results appeared "in print."

Iron implements and harness should be bought at Cales and Minturnae (five and seventeen miles from Teanum, respectively), spades and tiles from Venafrum (fifteen miles), sledges, carts, and baskets at Suessa (ten miles), Roman baskets at Casinum (twenty miles from Teanum), and so on. These places, within a twenty-mile radius of each other, are all at least eighty miles from Cato's home! It would be incredible to maintain, for instance, that one could not buy decent Roman baskets any closer to Rome than eighty miles and that the best craftsmen were Campanians and Samnites. Only three of the towns mentioned are in Latium, the very southernmost part! Cato wrote about the places he knew. This was the one time he was extensively away from home, within Italy, and with leisure time to study quality, compare prices, and record carefully what he learned.

Cato may well have lodged with some of these people. He knew them personally. "The best press-ropes," he says, "are made by Lucius Tunnius and Gaius Mennius, son of Lucius Mennius, of Venafrum" (CXXXV.3). He then gives the exact formula for making such press-ropes, which he must have gotten from the men themselves. In another place Cato says, "The best method for planting a cypress bed is that given by Minnius Percennius of Nola" (CLI.1). The specifications are exact; Cato must have been there to write them down.

Finally, there could be no other reason than familiarity for stating sharecropping contractual terms from Samnite Venafrum and Casinum in southernmost Latium, over eighty miles from Cato's home estate, and then neglecting to give those for any of the districts close to Rome or nearby Sabinum. Other portions of *On Agriculture* show a similar familiarity with these places, and in denial of any idea that Cato may have actually farmed there, these mention the cost of shipping products for six days, the length of time it would take from this area by freight to Cato's home district (CXXXVI.1, CXLVI.1, XXII.3–4, CXXXV.2).

In the year 215 Cato saw more vigorous campaigning, this time under the command of Quintus Fabius Maximus, who was given the army of the dictator Pera (Livy XXIII.31–32.1). Fabius was more to Cato's liking, but no acquaintanceship developed between them at this time. One was a lowly foot soldier, the other, the highest figure of authority at Rome. Affection and liaison came later, as Plutarch (III.4–7) and Cicero (*Cato* 10) show. Yet Cato was already highly capable.

Consonant with his combat training, Marcus was skilled in swordplay and javelin thrust and was swift of foot. Possibly he was ugly, because he tried to terrify the enemy by approaching with "fierce countenance, harsh cries and threatening speech." Plutarch (1.6) feels this technique was effective. But no matter how varied the campaigns or Cato's task in them, his habits remained the same. Others, caked with sweat and dust, drank "refreshments"—Cato drank water. If parched, he would substitute some vinegar, resorting to wine only if he were growing weak from thirst and exhaustion (Plutarch I.7).

The beginning of the campaign was unpretentious. Fabius, more cautious than most, performed the religious amenities on arriving in the new camp at Cales (Livy XXIII.36.9–10). He took the auspices (*auspicia*), attempting to divine the immediate future by interpreting the actions of birds, other animals, or natural phenomena as showing the will of the gods. The commanding general alone could perform this duty for an army (so an army succeeded "under the auspices" of a general); usually he took them before joining his command, as the first order of business upon election or appointment.[13]

Dire events must have caused Fabius to feel the original auspices were inadequate, for he took them afresh at Cales, where a succession of "ominous events," also seen as portents of the future, were reported. Each of these required certain religious ceremonies to neutralize them, but so dark was the outlook that Fabius used professional soothsayers (*haruspices*) to help discover the will of the gods. Even these continued, on the basis of their study of the entrails of sacrificial victims, to report nothing but difficulty.[14]

Meanwhile, Tiberius Sempronius Gracchus, consul-elect for 215 and colleague of Fabius, was hard pressed at Cumae—besieged by Hannibal, fresh from Casilinum—with only raw recruits at his command (Livy XXIII.36). The gods apparently willed that Tiberius should win alone because Fabius' preoccupation with auspices prevented his reinforcing the former, who triumphed over Hannibal's siege unaided.

Imagine the chagrin of one such as Cato, in the army of Fabius, furiously impatient to do or die for god and country, forced to sit and fidget while alien soothsayers pretentiously cut up sacrificial chickens! Burning for the foe's dying screams, he heard only squawking hens. Finally, after the Battle of Cumae, good omens were reported, and the army of Fabius crossed the Volturnus River action bound, but not, we may be sure, without observing the *peremnia auspicia* (confirming auspices taken on crossing a stream) for insurance (Livy XXIII.39).

The initial action for the troops of Fabius was not such as eager recruits might have wished. They attacked mere towns in Campania, albeit there were Carthaginian garrisons in them. It was hardly the same as engaging the army of Hannibal himself, which the troops of Marcellus now undertook at Nola, again with resounding success.

Once more the brilliant plebeian general outwitted Hannibal. His infantry used the long throwing-spear, surprising the enemy from a distance, as they expected the usual hand-to-hand sword and javelin. Even so, Fabius continued to burn farms and towns. He refused to place his troops in any position of danger (Livy XXIII.44–6; Plutarch, *Marcellus* XII.2).

Marcellus and Fabius disagreed basically on war policy. Nearly all generals after Cannae adopted the "Fabian" defensive tactics of dogging Hannibal, forcing him to be alert, meanwhile destroying supplies for his army by burning farms and granaries. Marcellus thought this foolish because the remedy would kill the patient. Italy would be exhausted before Hannibal was (Plutarch, *Marcellus* XXIV.2, IX). In 215, however, Fabius imposed his policy on the other because he, as *consul suffectus*, was the superior of Marcellus as *proconsul*. Doubtless he thought Marcellus' confrontation of

Hannibal dangerously foolish. Fabius had bitter cause to regret earlier insubordinations costing thousands of lives. He could not know that Marcellus was Hannibal's tactical equal. Therefore, after Marcellus' repulse of Hannibal, Fabius ordered him to leave but a token garrison in Nola and dismiss the remainder of the troops to Rome, in order to save the expense of maintenance (Livy XXIII.48.2).

This is specious reasoning that smacks of cunning! Fabius could not presume to supervise the tactical moves of a proconsul, but he could control the disposition of troops. The legions under the command of Marcellus at Nola were the two city legions enrolled in the emergency after Cannae. One might argue that the dismissal of these was admirable thrift in view of the approaching winter season. But there would be less reason to release those particular troops than to relieve the sixteen- and seventeen-year-olds or the six thousand enfranchised criminals under Fabius' own command, or the eight thousand slave volunteers under the command of Gracchus (Livy XXII.57.9–12, XXIII.14.3). During the campaigning season the number of legions had to be raised by six (XXIV.11.4). Unless Fabius was so dull-witted he did not know of the crying need for more loyal, experienced legions, obviously he used mere pretense here to deprive Marcellus of troops and therefore eliminate what he thought a useless trial of Hannibal's power.

Perhaps this thought of carelessness caused Livy (XXIII.43.7) to try, in another place, to vindicate Marcellus' military judgment, saying, "Marcellus had done nothing that could be described as risk; nor had he underrated the enemy."

Fabius and his troops wintered above Suessula in Campania. Then in the spring Fabius went to Rome for the elections of 214 B.C. His escort must have included Cato, because of Cicero's statement that after the election of Fabius, his fourth consulship, Cato set out with him to return toward Capua (*Cato* 10; Livy XXIV.7.11, XXIV.9.1).

The year 214 saw something of a return to normalcy. The proconsul Gracchus triumphed over Hanno and an army of eighteen thousand at Beneventum (Livy XXIV.15–16). Consul Marcellus again overcame Hannibal at Nola—this time so decisively that, but for a detail, Nola might have been Hannibal's Cannae (XXIV.17). Fabius mounted a siege of Casilinum. True, he was painfully aware of his exposed position and consequently sent for Marcellus to hold off attacks from the rear as he mounted the siege. Nevertheless, many soldiers were wounded from rash approaches under the walls. Fabius almost gave up the siege because of casualties and the necessity to save men. Marcellus persuaded him otherwise, while also salving his pride for the slight of 215, his dismissal from Nola. He presumed to chide the great Fabius, saying, "There are, to be sure, many places which 'great generals' ought not to attack. But once the attempt is made, however ill-advised, it ought not to be abandoned, because of the fickleness of reputation . . . " (Livy XXIV.19).

Some of the casualties at Casilinum were unnecessary. Human nature often reverses maturity and causes the man to play the boy. The soldiers had seen action before a number of towns. They knew full well the dangers of approaching fortified walls unprotected. Yet the presence of Marcellus was a catalyst that must have caused veterans to attempt acts of foolish bravery, just to "show off." Especially was this true of the plebeian and allied portions of Fabius' army, for whom the plebeian general Marcellus, thrice conqueror of Hannibal himself, must have been the glittering hero of the war. Our young recruit, Cato, was among them, tingling at the sight of another "Dentatus" risen from plebeian ranks to become the hero of the republic. Now was the time for him to outdo himself!

It must have been there, before the walls of Casilinum, that the young fellow fought nobly and then became a casualty. The "honorable wounds covering his breast," if indeed that numerous, would have been received while Marcus was one of the *velites* (light-armed soldiers), without body armor—before he began to wear a breastplate or coat of mail as one of the *hastati* or *principes* (heavy-armed soldiers; see above, p. 00, for *velites*). Certainly, they would not have been sustained in such number during these two years while he was yet a "stripling" and fighting with an army following "Fabian" tactics if he were a cavalryman (Polybius VI.22–23).

Velites took pride in calling attention to their distinctive helmet covers by daring deeds under the eye of the commanders. Some wore wolfskin; some, other pelts, but all different, so that they could be individually noticed in combat. Our young farmer proudly wore his wolfskin cap to the very thickest forefront of the battle and then fell, a victim of many honorable wounds.

This brave display served two purposes, in addition to the obvious one of making Cato a casualty. First, it indeed must have attracted the attention of Marcellus, and, together with the recommendations of Publius Valerius Flaccus, long a friend of Marcellus, convinced him to appoint Cato military tribune in his own command, which now included Sicily. Second, the wounds received by Cato were the cause of his being reassigned to Marcellus' army (Livy XXIV.21.1, XXIII.25.7, 31.4).

III *Promotion to a Commission (Tribuneship) in Sicily*

A stipulation had been made at the elections for 215 that sick or inferior troops from the army of the dictator Pera, Cato's original military unit, were to be removed from it and sent to Sicily. Livy nowhere shows that the order was meanwhile rescinded or the army of Pera disbanded, thus nullifying its operative instructions. The regulations could apply only to the "walking wounded" or temporarily ill, since they were obviously meant to convalesce and return to duty, thus suiting Cato's state of health. So it seems that Cato simultaneously received honorable wounds, reassignment to Marcellus and Sicily, and promotion to the rank of military tribune (Nepos I.2).

The situation in Sicily and the duties of tribuneship were quite different from those Cato had known in Italy. Tribunes were legionary commanders. Elected at first by the people, but later appointed also by consuls, they ranked as magistrates with authority second only to that of the consuls in the legions. There were six tribunes to a legion, and subconsular command of the whole legion rotated among them. Their subordinates were the centurions, four to each of the companies, two to a maniple, one to a century. Twenty of these were chosen on the basis of merit and twenty more co-opted by the first group. The legions, each of forty-two hundred men, were ordinarily enlisted and sworn in by the tribunes; then they were marshalled at the place appointed for assembly by the consul. This particular duty was unnecessary for Cato, since he joined the unit long after its original formation (Polybius VI.19–33).

Tribunes were allowed to keep horses, and space was allotted them for beasts of burden, so Cato's hard life must have been eased somewhat, now in his nineteenth year. Added ration allowances were made for the beasts, and the pay of tribunes was more than that of infantrymen. Another privilege was that of having one's tent fixed by legionaries, rather than by a personal attendant. The legionaries also saw to his baggage, protecting and, if necessary, covering it. Finally, four soldiers were always on guard before and behind the tribune's tent, ministering in all things necessary to his convenience and enforcing respect for his authority.

These honors, however, were accompanied by an equal number of weighty responsibilities. Command in the field and in camp was the function of the tribunes. At the break of day they had to hurry to the tent of the consul and receive the orders for the day. These instructions they in turn made known to the centurions of the legion companies and the decurions of the cavalry, assembled at the tribunes' tents. These noncoms, in turn, transmitted orders to the individual companies and squadrons at the proper time. Simultaneously, the tribunes had the duty of enforcing discipline. They had to inflict fines, demand sureties for them, punish by flogging and other means, and provide for every kind of necessary work and service within the camp. Usually the six tribunes divided the six months of active service by pairs, each pair supervising the camp for two months (Polybius VI.34.3–6).

The duties of the camp were primarily those of maintaining the protective entrenchment around the camp, providing for diligence in the guard, and stimulating bravery by distributing prizes and administering punishment. Citizens or allies whom Cato and the tribunes said were saved by certain soldiers had to show their gratitude by awarding the appropriate prize themselves and then acting as patron or father to the soldier (Polybius VI.39.1–11). These measures of recognition and punishment, according to the Greek historian Polybius, were the incentives driving Roman officers and men to persevere and to overcome all odds. The recipients of awards displayed them prominently from that day, as marks of their valor, hanging them conspicuously in their homes and wearing them in religious processions.

IV   The Conquest of Syracuse and Its Aftermath

Events in Sicily were crucial for Rome's war effort. The great city of Syracuse had been the ally of Rome through the lifetime of its ruler Hiero. His death in 215 resulted in factional strife that caused the murders of Hiero's successor and the intriguers for alliance with Carthage. The Syracusans then chose two Carthaginian agents as generals, and Rome, fearing the worst, sent the newly elected consul, Marcellus, with a legion to supplement the two already there and ensure that Sicily did not fall to Carthage. As he arrived, Syracuse began the war by an attack on a Roman outpost. Marcellus retaliated by sacking Leontini with a vengeance. His army then moved to the siege of Syracuse, together with the navy under direct command of Marcellus. Encamped north of the city, the army was commanded by the *propraetor* Claudius (Livy XXIV.27.4–6, 30.2, 33.3, XXIII.24.4).

The situation must have been difficult for Cato. He found himself under a strange commander and in an environment of steaming heat that was almost unbearable. True, the Romans had every expectation of success because of their numbers, equipment, and experience. They began the assault both by land and by sea, demonstrating a dual efficiency of command. Unfortunately, they reckoned without Archimedes' machines (Livy XXIV.33; Plutarch, *Marcellus* XIV–XVI).

Syracuse was built on the brows of a continuous circuit of hills whose sides dropped sheer from the city wall. It was approachable at a limited number of places. Therefore, the defense could concentrate effort in a few areas rather than around the whole perimeter. In those places, Archimedes had collected long-, intermediate-, and short-range catapults, ballistae, mangonels, and scorpions, so that no matter where the Romans stood, they were in range of one or another of these missile-throwing devices. If they came close under the walls, Archimedes had contrived cranelike beams with a long axis turning on a fulcrum so that through the arc of swing they could drop large rocks flush along the walls or many feet out, at the farthest reach of their circle. They were operated by moving lead weights up or down the length of the beam as counterweights, on the other side of the fulcrum from the rocks to be dropped. Other crane-booms were fitted with grappling hooks attached to chains swung from the outer ends in such a way that they could be dropped over and hooked onto objects outside the walls, lifting them straight up to be held indefinitely or dropped from that height. Used against live soldiers in armor, one of these machines was a terrifying thing. Even worse, the machine was capable of lifting entire ships or dropping 800-pound stones (Livy XXIV.34; Polybius VIII.5–7).

Against these, Appius and Marcellus, with subaltern Cato, proceeded. The infantry received short shrift. They were mowed down like wheat before coming close to the walls. When they did finally approach, mangonels and catapults fired arrows at high speed through loopholes in the walls with disastrous effect. If they came too close, the crane-booms dropped huge stones on them or plucked them bodily up from the ground, to be flung headlong on the rocks below. In this emergency Appius recalled the army to camp and held a council with Cato and the tribunes. Together they decided against any further attempt to storm the walls of the city, thinking that the sheer size of Syracuse would make even a partial blockade eventually successful because of the amount of necessary daily consumption.

Perhaps this council held by Appius was the first direct command decision in which Cato participated. Certainly, it was not unusual for the commander to consult his tribunes and then, on the basis of their advice, make tactical and strategic decisions. Doubtless the unusual circumstances of this campaign, with the attitudes of Appius and Marcellus, account for Cato's rapid assimilation of military command capability and technology. They climaxed in Cato's later, successful military generalships. No less valuable was observation of the naval operations of Marcellus.

The "eminent plebeian" again demonstrated his tactical technological ability by inventing the *"sambuca"* to attack the seaside walls of Syracuse. Called *"sambuca"* because of its resemblance to the musical instrument of that name, this collapsible tower was supported on two quinqueremes lashed together and consisted of a four-foot-wide ladder as tall as the height of the wall. Each side of the ladder had a protective breastwork much like an enclosed gangplank. A platform large enough for four men was fastened at a 135-degree angle to the top of the ladder, and this platform was supplied with a waist-high wicker screen, attached to the "gangplank breastwork," to furnish protection (Polybius VIII.4).

Ordinarily, the ladder lay flat between the two quinqueremes, half on each and protruding well beyond the bows. As the ships neared the wall, each side of the ladder was raised by ropes attached to pulleys at the top of the nearest ship's mast. The ends of the ladder were cleated down so only the top part rose as the ropes were pulled. Men were stationed on the bows of the ships to help raise and steady the ladder by means of poles, as the outer banks of oars moved the entire affair toward the wall. On arrival, the ladder platform would lean against the top of the wall, the ship would be anchored in place, and soldiers would pass from the ship over the ladders and into the city (Livy XXIV.34).

It did not work. The sailors were riddled by Archimedes' missiles as they approached, forcing them to seek the cover of night. Even then, scorpions fired through loopholes wounded many, while crane-booms dropped mighty stones, smashing the *sambuca* ladders and nearly ruining the ships themselves. Meanwhile, the booms with grappling hooks picked ships up by the bows, stood them on their beam ends or plucked them clean out of the water, and then dropped them, some capsizing, some completely wrecked. The total effect was utterly demoralizing for the crews.

Marcellus was forced to make the best of a bad situation with offhand, humorous remarks about Archimedes' use of ships as wine-ladling spoons wrecking his "*sambuca* orchestra" at this "Syracusan party." Yet it is typical of the man that he thus dissipated what might have been a crucial blow to the essential morale of his troops and kept up their will to overcome in spite of the setback. But these implied estimates of Marcellus' own reaction to the wreck of an ingenious tactical force and the obliteration of brilliant strategic planning seem oversimplified. In the light of later, inexcusable Roman reprisals in Sicily, it is perhaps more realistic to assume that the general's actual feelings were anguished humiliation and suppressed rage (Plutarch, *Marcellus* XVII; Livy XXIV.34).

Part of the army was now devoted to punitive military expeditions against other Sicilian cities, while the remainder patrolled the Syracusan blockade. There is no way to determine, on the face of it, which portion of the army Cato was assigned to.

The other Sicilian cities did not fare as well under attack as Syracuse. Helorus and Herbesus surrendered; but Megara, which resisted and was taken by assault, was then sacked and devastated as an object lesson, says Livy (XXIV.35). Doubtless its ruin was soothing balm for the Roman general's wounded ego. Unless Marcellus was a dullard without historical knowledge—and his later emotions over the spoil of Syracuse because of her illustrious history show he was not—he must have known that such "object lessons" would serve only to inflame the foe. Such was the case here.

While Marcellus was yet in the field, a Carthaginian force of twenty-five thousand men marched under Himilco from its disembarkation point to intercept and defeat him. Ten thousand men slipped from Syracuse at night to join them, but these were surprised by Marcellus, returning before the pursuing Carthaginians. The Syracusan cavalry, with its leader Hippocrates, escaped, but the remaining eight thousand Syracusans were slaughtered by the Romans. Marcellus's "humanity" here again seems to have ordained that no prisoners be taken (Livy XXIV.36; Plutarch, *Marcellus* XVIII).

Himilco marched to within eight miles of the city while his fleet under Bomilcar occupied the great harbor of Syracuse. Neither force remained there because of the arrival of thirty Roman quinqueremes with the First Legion at the city of Panormus. Himilco advanced to intercept this force, hoping to prevent a juncture of the two Roman armies, but he took the wrong route. The Romans marched by the coast road and joined forces with Appius, while the conjunction of the two Roman fleets vastly outnumbered the fleet of Bomilcar. Bomilcar returned to Africa. Livy shows the decision of Cato's first tribunician council to have been sound, when he mentions part of the reason for Bomilcar's withdrawal also was a shortage of supplies in Syracuse.

The combination of the two armies made it impractical for Himilco to remain at Syracuse. He thenceforth stationed himself so as to encourage the greatest amount of rebellion against Rome by the allied towns. Morgantia rebelled successfully, as did several others. An attempt at rebellion in Henna was thwarted in a way that shrieks for notice and documents the brutalization of liberal Roman citizens by years of warfare.

Military discipline and the chain of command require that supreme generals be the army's conscience. All below are allowed the alternative only of obedience, not of insubordination on moral, or other, grounds. Therefore Marcellus was the Roman moral lord over Sicilian affairs. Plutarch calls him humane (XIX.2, XX.1). After conquering Syracuse, he says, the general was lenient to a fault, forbidding all outrage against citizens and only hesitantly allowing booty to be made of property and slaves. We are further told that Marcellus was the first to teach Greeks the noble justice of the Roman race by his gentle forbearance in triumph.

This "model of civility" had already razed Megara to the ground and taken no prisoners of eight thousand trapped men at his mercy. Perhaps the historians of Rome justify these as acts of war—but Henna! There was a tale of indiscriminate butchery! Unarmed men and helpless women and children fell under the swords of the Roman garrison. Livy says the troops' crazed lust for blood was only increased by the weak and unresisting nature of the victims. He seems to place responsibility with the commander and yet to exonerate him when he says, "Marcellus expressed no disapproval, allowing the troops to plunder in the belief it would stop the betrayal of Roman garrisons in other towns." In other words, one may regard this too as an "object lesson," if he so chooses. The historian concludes: "Thus Henna was held—by a criminal act or a necessary one, call it what you will" (XXIV.37–39).

So do the chroniclers of war avoid the moral issue and teach to schizoid man a double view! One can be both hero and murderer, cloaking his darkest deeds in historical "necessity." Even Plutarch—that great moralist—bids us regard Marcellus as a creature who at once displayed great impetuosity and high temper in war and otherwise was modest and humane—a lover of Greek learning (I.1–2). Thus were ancient students taught to reason The Good with historical bifocals. Seen one way, a man could order mass homicide in the name of military expediency quite apart from moral assessment. Because he acted from "necessity," the same man could be called a model of propriety in his private life. The ghastly charade goes on: History is peopled with such "compulsive" maniacs, each given the badge of humanity by historians waving pen-like wands.

Sicily was Cato's secondary school. Now twenty years old he, like many another youth whose education has been amputated by war, was still highly impressionable. Throughout his later life Cato had an ugly, malformed sense of the necessary and the expedient, untempered by any consideration of mercy and utterly prodigal of human life. Beyond a reasonable doubt he received that mental deformity in Marcellus' Sicilian classroom. Sensitivity was ripped from his heart by the witness of actions like that at Henna.

Henna and the Roman bloodlust Livy describes can only be understood as a result of prolonged, desperate war. These soldiers were proper citizens in peacetime, educated to respect the rights of others and honor the law. Yet now, at an order from their commander Pinarius, they became merciless butchers. Frustrated and terrified by Hannibal and then by Archimedes; doubtful, yet hysterically sure Rome deserved their deaths; hating, but also fearing the enemy—these despised invaders in a foreign land had now become "The Aggressor." Their liberal image was shattered by the free Greeks fighting for their homeland. The Romans became little more than alien lunatics assaulting peaceful citizens. Participant and observer alike could not survive that experience unchanged. They would have to reconcile Henna with reality and continuing existence and therefore treat it as normal or rationalize it as temporary insanity or as extraordinary military necessity. None of these was realistic, seeing the unarmed victims.

So Cato's morality became a thing of expediency. If one could reconcile an event or action as necessary in terms of some preconceived or agreed objective, that reason alone also made it "moral." The end justified the means, and morality in terms of an elusive, objective kind of "good" was to be ignored.

Appius, the other commander, left for Rome in order to stand for the consulship, and Marcellus besieged Syracuse over the winter. In 212 Marcellus was finally able to break into the city by a combination of trickery and valor. While he was engaged in negotiations with the Syracusans over a Spartan prisoner, an attendant idly counted courses of stone in the adjacent wall, thereby discovering it was low enough to be scaled by relatively short ladders. This information was husbanded by Marcellus and combined with further intelligence from a deserter that a festival of Diana was to take place in the city. That seemed to furnish the opportunity, for with food in short supply more wine was to be offered the people than usual. Wine on empty stomachs would cause sleepiness and lack of caution among the guards, allowing the Romans to approach the walls under cover of darkness (Livy XXIV.39, XXV.23; Polybius VIII.37).

Marcellus conferred with a few trusted tribunes, who in turn chose capable volunteers among the centurions and soldiers. Without doubt Cato was a participant, since he was originally chosen for Sicilian duty because of his bravery, among other things. An advance party of about one thousand men was chosen in this way, and they secretly prepared the ladders for a swift, silent ascent of the walls. All the troops ate and slept early, so as to be ready for a night campaign (Plutarch XVIII).

Late at night, when the Syracusans had fallen into a drunken sleep, the Romans awoke at a signal, quietly placed their ladders, and mounted the wall, one by one. A thousand men crept silently up and then lined the top of the wall. Soundless mirth wreathed their scarred faces with homely grins, and their shoulders shook with swallowed laughter as they took possession of the great Hexapylon gate. The sound of a trumpet signalled the onset as the entire Roman army prepared to follow onto the walls, and Marcellus commanded the breaking down of the gate itself. By dawn the gate was forced and the Romans occupied "the new city," the so-called Epipolae (Livy XXV.24).

As he stood on the heights of Epipolae and looked down at the city below, Marcellus is said to have wept at the fate of the great metropolis that was shortly to undergo pillage by Romans. Plutarch (XIX.1) says he wept because of the greatness and beauty of the city, which was to be so forcibly altered. Livy, conversely (XXV.24), says Marcellus wept because of the joy of accomplishment and because of grief at the illustrious history of the city now to be reduced by Romans. For, according again to Plutarch, not a single officer—not even a disciplinarian like Cato dared oppose the soldiers' demand for plunder; many actually urged the city be burned and razed to the ground.

This literary refrain—the great commander weeping over a helpless city, yet signalling its destruction—is the height of historical doggerel and the depth of biographical favoritism. Tears showed he was a "fine fellow," but factual analysis drives one to the cynical conclusion that they were a human hunting license. Sorrow means genuine contrition; one who is truly sorry must be forgiven. By this forlorn reasoning, we fail to progress socially because we cannot help ourselves. Reformers are told human nature will never change, and one can be only as good as his nature will allow. So we weep and destroy; we ruin and cry, commiserating with each other through crocodile tears as we kill. If this is true, one wonders why history was ever written in the West. The plot is ever the same; curtain rings down on curtain as the weeping murderer is played to infinity.

Our lachrymose hero's grief was premature. He discovered to his dismay that the Epipolae was but an isolated section of Syracuse; there were two fortified citadels, both walled against the inside as well as the outside of the city—the Euryalus and the Achradina. The latter was the entire old section of the city, and the former was the westernmost citadel. Two forts were yet to be captured instead of one. Marcellus was forced to build a fortified camp between Tyche and Neapolis on the north and south, and Euryalus and Achradina on the east and west. He used bricks from adjacent houses to wall the camp against surprise attack in the close quarters of the city. There Marcellus received a delegation from Tyche and Neapolis, imploring him not to burn and kill in these quarters of the city. His reaction to that entreaty gives the lie to Plutarch's idea of Marcellus' humanity (Livy XXV.25).

Plutarch, as mentioned previously (p. 30), attempts to prove the essential humanity of Marcellus by citing his refusal to allow killing or enslaving Syracusans at this juncture. Livy directly contradicts him, saying that the delegation from Tyche and Neapolis caused a council to be held, at which it was agreed unanimously that no free man should receive bodily injury but that everything else was subject to plunder (XIX. 2). In other words, a second tribunician council was called, and it was probably the tribunes and centurions, rather than Marcellus, who were humane. The order was given as a result of the council, not at the individual discretion or initiative of Marcellus. The uproar of the ensuing pillage, though without bloodshed and including only Epipolae, Tyche, and Neapolis, rose to such a volume that the commander of Euryalus lost heart and withdrew his garrison, allowing the Romans to occupy it. Marcellus was then able to concentrate on Achradina. The Syracusans and Carthaginians tried to break that siege by attacking from the rear on two sides while the Achradina garrison made a sortie, but they were easily repelled. Unable to take Achradina, Marcellus was forced once again to blockade, while the Syracusans began gathering volunteers from all Sicily for a final great effort and the Carthaginians awaited events (Livy XXV. 25). Then the Syracusan weather and environment began to take effect.

It was autumn. Steaming air rose from rotten swamps. A foul breath, it misted the shining sea and fogged the sun. Swords blistered flesh at a touch. Helmets became inverted boiling pots, and blazing breastplates fried men's hearts. Lust paled like a match in the oven sky, as the "Conquerors of the World" lay gasping each breath burnt by the sun.

The fetid atmosphere bred disease, which soon spread to plague proportions. Whether it was dysentery, influenza, or malaria, the dread contagion was transmitted from the dead to the sick and then to the whole, until there seemed no hope. Even isolation of the sick was tried, with no effect. Death was everywhere. As the corpses became too numerous to bury or mourn, natural refinements were forgotten, dignity and compassion became unthinkable luxuries, and the stench of putrefying bodies added to that of disease. The Romans seemed to fare better than others, as they were more accustomed to the environment by that time, and they transferred all troops inside the city, under the shelter of roofs and the relative coolness of brick walls. Sicilians, who had seen the malady before, deserted from the Carthaginian army and fled to nearby towns for relief and protection. But the Carthaginian army, with its commanders, perished to a man (Livy XXV. 26).

Ancient authorities, with their double historical view, ignore the bitter irony of this impasse at Syracuse. Universal, impartial death made fellow sufferers of everyone. Friend and foe must have cooperated in matters of mutual necessity and distress, or the funeral processions mentioned by Plutarch would have been impossible. Yet once the plague abated, they were again at each other's throats, creating the death that had so lately humbled and made fellows of them all, as though there were a subtle distinction between deaths and one must be saved from a certain kind so that he could die more properly in the other way!

Further, the Sicilians had shown the better part of valor—that of flight. It seems not to have occurred to the Roman and Carthaginian armies. Out of a delicious sense of order or duty, they stayed in one place, though they knew it meant an inglorious death. They were foreigners, not homeland defenders. Yet some monstrous fiction of home defense, some whimsical extension of "security" pinned them there to die like insects on a board. Four hundred miles from Rome, they could hardly suppose the survival of their families depended upon their faithfully puking their lives away in a Sicilian swamp! This was the game of international affairs, in which the stake was power and the pawns were pride and honor. The might of Rome, extended through these dying men, asserted her image overseas—a grisly triumph of national "honor" demanding thousands of lives so that Rome could be lord over Sicilian Greeks. Since the entire Carthaginian army perished for the same sort of nonsense, Roman pride won by default, and a banner could be unfurled over that island proclaiming "Roman"—a fiction of international extension as elusive as foreign friendship. It committed Rome to a policy of continual military presence in Sicily, to maintain the false label, "Roman." Ultimately, the decimation and brutalization of Roman people was undertaken to establish those kinds of labels all over the world, not in the name of any humanity or refinement. Cato was there, young and impressionable, a tribune partaking in command decisions and learning that human life was cheap and expendable where the establishment of world power was involved.

Finally, in that fateful summer of 212, the wind began to blow smartly from the east—heavenly relief! However, it prospered a voyage of Bomilcar from Carthage with 130 warships and 700 transports loaded with supplies. These were meant to relieve the Achradina and possibly lift the siege. But, according to the same source, the strong east wind prevented the fleet's rounding Pachynum promontory so as to land in Syracuse. (This seems incredible, since the whole journey from Carthage to Pachynum promontory was virtually due east.) The transports were ordered to Heraclea, one hundred miles to the west of Pachynum, and there they stayed. The warships found anchorage in a bay facing the south, on the west side of Pachynum. News of this fleet and its possible supplies, along with the welcome east wind, heartened the Syracusan defenders of the Achradina, but they were stricken on hearing of the fleet's inability to pass Pachynum. Their commander, gambling that the whole defense depended on that fleet, risked all to travel to Bomilcar and encourage a renewed effort. Marcellus, meantime, not wishing to be caught between two forces, sent a Roman fleet to neutralize that of Bomilcar. It took up station on the east side of the promontory with orders to engage the enemy if he tried to round the point. Though the Roman fleet was smaller, it was on the east side and thus had the weather gauge of the Carthaginians, minimizing the difference in numbers (Livy XXV.27).

When the wind abated, Bomilcar put out to sea, but the Romans approached him to windward, forcing him to sail straight out to sea rather than risk an engagement. Out of sight of the Romans, he came about and set course for Tarentum, having sent orders to the transports at Heraclea to return to Carthage. The whole maneuver had been in vain. No supplies arrived in Syracuse, and her commander was without means of returning to the Achradina. The fortress had been left in charge of mercenary generals who were now assassinated by the natives to facilitate making peace terms with the Romans.

The negotiating terms worked out with Marcellus stipulated that Rome should have everything that had belonged to the Syracusan kings, but all the rest should be secured for the Sicilians, who should also keep their liberty and their own laws. When the mercenary soldiers and Roman deserters who were their allies heard of negotiations, they began killing Syracusans out of mad fear that they would be turned over to the Romans as prisoners and meet a horrible fate. They soon learned, however, that Rome was willing to forgive their former enmity and errors if they now would commit a sin in Rome's favor—the treason of betraying the citadel (Livy XXV.28).

Apparently Rome, and in her name Marcellus, was glad to forget such nonsense as honor and wink at treason in order to attain a military objective. Of course they would continue to insist that they were fighting for principle, but those kinds of considerations could be set aside for a time. The military objective, after all, served the goal of power; the principles—such as honor, pride, loyalty, and all that—were the means used to achieve that goal, means wielded at discretion by the clever commander. Expediency was the only deity worshipped by the military, so that one might win and merit the heaven of successful power. In the light of these influences, it is amazing that Cato emerged from his training with any ideals at all!

Once the treason was successful and the citadel gained, the mercenaries were rewarded for their "loyal treason," the deserters were allowed to escape, and then the terms of negotiation were conveniently forgotten by Marcellus. Now that the Syracusans were defenseless, it was once again convenient to remember "principles" and punish "wrongdoers." Rome had undertaken to guarantee, it will be remembered, that all property other than royal should be secured for Sicilians. Now the great commander called a third council, to which Syracusan envoys were invited, and set forth the final principles by which he would decide the fate of the city. One may imagine Cato and the tribunes listening attentively to the great plebeian who had achieved sweet victory (Livy XXV.31).

The man uttered pious phrases that made mock of faith and morality and established the pure relativism of an ethic asserting the justice of the power that wins. Marcellus said, in effect, that the Romans had spent three long years murdering Sicilians in order to prevent their falling under the dominance of other murderers! That, surely, was the way it must have sounded to his listeners, who knew the truth of what had been going on at Syracuse. Actually, he said Rome had besieged the city not to make it the slave of Rome, but to prevent its becoming a slave to foreigners and deserters. Obviously, the man chose to pretend that Romans were not foreigners. Now, since the Syracusans had not acknowledged the Romans as their benefactors in this thing or deserted to their side and betrayed their city to them but had instead chosen to protect themselves against the Roman "protectors," mere submission was not enough. There must be a sack and pillage of the city in order to atone for Syracuse's sin of self-defense against the Roman siege.

Even bifocaled Livy admits that many brutalities were committed
in hot blood and greed of gain during the ensuing carnage (XXV.31).
A special *quaestor's* guard had been set over the royal treasury,
for abrogating that part of the original negotiation, of course, did
not come under the head of "expediency." Also, the houses of the
Syracusan traitors who had deserted to the side of Rome were
guarded, since they had shown the moral courage to betray their
city. During the pillage, Archimedes was killed by a soldier as he
bent over his research calculations. This, the sources all agree,
Marcellus deeply regretted. In the light of factual analysis, Marcellus' precautions in behalf of the mathematical genius of the ancient
world probably left something to be desired.

Three versions of the death of Archimedes all agree that a soldier
committed the deed without knowing who the great scientist was.
When the news was brought to Marcellus by this man, sources say
the general turned from him as from a polluted person. He probably
turned in dismay at his own neglect. Marcellus knew that Archimedes was in the fortress when he ordered it to be given over to
pillage. He had shown concern for Syracusan traitors who had deserted to Rome by placing guards over their homes, demonstrating
that he had consciously thought of protective measures. He had,
further, shown where his heart lay by sending a quaestor's guard to
secure the royal gold. Showing all this foresight in the case of relatively unimportant persons and matters, yet not taking the precaution of guarding the person who surely must have dwarfed all others
at Syracuse, is sufficiently pointed evidence that one may say Marcellus deliberately neglected measures for the protection of
Archimedes—save a verbal statement of warning. His own example
through the years in Sicily had taught wild lessons of vindictive and
incendiary behavior. Common soldiers would not be slow to heed
that example during the sack of Syracuse. One can conclude only
that Marcellus hoped his embarrassing technological humiliation at
the hands of Archimedes would be forever avenged by the anonymous demise of the scientist. Again, one cannot help noting that all
subalterns present when the orders for the day were given to the
tribunes were as aware of the presence of Archimedes as Marcellus
and knew the orders to pillage without special guards for him
amounted to a death sentence for the scientist—excellent training
for the kind of person young Cato was to become! Further, the
pretense of grief afterwards taught the grim kind of hypocrisy that

was to become characteristic of all Roman militarism. No less so was the attempt to seek out, decorate, and so dishonor the family of Archimedes after his death. That was a mockery of image making (Plutarch XIX; Livy XXV.31; Cicero, *de Finibus* V.50)!

Action on the later accusation brought by Sicilian envoys against Marcellus in the Roman senate was one of the most farcical events for that august body in this early period of the republic. The entire defense of Marcellus was based upon the one point that Syracuse by its actions had made itself the enemy of Rome and as such deserved everything that had befallen it. Conversely, everything Marcellus had done was justified in the interest of winning, it being understood that no one questioned the essential justice of Roman victory. The senate, involved in a life-and-death struggle with Hannibal and presided over by Marcellus himself, recently elected consul for the fourth time, could hardly be in the position of denying those arguments. Marcellus was acquitted, and the Roman policy of justifying any behavior in the interest of victory was plainly established (Plutarch, *Marcellus* XXIII; Livy XXVI.30–31).

After the capture of Syracuse Marcellus made a general settlement of Sicily. He shone as a diplomat: Delegations from all over Sicily waited upon him, and he granted them terms in accordance with their history of relations with Rome. Those who had remained friendly or become allies before the capture of Syracuse were confirmed as loyal allies. Those who were frightened into friendship by the fall of Syracuse were treated as enemies. One may surmise a certain ingenuity of interrogation, analysis, and deduction in all this. Doubtless the city representatives came to lie, if necessary, so as to obtain favorable terms from Rome. Marcellus had to discover truth through their lies (Livy XXV.40).

This part of the training of Cato may be one of the most important, as far as his service to Rome was concerned. Nothing indicates that he learned diplomacy anywhere else than at this point in his Sicilian service. He had a chance to observe Marcellus at work in that capacity, and it must have been quite an experience. Cato's later career is proof of the excellence of Marcellus' tutelage. He was able to bring a number of hostile Spanish tribes into alliance with Rome by diplomacy during his consulship there and to persuade others to ally themselves with him when his army was threatened with extinction. During the war with Antiochus the Great in Greece, Cato brought the cities of Corinth, Patrae, and Aegium into the Roman orbit by diplomacy. That was no mean feat, as they were all restlessly anxious to join the other Greek cities in alliance with Antiochus. The other Roman envoy was Flamininus, a philhellene. Cato was prejudiced against Greeks and yet successfully sealed alliances with them in the name of his country. So much for his diplomatic ability and its Sicilian classroom (Plutarch, *Cato* X, XII; Livy XXXIV.11).

At the end of summer in 211 B.C., Marcellus returned to Rome, though his army and Cato remained in Sicily until 210. The extent of the pillage and the amount of spoil derived from Syracuse are to be inferred from the accounts of Marcellus' unparalleled ovational procession through the streets of Rome. The opulence, luxury of apparel, and splendor of the belongings of the kings are occasion for comment in all of them. A case for criticism is found, however, in the fact that Marcellus brought statues of the gods from Syracuse and carted them as well through Roman streets. Polybius (IX.10) feels this was foolish because it offered simple folk a taste of luxury and made them long for values other than those that he believes gave Rome her strength. Plutarch (XXI–XXII) says Marcellus became repugnant to the nobility but popular with the common folk—the former, he says, because the patricians thought it in bad taste to lead gods about as captives, like human prisoners, and because it turned the thoughts of a people used to war-and-agriculture to idle disputation about art and artists. Conversely, Marcellus was popular with the common folk, who appreciated his adorning the city with objects that had Hellenic grace and charm and fidelity. Livy believes the statues began Roman admiration of Greek art but simultaneously started the spoliation of shrines and temples that ultimately turned against the very Roman sanctuaries themselves (XXVI.21, XXV.40).

So far as the pronouncements of Polybius are concerned, the argument that exposing people to a sight of luxuries from a conquered land would cause them to want to emulate the vanquished and thus lose the qualities that brought them victory is questionable. History seems to show that there is no way to isolate a people so completely that they will not be affected by the outside world, especially if they have conquered and administered it. Sparta, for instance, followed the ideal of Polybius, forbidding the importation of luxurious spoil, yet her people were changed by simple exposure to the sight of it on their militaristic excursions outside Sparta and in the end seem to have acquired a greater greed because of the deprivation at home. Further, there is cause to argue whether the mere sight of luxuries creates a desire for them or whether desire is itself an indication of deeper motivations. Early heroes like Dentatus were not tempted.

The arguments of Plutarch defeat themselves. In the same place that he makes Marcellus the bane of the nobility and the darling of the masses, Plutarch says also that before this time, Rome neither had nor knew about such elegant and exquisite productions as these statues, nor was there any love for such graceful and subtle art. Instead, he says, Rome was full of barbaric arms and bloody spoils. Yet now, in a flash it seems, the common folk of Rome—not the nobility, but the common folk—became such experts on art that Marcellus was popular with them because he adorned the city with objects that had "Hellenic grace and charm and fidelity," and they became idle and full of glib talk about arts and artists, so that they spent a great part of the day in such clever disputation. Nowhere but in "Plutarch's Rome," one might say, could common folk by some mystifying instant osmosis become art experts of that competence on sculptures the like of which they had never before seen. Perhaps that is enough to say of Plutarch's evidence.

The moderate statements of Livy are more acceptable—they may even be near the truth of Roman reaction to Marcellus' spoils. It stands to reason that this first exposure to Greek sculpture inspired an admiration for Greek refinement. It did establish a sort of one-upmanship, indubitably, that caused generals to confiscate *les objets d'art* competitively, cart them off to Rome, and adorn temples and dwellings with them. Livy also says, later (XXVII.16), that Fabius showed "nobler restraint" in dealing with divine statues, an implied criticism of the behavior of Marcellus.

All this "business about statues" had significance in the life of Marcus Cato. Two of the commanding "identity" figures of his youth, Fabius and Marcellus, were preoccupied with statues, and that doubtless influenced Cato's attitude. Like theirs, Cato's view of such ostentation was a hypocritical one. He used to say that the only images worth anything were those of the most exquisite workmanship carried in the hearts of one's fellow citizens. To those who expressed amazement that so prominent a man as he had no statues of commemoration, Cato haughtily replied, "I would rather have men ask why I have no statue than why I have one." Further, in his later consulship Cato warned that Rome's conquests increasingly brought imports of "the treasures of kings . . . with all the allurements of vice . . . and I fear these things will capture us rather than we them. Tokens of danger were those statues brought to this city from Syracuse." Yet Cato as censor, opposed by the senate, used Roman funds to build the *Basilica Porcia* in the forum and offered no objection when the people raised a statue in honor of his conservative censorship. Cato had learned his "hypocrisy lessons" well (Plutarch, *Cato* XIX; Livy XXIV.4).

The Sicilian army and Cato had a rather tough time of it after Marcellus departed. They resented not being allowed to leave Sicily with Marcellus and the more difficult, less oppressive mode of life they had to live now that there was supposed to be peace. Cato, as tribune and necessary participator in the administration of legionary punishment, must have been closely involved in the situation of near mutiny among Roman troops in that year. The men, out of rebellious discontent, were growing slack in their duties. Marcus Cornelius Cethegus, the praetor in charge, succeeded in restoring order by a judicious mixture of sympathy and severity, once he arrived. Again, both the "sympathy," perhaps manifest through awards of various types, and "severity," or punishment, would be administered through the tribunes (Livy XXVI.21).

This "time of Sicilian troubles" taught the young officer Marcus how to mix exactly the right amounts of discipline and camaraderie to inspire maximum effort from Roman soldiers. Again, it required a certain pungent hypocrisy, for the ideal attitude of behavior one must project and officially expect was not the reality one must practise to get along with actual people. The parsimonious habits of Cato himself have been mentioned. These were his ideal, and he projected them critically toward the conduct of others both at Rome and in the field. Thus, for instance, he accused Scipio later of corrupting the soldiers with booty when their salaries exceeded their needs. One might assume, then, that Cato officially condemned any donative above salary as "corruption." Yet the pernicious ethic he had learned so well from Marcellus—the end justifies the means— was a rule of thumb he applied also to the command of troops. He allowed the soldiers under his own command in Spain to collect great quantities of booty and gave them each a pound of silver besides, saying that it was better to have many Romans with silver in their pockets than a few with gold. Cato was also more inclined to be generous with allies than even his own officers would approve.[15]

Whether from this surprising and contradictory policy or from the personal amenities he must have maintained toward his men, Cato had learned how to elicit both affection and consequent maximum effort from soldiers. An attendant of his in Spain hanged himself rather than appear in disgrace before Cato, hardly the act of one indifferent to the wishes of his commander. Another incident of praiseworthy daring and instant volunteering on the part of a whole company of men from Firmum, in the command of Cato during the war against Antiochus, speaks also of his ability to inspire loyalty in men. Since Sicily is the one place Cato had extended exposure to men who were at first content in the service of Marcellus and then unhappy and dissatisfied under other circumstances, his rapport with men was learned there (Plutarch, *Cato* X, XIII).

Doubtless the impressionable tribune saw how unfair the distribution of spoil in a general pillage could be and how unlikely it was that men having little part in the attack could gain a lion's share of the booty. Also, he would have learned how important a generous or significant donative from the campaign commander could be to the morale of the troops. Either or both would be a justification for the surprising statement that it was better for many Romans to go home with silver in their pockets than a few with gold.

The entire Sicilian action was terminated in 210 B.C., and Cato returned to Italy at that time. The homecoming must have been, like his earlier departure, cheerless. Only his overseer, domestics, and household gods were there to greet him. In the emotional vacuum of that atmosphere, one can assume that Cato reverted to type and performed the steps on his checklist for "proper homecomings." He saluted the god of the household, then inspected the whole farm within two days, and finally called in the overseer to go over the accounts and the work with him. Admonishing him for the work left undone, Cato would have next issued instructions as to what work to do immediately and in the future. The following day he must once again have worked in the fields as before (Livy XXVI.40; Cato II.1–2).

CHAPTER 2

The Country Boy Goes to Rome

I Campaign under Fabius at Tarentum

MARCUS Cato was twenty-four years old in 210 B.C.; he celebrated by involving himself in affairs and becoming acquainted with an increasing number of politicians. Two sources
insist that he took service with Fabius Maximus at Tarentum the
very next year. Modern authorities seem agreed that Cato did not
fight at Tarentum because the only reason for saying that he did is
that of setting a time and place for an instructional meeting between
Cato and a Pythagorean philospher, Nearchus. This man, by a tradition imputed to Cicero, preached the message that the simple life
was best, while Cato listened.[1]

There are reasons to believe Cato actually did serve at Tarentum
in 209 B.C. under Fabius. Perhaps the best proof is the agreement of
two ancient sources, Cicero and Plutarch, that he did and the denial
of such service only by modern, tertiary sources. Service with
Fabius was the politic thing to do. Marcellus' ovation and the conservative reaction to it must have shown Cato that he was identified
with the wrong crowd. The best way to erase that image swiftly
would be to serve under Fabius at first opportunity, for he, more
than any other, was "Mr. Conservative" at Rome. Cato probably
went to Tarentum voluntarily, without a commission. Cicero (*Cato*
10) implies he served both in 214 and 209 B.C. under Fabius as a
private soldier. Yet if one is correct in assuming he was there to
establish an image, Cato would have made himself known to the
leaders of the army, particularly to Fabius. There is one rather
flimsy bit of evidence in one source that he did attempt to achieve a
reputation that would merit more than mere notice.

Some of the siege techniques used by Fabius at Tarentum were
very similar to those of Marcellus at Syracuse, especially the de-
ployment of ships to attack from the sea. Those described by Livy

(XXVII.15) as carrying engines and ladders up to the walls bear a striking resemblance to the *sambucae* invented by Marcellus. It is entirely possible that Cato had something to do with their implementation. He would be one of the very few military personnel who took service with Fabius at Tarentum just a few months after returning from the arduous Sicilian campaign. Similarly then, he would be one of very few in a position to tell Fabius of that siege technique. Cato might, finally, be the only one with both the ideas and the technological ability to carry them out by building engines on ships. The ideas and engineering skill were a part of his capability, and Cato later showed great skill with ships (Livy XXXIV.8.4–7). The exacting descriptions and details he noted when on winter leave in 216 and 215 B.C., connected with such things as presses and mills, show his technological ability, for the present. The ideas came from Marcellus.

The actual encounter at Tarentum was aborted by treachery. The city was betrayed into Roman hands. Despite the ease of the campaign, however, Roman soldiers became bloodthirsty butchers again once they got inside the walls. Livy gives his characteristic bifocal view (XXVII.15). He talks of the "noble restraint" of a victorious Fabius in the matter of leaving the statues of the gods alone. Then he hints that the same man may have allowed indiscriminate slaughter of Bruttians just to prevent the story of betrayal of the city by treason from getting out and to make it seem as though the capture was by force of arms alone. Finally, Livy languidly documents the massive murder of unarmed as well as armed men and the succeeding plunder of the city. The historian seems bereft of any moral discrimination whatever, as he indifferently discusses the massacre in the same place where he speculates on "nobleness" in the man Fabius (cp. Plutarch, *Fabius Maximus* XXII.3–5).

Plutarch at this point comes to the rescue. He indicates the moral fallacies of Fabius' behavior, saying that his ambition proved stronger than his principles in the matter of the Bruttians. He further calls him unfaithful and inhumane. Then Plutarch says that Fabius, though he left the majority of the gods' statues in Tarentum, did haul a gigantic statue of Hercules to Rome, beside which he made an equestrian statue of himself. Plutarch's motive here is that of aggrandizing Marcellus, whom he calls extraordinarily mild and humane, in the same place (cp. Pliny, *NH* XXIV.18).

Cato's presence at Tarentum is further established by the business of these statues. He deliberately chose to identify with Fabius and the conservatives rather than Marcellus and the people. That much is plain from his later consular denunciation of Marcellus' looting of Syracusan statues. Seeing the heroes of his childhood, Cato had little choice in this. It would be difficult to understand his surprising and contradictory attitude concerning statues and memorials if the only model of behavior in his army background were Marcellus, whom he now ideologically denied. But the moral aberration of Quintus Fabius Maximus—the grandest aristocrat of them all—and his vanity in placing a statue of himself by that of one of the gods makes Cato's failing completely logical and understandable.

The meeting between Cato and Nearchus the Pythogorean, which is the occasion of modern doubt, should not in itself cause such discomfort. It has been shown before that Cato was a loquacious weekender at the houses of Campanians and Samnites during his army service in 216 and 215 B.C. (pp. 19–21). His conversational charm during social meals in the long country evenings of his later life is a tradition (Cicero, *Cato* 46). His talking with a Pythagorean lodged in the same building should not seem strange. Cato would not regard Pythagoreans with the same reserve and suspicion he held toward Greeks in general. Cicero shows this when he had Cato use the term "Italian philosophers" of Pythagoreans, because of the long residence of Pythagoras at Croton in southern Italy.

Nearchus summarized attitudes of the Pythagorean philosophy by saying that pleasure is the greatest incentive to evil and that the body is the chief detriment to the soul, from which the soul can release and purify herself only by reasonings that divorce her from bodily sensations. Surely Cato found nothing contradictory or uncomfortable in that! It served only to confirm the ideals he had already appropriated from his identity heroes. Little is accomplished by debating whether this conversation was impossible because of Cato's inability to speak Greek. Tarentum had been a subject of Rome for nearly seventy years by this time. It is likely that Nearchus could speak Latin, if Cato could not speak Greek. The argument that Cato did not learn Greek until later in life, furthermore, must be reconciled with his negotiating peace in 191 B.C. with the Greek cities of Corinth, Patrae, and Aegium under Manius Acilius in the war with Antiochus. He would then have been forty-three years old—hardly in his "later life." Plutarch (II, XII) says that although Cato spoke through an interpreter with citizens of

Athens, he could have spoken with them directly but disdained the image of being that familiar with things Greek. Nothing seems to contradict the confrontation between Cato and Nearchus but modern intransigence.

II *A Public Career in Rome: Cato's Style*

It was during the period after the Tarentine campaign, 209 to 207 B.C., that Cato's friendship with the Flaccuses must have caused him to establish summer quarters in Rome. Plutarch says that Valerius persuaded him to do this and that he then engaged in public life at Rome, taking up his abode there. He had the patronage of Flaccus and a speaking acquaintance with Fabius Maximus, as well as full knowledge of the popular leaders such as Marcellus, if he wished to use it. Yet Cato's own style and characteristics seem to be all that he needed to establish himself very well indeed. Now the eloquence Cato walked miles in the dawn hours of his youth to achieve began to bear fruit.[2]

There was about him an orphan look—a gaunt homelessness—that drew friendship. He was everybody's cousin, and his ways smacked of gran'pa's cabin: neat, quaint, and parochial. Homespun clothes, hungry eyes, healing scars, and calloused appearance made Cato a figure of instant sympathy in the newly sophisticated city. His language was that of the country court and the farmers' market—archaic Latin and rustic aphorism—yet it was peculiarly effective. It was unrefined and artless, but direct and sincere. Cato's homely phrases rang of ancient days; his stern, grey eyes froze others' facile words, and his spare, sinewy frame was like Cincinnatus at his rusty plow, leading Rome again. All this was irresistible to the people; it wrung their hearts and moved them to tears.[3]

Plutarch says (VI) that Cato's discourse was pleasant and compelling, graceful and powerful, facetious and severe, sententious and belligerent. Cicero adds (*Brutus* 16–17; cp. Gellius VI.3.53) that he was adroit, witty, elegant, and concise; therefore, he could be withering in rebuke, scintillating in epigram, and acute in analysis and demonstration. Then he says that Cato used admirable material in his written speeches and set it forth in faultless diction. It seems the chief characteristic was a certain winning, unadorned simplicity that nevertheless contained sparkling eloquence. This style Cicero likens to "Attic simplicity" and parallels it with that of Lysias, the most prolific Attic rhetorician before Demosthenes, except that Lysias had a certain "sparseness" that Cato did not. Cicero would only refine Cato by adding rhythm and transposed word order, whereon he would compete with the best of "modern" orators. Cato practiced and deliberately sought terse simplicity. He was later proud of Athenian astonishment at the pungent speed of his discourse (Plutarch XII.5).

Perhaps this deliberate brevity was the reason that men sought Cato out and patterned their styles after his. Terse Latinity appealed to the pragmatic Roman mind, and they clamored to imitate him as he had once sought to copy Manius Curius Dentatus. History seems to record that they were successful because the style became popular and there was a prevalence of "packed brevity" in the Latin usage of writers such as Sallust, Caesar, Horace, and Tacitus. Yet in the time of Cato that success was not apparent. Many seem to have despaired of the struggle, believing one must live Cato's kind of life in order to achieve his laconic speech. It proved impossible for them to do that.

Cato himself derisively called his imitators "left-handed Catos" because of their inability to sacrifice enough to live like him, as well as talk like him (Plutarch IV, XIX). Many had lost the knack. Roman citizens in this period of increasing urbanization may well have forgotten how to fashion things with their own hands. Affluence and supply had made them dependent on craftsmen. Almost as impossible was eating a cold breakfast and frugal dinner of thirty penny's worth of fish or meat and washing it down with sour slaves' wine, the rest of the time eating bread alone for these two meals. Those who were fond of clothes as status symbols found it impossible to copy Cato's clothing budget. The ostentation of sumptuous dwellings made it difficult for others to live like Cato, for he refused to pay for plastering on his walls, believing the simple wood siding sufficient. Yet more would such people find it difficult to rise before it was light (Plutarch VIII.9).

There is no reason to suppose, with Plutarch, that this period of Roman history from 209 to 207 B.C. already saw people enervated by luxurious pleasures. Therefore the contrast between Cato and the rest of the citizens could not have been so dramatic as the biographer thinks. Again, Plutarch himself furnishes the lie to his own documentary. In the life of Marcellus—again the matter of statues—Plutarch talks of the barbarian nature of Rome before the ovation of Marcellus. Now, two short years later, the reader is called on to believe that there was a kind of corroding ease of life in a city so totally at war that there had been emergency subscriptions to supply the very monies needed to outfit troops. If the generalization were confined to Cato's later years, there might be more justification for it.[4]

Any credence attaching to the idea that apprentices must live like Cato in order to speak like him should be dispelled by the knowledge that his terse Latinity was generalized and then perpetuated in the works of other authors. Yet there was one stylistic feature in which the urban removal from rural custom and knowledge made an important difference if one wanted to be like Cato: the rustic, countrified aphorism. "Fellow citizens, it is a hard matter to save a city in which a fish sells for more than an ox," Cato exclaims, and unless people knew the comparative values and utility of each at first hand, the aphorism would fall on deaf ears and be without effect. In the same place, his likening the Romans to sheep, who cannot be led individually but who in flocks follow their leader, would fail in its effectiveness unless one knew the sheepfold. Similarly, Cato's own predisposition to favor land located near the sea would cause him to impugn a man who had recently sold such an estate, saying, "That man disposed with ease what the sea could not wash away." But again, unless one knew farming and the value of such land, he could hardly appreciate the saying. These pungent statements would not be used by one who had no first-hand acquaintance of the country, but neither is there a sign that such sayings were essential to the style of brevity (Plutarch VIII. 1, 2, 7).

Aside from the particulars of style and mode, plainly Cato considered forensic oratory—the kind in which he now began to excel, before his political career—extremely important. Cases in court were a means he used consistently to impeach and convict malefactors in office. Because of this, he incurred much enmity and was as often a defendant in court as he was a prosecutor. Further, he aided others in both defending themselves and bringing actions against his own political enemies, a device more commonly used in the middle and late republic. Plutarch says (XV) Cato was defendant in at least fifty cases, so the total involvement must have numbered twice that—a very active life of litigation.

Politics were not the only reason for court appearances. Cato viewed court also as a place for the vindication of honor. He is known to have told a young man who got a favorable judgment against an enemy of his father that such verdicts were a more fitting service to the memory of parents than the religious sacrifice of lambs and kids. Those are strong words for a man as devout as Cato and show how much he thought of the court as a means of establishing truth and honor. Perhaps that is part of the reason Cato acquired the name of "Roman Demosthenes." The styles of the two men were dissimilar, Demosthenes being lengthy and dramatic while Cato was profoundly simple and brief. Perhaps more of a clue to the epithet is Cicero's indication that Cato used admirable material in his speeches and set it forth with faultless diction; surely that trait was characteristic of both orators. So also, was eloquence, except that one must be careful to define the differing conceptions of eloquence in each age. Historical truth seems to have been a goal for both Cato and Demosthenes. Cato's later speech, opposing repeal of the Oppian Law, is surely an eloquent appeal to history and past custom—the authority of the past against present female extravagance (Plutarch XV, IV; Livy XXXIV.2–5).

It is at this point in his biography of Cato's career that Plutarch (V) again pauses to moralize. This time he states an opinion about the man's callous attitude to such as animals and slaves. In a section where self-denial leads to the purchase and keeping of slaves that are strong rather than attractive, Plutarch laments over Cato's well-publicized compulsion to get rid of old slaves rather than to continue feeding them as charity cases. This equates slaves with beasts of burden, he says. Therefore, he further opines, Cato had a mean nature. One could easily agree with that and yet wonder about Plutarch's standards and priorities once more. The tone of this entire section of the biography is one of approval. Plutarch, in other words, likes the character of Cato but will not approve the behavior that character leads to. Seeing the total personality of Cato, one could easily predict this kind of moral blindness about old slaves. It is as though Plutarch had no psychological insight at all—yet his treatment of some illustrious men, both Greek and Roman, and his famous moralizing show that he had very incisive ability to read character, at times.

Further, there is the matter of bifocalism once again. Plutarch showed in the lives of Fabius and Marcellus, to mention just two, that he could document mass murder and blood craze ordered or condoned by these two and yet in the same breath speak of their "nobility"; and in the case of Marcellus, he presumed to argue for "gentleness and humanity" as well. Now he professes moral shock at the discharge of old slaves, styling Cato "mean-natured" because of it. In other words, if Plutarch had any sense of objective ethic at all, he applied it only where he wished in order to make some seem more, some less, great.

Even more ludicrous is the biographer's application of this "Catonic" standard to animals. "Beneficence and Charity," Plutarch says, "flow from the gentle heart. A kindly man will take good care of his horses and dogs when they are worn out with age, regardless of the inconvenience." He then goes on to speak of Athenians and their kindness to an old mule that had worked on the wagons hauling stones to build the Parthenon. Despite the mule's being turned out to pasture because of age, it came back to the works of its own accord, trotting along with the wagons and leading them up the steep incline to the Acropolis. The Athenians were so charmed by this brute loyalty that they passed a decree that the animal be maintained at public expense as long as it lived. This again is directly contrasted to the deliberate economy of Cato, who left his faithful horse in Spain after the creature had carried him through all his consular campaigns in that country rather than charge Rome for its transportation. The story is followed by what the biographer seems to hope is a moot question: Does this mean greatness of spirit or littleness of mind?

The answer to this question, so far as the character of Cato is concerned, is obvious. He simply did not equate animals with Roman citizens; he would not tax the one to support the other. If it were a question of personal expense, one may be sure that Cato would have weighed the economics. Had the horse been a magnificent charger whose worth was considerable, Cato would have brought it back. No doubt Plutarch thought it was such a creature and lamented accordingly. But in view of Cato's thriftiness, it is as likely to have been a flea-bitten nag barely adequate to the task at hand, surely not worth hauling back to Rome. One wonders if Plutarch would have sounded the mighty histrionics over such an equine disaster. Moreover, the biographer exhibits aristocratic blindness. He is unaware of the poverty among slaves and low-class freedmen at Athens during the age of Pericles. Yet Aristophanes' comedies plainly set it forth for all to see in lampooning the sort of people who served on the juries to earn three obols a day so they could eat. Is this Athenian bigotry of "animal welfare," then, greatness of spirit or littleness of mind?

Finally, it has been shown that the military campaigns of Cato in Sicily and Italy, under Marcellus and Fabius, did more to dehumanize Cato and deprecate life than anything else. Not many of even the sternest moral fibre could experience four bloodlusty, wholesale massacres as Cato already had and emerge with their human values and doctrines of life unchanged. To say that Cato's treatment of old slaves and animals was caused by his thrifty nature is a vast oversimplification that looks only at the surface. Any nation whose history is as drenched in continuous bloody war as Rome's will in the end experience a cheapening ideal of life and human valuation. Cato's views, with those of Fabius and Marcellus, his instructors, are a living testimonial to that fact. Yet the ancients show little appreciation of the principle, except when they choose. Plutarch, indeed, does call attention to the barbaric arms and bloody spoils, the memorials and triumphal trophies that made Rome a virtual "precinct of much-warring Ares." But he does so to prove the civilizing effect of Marcellus' looted Syracusan statues and the consequent greatness of that man's nature—he who had just ordered the massacre of tens of thousands of fellow human beings, albeit they were Greek enemies. It is therefore impossible to know whether Plutarch's description of Rome as "bloody with spoil" is accurate or exaggerated for effect. In any case, much more than thrift was behind Cato's attitude to servile or bestial life.

III   *Voluntary Tribuneship at the Battle of Metaurus River*

The clamor of imitators, the influence of Valerius and possible approval of Fabius, along with the admiration of sincere friends, made Cato an increasingly important figure at Rome. His action at the battle of Metaurus River in 207 enhanced this reputation. It is almost certain that Cato's service in that campaign was again voluntary. No shred of evidence backs the modern opinion that he was elected tribune of the soldiers for that year. His name is missing from all the lists (*fasti*) where it would appear if he had been elected. On the other hand, Nepos unmistakably places Cato at the Metaurus under the command of Gaius Claudius Nero— unmistakably because of his accompanying statement that Cato won high praise in that battle. Beyond a doubt he was there. Similarly,

Plutarch (III) says that after Cato settled in Rome (in 209 B.C.) and before he became quaestor (205 B.C.), he was made a military tribune. But Plutarch's word *'étyche* does not mean he was elected to that office. Nepos' indication that Cato simply joined the army of Nero is the likely alternative, and he was given the commission of tribune, if Plutarch is to be accepted. Nero must have known something of Cato, making the appointment on the march north from Canusium.

Nero had undertaken a daring separation of forces after intercepting Hasdrubal's message to Hannibal. He marched north by forced stages from Apulia with a part of his army, seven thousand men, to join his colleague, Marcus Livius Salinator, in fighting and defeating Hasdrubal so as to prevent the union of the two armies (Livy XXVII.43.1–5, 11). It called for haste, lest Hannibal find out what was afoot before Hasdrubal could be surprised. So the camp opposite Hannibal must be maintained as though it were fully manned, while seven thousand of its men slipped out at night to march north. The march was 250 miles long, and they covered it in seven days. Nero had sent word to the senate of his intentions, and then messengers along the line of march implored towns to be prompt with necessary food and supplies. More was in fact offered by hopeful men along the way than the troops needed. The army of Nero grew during the march as volunteers who were physically capable and experienced were enrolled among the men of Nero (Appian VII.52; Dio XVI; Livy XXXVII.45, 46).

This was the way in which Cato joined the army of Nero. Living in Rome and active in affairs, he would have heard from senators what Nero was about and judged for himself the possibilities of the action. He then repaired to his farm to fetch the supplies he would need and perhaps extra rations for others, since the call had been for provisions along the way. From his farm Cato probably did not have far to go. Nero's line of march—south toward Lucania for deception, then straight north to Larinum in Samnium, through the country of the Frentani, Marrucini, and Praetutii, and so to Sena—may not have passed very far from Cato's country estate in Sabinum. The Marrucini were residents of the eastern Sabine territory, and the Praetutii were natives of Picenum. Cato had a fast friendship with the Picene men of Firmum. It is likely that he now felt called on to aid the army of Nero that was marching through neighboring areas and might be protecting his own home territory from Hasdrubal. So

Cato joined, bringing supplies, and his name and reputation got him a commission as tribune.[5]

The young officer won high praise at the battle of Metaurus. Nero sneaked into the camp of Livius at night, all his men bunking up with others of the same rank in that camp, so as not to add to the number of tents or the size of the camp, or otherwise to indicate that the army of Livius had doubled in strength overnight. The strangers were received with joy, all the men jubilant over the prospect of major victory. But everything depended on the element of surprise; Hasdrubal must not discover by any external sign or by word from Hannibal that he faced superior numbers. The next day Cato attended a council of war, at which many favored delaying battle so that the men of Nero could rest from their breathtaking march and Nero could familiarize himself with the enemy. Nero, however, rose to differ violently with this view, saying that any delay would forfeit the surprise they had worked so hard and marched so far to achieve. Rumor travels swiftly; at any moment Hasdrubal might hear whispers from some quarter that would destroy everything. Attack at once (Livy XXVII.46; Dio XVI)!

That decided it. Orders for action were given, and the army moved out into line. Hasdrubal's army was already drawn up in front of his camp. The man was a wily commander. As the Romans formed up, he observed some battered shields in their front line he had not seen before. There seemed to be more horses in the lines than before, and they had a more stringy look than the rest. These signs caused him alarm, and he sounded the retreat so as to reconnoiter. Scouts were sent to the river watering place to see whether any soldiers had a specially weather-beaten look. Others looked to see if the camp had been enlarged anywhere and to listen for trumpet calls when the troops were mustered. None of these indicated cause for worry, except the trumpet call. Scouts reported that the trumpet had sounded twice in the consul's camp. That, to Hasdrubal, meant there must be two consuls present, and he suspended all plans of combat to reason it out (Livy XXVII.47; Dio XVI).

Hasdrubal's knowledge of Roman custom told him one consul should be in the south before Hannibal. The problem was how that consul had got away from Hannibal so that there were two in the camp he himself now faced. Either, he reasoned, Hannibal had suffered such a reverse that he could not pursue, in which case everything was lost, or Hasdrubal's message had been intercepted.

Both alternatives meant he faced an army entirely too strong to gamble on fighting. In that case he must leave with all haste. Hasdrubal ordered the illuminating campfires extinguished, and his army packed silently. Under cover of full dark they moved out, but in the confusion their guides escaped, the men were exhausted from lack of sleep, and the column got lost. They followed the bank of the Metaurus river by dark, but it wound through deep gorges, and they were losing time. Hasdrubal was forced to order a halt until daylight. Even then, the winding gorge of the river allowed no crossing, and he frantically began building a fortified camp (Appian VII.52).

The arrival of pursuing Romans—first Nero with the cavalry, then Licinius, the praetor, with the light-armed troops, and then Livius with all the infantry—forced Hasdrubal to fight. His strategy was excellent: He chose a narrow place for the engagement, so that the superiority of numbers would be of little effect, and then massed his force with the elephants and veterans in front. It is difficult, because of the variations between three accounts of the battle, to say just how the details of the fighting went. All are agreed that the elephants were a hindrance to both sides. Polybius (XI.1) says six of them had to be killed by their drivers, and four were recovered by Romans afterward. The fighting was extremely heavy, but there is a hysterical difference in the casualties mentioned. Livy says fifty-six thousand Carthaginians were slain and fifty-four hundred captured (XXVII.48–9); eight thousand Romans and allies died. Polybius, on the other hand, says ten thousand Carthaginians were killed and two thousand Romans (also, Appian VII.52; Dio XVI).

The main deciding tactical factor in the battle was Nero's withdrawal of idle cohorts from the Roman right, where a hill prevented their being engaged with the Gauls on that flank, his marching with them around the rear of the Roman formation, and then using them to attack from the Roman left on the right flank of the enemy. That soon collapsed, and he then could attack Hasdrubal's formation from the rear, forcing it to give way. Thus was the battle won. Hasdrubal is mightily praised by Polybius for taking every precaution and measure to ensure success, but when defeat was known to be inevitable, spurring his horse into the thick of battle so as to lose his life in the encounter. Since he previously insists that a commander should above all protect his own life because of those dependent upon his welfare, one knows that Polybius believed Hasdrubal had done all that and could be forgiven for taking his own life in this extremity, a remarkably shortsighted view for one who is supposed to be a genius in analytical and objective historical writing! Hasdrubal could not have been certain that Hannibal was dead or defeated, and therefore he might have foreseen the grief and loss of morale his death would cause in Hannibal's army. He had no right to take his life; had he disengaged and fled with but a company of men and then joined Hannibal even without an army, the Carthaginian cause would have been better served (Appian VII.54).

Cato had now participated in the second great victory of Roman arms in the eastern theater of the war. He was a veteran of Syracuse and of Metaurus. The second, in particular, would be a great political asset because of the unbelievable anxiety that had preceded it. Livy is very dramatic about this (XXVII.51), carefully tolling the factors one by one: Since it had received word of Nero's hair-raising dash across Italy, the senate had been in continuous session, and not one senator had left the chamber; the magistrates had been with it in suspended apprehension; the people had not left the *Forum;* the matrons had been wandering from one temple to another, importuning this god and that with endless entreaties for victory. Then, like a small ripple growing to a wave, swelling to a roar, distending to a screaming shout of delirious joy, came the word of victory along the streets to the center of the city. Three days of thanksgiving were decreed, and everyone crowded the temples. The worst seemed over; it was only a matter of time. Polybius (XI.3) and Livy emphasize that Romans now, for the first time, renewed business and arrangements as though the war were over.

Everyone who could remember that gladsome day would also reflect to Cato's credit the saying of Nepos that he won high praise at Metaurus (I.2). It may be that this, as much as anything, sponsored the further increase of the man's reputation. That is central to Cato's next life phase.

CHAPTER 3

Master of Supply for the Invasion of Africa and Aedile at Rome

THE quaestorship of Cato is one of the most contested areas of his life. Among the issues are a quarrel about whether Cato began his famous debate with Scipio Africanus during this official tenure and a contested dispute about the exact dates. Several problems are involved, in turn, in the question of dates. The main juxtaposition is that of placing Cato's quaestorship in 205 B.C. during Scipio's consulship or in 204 during his African proconsulship. The debate here is summarized in the footnotes. Examination of the evidence leads to an overwhelming conviction that Cato was quaestor in 205 B.C., associated with Scipio as consul, and that his quaestorship was prorogued through 204, 203, and 202 to 201 B.C. This solution, advocated by Dietmar Kienast and others, is the only one that seems to include and account for all the evidence. It was, as quaestorships are, an association with a particular consulship—that of Scipio during the conquest of the Carthaginians.[1]

I The Politics behind Scipio's African Campaign

Some authorities affect to see family coalitions, interest groups, and power blocs behind the events of 205 B.C. Scipio's return from Spain forged such a combination in Roman politics, by this view, and it was an expansionist, imperialistic circle centering around Scipio's well-known wish to invade Africa. Its natural foe was anti-expansionist and isolationist—conservative in the sense of Italy for Italians. Its born leader was Fabius Maximus, who was now quite old. The threat of restrictive action by the Fabian group is supposed to have influenced certain of Scipio's actions. Surely 205 B.C. is too early to prove a structured stability of foreign policy or a group orientation that would transcend natural individualism. The pres-

ence of interest groups can certainly be asserted, but these were, as
the label implies, subject to momentary revision and absolutely to
annual reevaluation. They did not, according to the evidence displayed in detail below, assert any kind of continuity or stability in
foreign affairs.[2]

Scipio felt he had a popular mandate from the people to end the
war by invading Africa. The historical accounts show this was true,
because of his public following (Appian VII.55) and forcefulness, but
also generalize that the people thought Scipio should bypass the
drawing of lots for provincial commands and simply take Africa as
his sphere of action, or *provincia*. His colleague, P. Licinius Crassus, was *pontifex maximus* and could not leave Italy because of his
religious duties. There seems to have been a general knowledge
among the electorate that with Spain now neutralized, the second
theater of war besides Italy would be Sicily and Africa. They had
anticipated Crassus' confinement to Italy, and that is the reason for
their feeling that a vote for Scipio was a vote for the African command (Dio XVII.52). When the election had taken place, the senate
routinely defined the consular *provinciae* as Bruttium—against
Hannibal—and Sicily. The drawing of lots was bypassed because of
the religious duties of Crassus. That, at least, is the statement of
Livy for the year 205 (XXVIII.38, 40). Then things seem to have
changed.

A second discussion in Livy (XXVIII.40) of the *provinciae* early in
205 B.C. states that it was common talk that Africa was to be assigned to Scipio as a new *provincia* without the casting of lots.
Scipio, in full knowledge of popular feeling, kept saying he had been
elected to finish the war and could do so only by invading Africa. He
is reputed to have said also that he would accomplish the necessary
redefinition of *provincia* to include Africa by popular vote, if the
senate refused its approval. The matter of redefining the sphere of
action was then debated in the senate, and Fabius led the resistance
to Scipio's plans. Both he and Scipio gave speeches. Livy
(XXVIII.40–45) says Fabius rallied the minor nobility in the senate
by coercion, stating that they failed to speak out because of fear or
else to curry favor—another instance of unethical leadership by the
senior statesman that was to backfire. Fulvius, consul four times and
censor, forced the issue by asking Scipio whether he would in fact
abide by the decision of the senate in this matter or bring a bill
before the people's assembly if the senate decided against him.

Scipio sidestepped by saying he would do what was in the best interest of the state. Fulvius then locked the senate in an impasse by refusing to express an opinion at all unless Scipio agreed to abide by the senate's decision, and he called for the protection of the people's tribunes in that refusal. Scipio retorted that it was not legal for the tribunes to veto senatorial opinion in the house. The tribunes pronounced that Fulvius was essentially right and they would back his refusal to say anything if, as seemed likely, it meant nothing. Scipio had then to decide, obviously, whether he would commit himself to the senate's decision or reserve the right to take it to the people. He asked for a day in which to confer with his colleague.

It seems almost too obvious that Scipio spent this day in careful assessment of his strength and his consequent options. Some authorities insist either that the opinion of the tribunes is a spurious addition to the events or that it solidified the opposition to the point that Scipio dared not risk a vote of the people any longer. Neither alternative is to be preferred. Far more likely is the historical tradition itself, that the events occurred essentially as Livy depicts them. Scipio, rather than risk the massive displeasure of the senate and its possible failure to support his African campaign, paused to assess his actual chances of submitting to senatorial vote on the issue. Some rather sharp arm twisting and horse trading must have transpired behind the scenes during that day because facts surface later that were no part of the official dispositions for the year. They were instead a part of the political compromise offered by Scipio so as to ensure a favorable vote in the senate. Parts of that compromise involved young Cato, his quaestor.[3]

II *Mustering Supplies and Troops for Scipio's Invasion of Africa*

Scipio undertook to promise the senators, behind the scenes, that an invasion of Africa under his command would cost the government nothing in terms of troops or ships. He would raise and build all that was necessary by private subscription and volunteers, provided the senate redefined his provincial command to include Africa. Scipio must have met privately with his *quaestor*. Cato, before pledging all this to determine whether it was possible. All of the support for this voluntary enterprise ultimately came from within an area with a radius of eighty miles from a center just north of Rome, leading to the assumption that it was planned to be an organized canvass such as could be performed by Cato with the help of other officers. He would be functioning for the most part in familiar territory relatively close to his home district. Sabinum, for instance, and next door Umbria supplied virtually all seven thousand volunteers for the army and most of the rowers for the fleet. A lot of these, in turn, came from three Sabine cities—Nursia, Reate, and Amiternum—and the rowers came largely from three Sabine tribes: the Marrucini, the Marsi, and the Paeligni. Adjacent Umbria contributed many military volunteers, and the city of Camerinum, just twenty miles from Nursia, gave a whole cohort of fully equipped men, though it was an equal, federate city under no obligation to levy men for the military. All this was voluntary, not part of the regular annual levy to which subject cities and territories were obliged to contribute.[4]

The bulk of the necessary hardware came from cities in Etruria: wood for keels, garboards, cordage, rigging, linen for sails, hand mills (windlasses), helmets, spears, javelins, lances, axes, shovels, shields, and foodstuffs. Perhaps one of the officers had his home in Etruria and knew where to canvass for these (Livy XXVIII.45). It was facilitated by the personal success and appeal of Scipio. People wished to support him.

This compromise decided the senators. Advance tallies showed Scipio had the votes to win, so he submitted to the senate's pleasure in the matter of the "African amendment." What happened then is a mystery. Livy explicitly says the senate by decree (*decretae*) allowed Scipio to cross to Africa in the interests of the state (XXVIII.45.8). This amended *provincia* must have been the one renewed in 204 (XXIX.13.3), the first year of Scipio's "African proconsulship." In anticipation of this, Pomponius, elected praetor for 204, was assigned the Sicilian *provincia*, preempting that command. Yet Livy next says that Africa had not been openly assigned (*decreta erat*) as a province for reasons of security (XXIX.14.1) and Fabius knew nothing of the affair. The latter, after the elections of 204, brought an indictment against Scipio for having left his province (Fabius must have still thought it was Sicily alone) without senatorial orders, because he thought Scipio had left for Africa (XXIX.19.6). When Pomponius' investigating commission returned, the senate superfluously voted for the African expedition and necessary troops (XXIX.22.11; Dio XVII).

Many things are contradictory here. Fabius did not know of the original compromise formed by Scipio for the African amendment. Either there was a secret caucus by a majority of the senate but excluding the Fabians, or no such family coalitions as the Fabian group existed, and consensus was achieved without Fabius' personal knowledge. The first alternative is unlikely; the senate would have to keep a secret from a large minority. The position has been taken here (p. 57) that such power groups or "blocs" did not yet exist in a continuous sense. They may have been formed temporarily on the basis of mutual interest, subject to reinterpretation. That would explain the unity in bitterness among the leaders of the senate against Scipio, brought out in the affair of Locri, and Scipio's senatorial vicissitudes, without "power blocs."

The issue was now decided, and it remained to conduct the canvass mentioned already above and marshall the men and materials at shipyards and staging areas. Cato the quaestor-quartermaster was extremely busy during the days of feverish preparation thereafter. He, Laelius—a gifted admiral who had served with Scipio before— and the tribunes of Scipio's army had to perform all these duties while also supervising the shipbuilding activities that Scipio personally pushed so as to hasten departure. Cato was a handy and capable quaestor for this because of his knowledge of building, engineering, and rigging things. Even so, without Laelius and the skilled Etrurian shipwrights who furnished the material and aided with the building, it would have been impossible to finish the twenty quinqueremes and ten quadriremes they built within the forty-five days Livy mentions (XXVIII.45.13–21), with all equipment. So swiftly did they build that they had to use green lumber. Livy says that the ships were completed from timber that had been felled for the purpose, and for that reason they had to be beached and careened at Panormus next winter in Sicily to allow the wood to cure (XXIX.1.14).

Cato continued to supervise the loading and the marshalling of supplies (Livy XXVIII.45–46; Dio XVII). It was difficult, there being seven thousand men to be embarked, three thousand shields, a like number of helmets, and fifty thousand pikes, javelins, and spears. There were well over a hundred thousand pecks of wheat for the soldiers, plus allowances for travelling rations for minor officers and rowers in the fleet. Then the force finally sailed for Sicily (Appian VIII.8).

III   *The Stay in Sicily: Cato's Responsibilities and*
Quarrel with Scipio

Cato now returned as a higher officer to the land where he had
served his first commission. That first service was to be important
still. The compromise agreement stipulated that the regular forces
of the Sicilian province were to remain intact. Scipio built his invasion force from the seven thousand volunteers he brought with him.
Ultimately, he chose also to use two legions of the despised armies
that had lost at Cannae and been sent to Sicily. They had been
allowed to serve with Marcellus during the siege of Syracuse. Scipio
especially picked and set apart the veterans of that battle because
they would be most skillful in siege and assault operations before
Carthage. Here again, Cato would be of great aid to the commander
as an officer of Marcellus during that campaign and one who had
great skill with machinery of all kinds. Very likely he knew some of
the veterans now chosen as an "assault team" personally, from the
days of the Syracusan campaign. But they had little time for rem-
iniscing. Supplies brought from Italy had to be conserved for the
African invasion, so the foodstuffs had to be off-loaded from the
ships so they could be careened, and warehoused. Then Cato had to
travel all over the island, requisitioning grain from the Sicilian states
and quartering the Roman troops in various towns, seeing that they
were billeted and supplied properly for the winter. Scipio made the
task easier by ensuring good will among the Sicilians: He returned
judgments against Italians who since the conquest had continued
illegal possession of Sicilian property (Livy XXVIII.46, XXIX.1,
24.13; Dio XVII).

The Cannae legions were each of a strength of sixty-two hundred,
and Scipio had none of the prejudice shown by the senate against
these men, knowing, since he had been tribune there, that Cannae
had not resulted from their cowardice. He even chose allied infantry
and cavalry from the army of Cannae to participate in the African
invasion. They were elated at the prospect of earning their way back
to Italy by invading Africa and defeating Carthage. An additional
squadron of horse was furnished by the ingenious method of draft-
ing men and material from native Sicilians and then offering substi-
tutes if the Sicilians would train and equip them.

Having secured billeting and supply warehousing and requisition, it seems Cato partook in African raids. The green quinqueremes and quadriremes were still beached; meanwhile, the old

fleet assigned to Scipio was not in good shape. Thirty ships formerly commanded by Servilius the year before had to be patched up and repaired before they could be used. It must have been another task for the quartermaster, *quaestor* Cato, because the ships' mission was to perform a raid on the African coast to secure additional supplies and booty. This required the services of his office once again. The raiding party took troops as well as crews to ensure success on marauding strikes at the African countryside. It was at this time of building, patching, and sailing ships that Cato learned the navigational ability he displayed during his later consulship. Likely he was tutored in that art by Laelius, another gifted plebeian who was sponsored by Scipio, during this and the later African voyage. Laelius was a qualified admiral of the fleet, having commanded the navy during the conquest of New Carthage in Spain (Livy XXVI.42, 43, XXIX.1.14; Appian VIII.8; Polybius X.9.1–5).

The raids were highly successful, spreading destruction, panic, and gloom to the hearts of Carthaginians. The ships landed at Hippo Diarrhytus, just forty miles from Carthage itself. No one expected them. The Carthaginian fields and wagons were laden and unprotected. Roman ships were soon filled with spoil and supplies. Further, valuable messages were brought to Laelius by Masinissa, exiled king of the Numidians, counselling haste. These Numidians were eventually to furnish invaluable cavalry to the Roman enterprise before Carthage (Livy XXIX.3–4, 6).

Though Scipio would have liked to launch the invasion of Africa on hearing of the encouragements of Numidians, his plans were stalled temporarily by the recovery of Locri, in southern Italy. A force of three thousand men under the tribunes Sergius and Matienus was sent there on the promise of capturing the city through treachery. It supplemented the armies of propraetor Pleminius at Rhegium. Securing the city was not enough. There were problems with Pleminius later, and Scipio had to go there himself to settle the issue between his tribunes and Pleminius. The propraetor so abused his prerogatives as commander and governor that it became a cause of scandalous complaint to the Roman senate itself. The affair was then used by Scipio's enemies to form a commission to question his aptitude to command (Livy XXIX.6–9, 16–18, 21–22; Dio XVII).

Plutarch (III) has a tradition that it was in part Cato's open criticism of Scipio's method of dealing with troops while they were in

Sicily that caused the senatorial investigation of Scipio. According to this account, Scipio replied to Cato's remarks sharply, saying that he had no need of a parsimonious *quaestor* when on the way to war. Cato thereon left Sicily, Plutarch says, and joined Fabius Maximus in denouncing Scipio's life-style as well as his laxness in discipline. It was because of this attack, the biographer implies, that the senate decided to investigate.

Modern authorities say that Plutarch's account is a fabrication, particularly as it mentions nothing of Pleminius and assumes charges of moral turpitude and military discipline were sufficient cause for official inquiry. There can be no doubt that Plutarch is wrong on that count, at least. He enlarges on the moral and ethical differences between Fabius and Cato on the one hand, and Scipio on the other. Personal habits of a man with Scipio's reputation could hardly have been cause for official complaint, much less investigation. In the matter of discipline and conduct toward troops, the practices mentioned as cause for question are little different from the methods used previously by Marcellus and those that were to be used by Cato himself, as documented by Plutarch personally. They could hardly be urged as serious indictments calling for official investigation.[5]

Further, the departure of a quaestor from his appointed commission would be more serious than the faults Cato purportedly charged his commander with. Desertion would be tantamount to treason. Consul and quaestor were supposed to cooperate very closely in discharging the obligations of the consul's *provincia*. Nepos depicts the proper relation between them (I.3), pointing out that Cato did not live with Scipio as the intimacy of their association demanded. Cicero (*In Caecilium Divinatio* 61) shows that the ideal required consul and quaestor to live much as father and son. Cato was not the sort of person to violate the legal requirements of such a commission, however unable he may have been to live up to its social obligations. After all, it would be hard to treat a man just two years older, with only a little more military experience, as one's father. There may have been some jealousy in Cato's heart.

Though the differences between Scipio and Cato about life in camp were not sufficient cause for a reprimand, and especially not for a desertion of commission by Cato, Plutarch (III.4–8) is not all wrong. The idea of verbal altercation betwen the two men that he preserves, at least, must be correct. But vocal disagreement would be of little point if it were mere grumbling in barracks. Conversely, a straight technical interpretation of his commission would forbid Cato to voice complaints against his appointed commander in the hearing of common soldiers. That seems the view Cato would take of it, at any rate. The question is, when and under what circumstances during the Sicilian service did Cato oppose Scipio's methods stringently enough to cause the historical tradition Plutarch exaggeratedly records, yet not legally to breach his commission or military protocol?

Plutarch must be right in placing Cato's criticisms during the senatorial investigation of Pleminius. That was the only time during the Sicilian service when he could have received an impartial hearing from officials not involved in the provincial undertaking. The most obvious time Cato could have mentioned "problems" of this sort would have been when he took commissioners on inspection of the arsenals, magazines, and war equipment (Livy XXIX.22), his own peculiar department of the African invasion preparations. It is even possible that the praetor's commission held hearings while it was in Sicily. Livy (XXIX.20) says its method of investigation was to hold inquiries, determining Scipio's guilt or innocence that way. Yet it was empowered to arrest Scipio and suspend his command only if it decided he had ordered the deeds at Locri, and that issue had already been settled. The Locrians (XXIX.21) exonerated him of complicity in Pleminius' acts. The commission continued on its investigative journey anyway, says Livy, to see for itself whether there was any truth in the gossip about Scipio's personal life and his military discipline (Dio XVII.62 differs somewhat).

Technically, the jaunt to Sicily undertaken by this commission was unofficial and extralegal. The group had already discharged the function for which it was created. It had no authority to take any action with respect to Scipio in the light of what it had previously discovered. Their continuing perseverance has to mean that there was considerable wonderment in the senate about the accusations made by leading senators against Scipio's life and his military methods. It also means that the commission considered an inquiry into these things a part of its business. It had, in other words, received the impression that it must be able to answer the anti-Scipionic, or anti-African, element in a way that would be predictive of the success of the invasion. Thus Scipio's brave show, demonstrations, and war games for the commission would hardly be enough, even when supplemented by Cato's tour of the arsenal, unless there were some way they could determine by deeper inquiry that Scipio's personal habits and methods were beyond reproach. If in this atmosphere Cato spoke out in the way Plutarch quotes, it would at once identify him with the Roman group questioning Scipio and abundantly account for Scipio's wrath, without necessitating Cato's leaving Sicily. It would also mean that there was plentiful evidence to counteract Cato's damaging statements.

Plutarch is nearer the truth than is often supposed. He connects verbally damaging statements made to a commission investigating personal and military aspects of Scipio and Cato's possible identity with the pro-Fabian group at Rome. He errs in thinking Cato would desert his commission and return to Rome in order to make a political charge against Scipio and in assuming that the senatorial commission's Sicilian visit was a part of its official function, rather than a mere side trip with secondary importance. The latter is hardly surprising, since the committee at its return reported on personal and military matters, praising Scipio, his army, and the fleet. The senate voted for the invasion, empowering Scipio to select any forces he chose from the Sicilian army for that purpose (Livy XXIX.22.11). Later annalists reporting the doings of the commission in governmental records that stated the reason for going to Sicily would receive the same impression as Plutarch, unless they troubled to read back in the account to the written commission (cp. Dio XVII.62).

Scipio exercised no sanctions against his quaestor, merely deriding his parsimonious ideals. He could hardly afford to dispense with the services of a man so efficient in his job as this particular quartermaster or to forego the leadership of one who so readily identified with the older "Marcellan" soldiers he had separated as an assault team, especially on the eve of invasion. Without doubt, also, Scipio's leniency toward Cato's breach of military etiquette resulted from gratitude for the invaluable work the latter had done in making Scipio's "African amendment" possible: supplying men and material without an official levy by canvassing his home and neighboring territories. Thus not only did Cato escape censure for his temerity, but he also participated in the glorious enterprise against Carthage and, indeed, commanded a part of the invasion flotilla's naval escort (Livy XXIX.25.10).

The quaestor was immediately pressed into further responsibility. Orders went out from Scipio that all men and material should rally at Lilybaeum, the westernmost port in Sicily (Livy XXIX.24). That became the staging area for the invasion. Cato had to supervise the transshipment of all supplies to that place and to see to the requisition of merchant vessels needed for troopships and freight. These were secured by simple seizure of both ships and crews docking anywhere in Sicily and their impressment in Roman service. Four hundred vessels were gathered in this way, in addition to the naval ships of war. The harbor was too small to contain them all, and they spilled over into the sea. Similarly, the town was unable to accommodate the sheer number of soldiers sent there. The Cannae legions mentioned before were each sixty-two hundred strong. The sick and aged were replaced by volunteers brought from Italy. That contingent, in turn, had been seven thousand men. Add the horse Livy mentions, and it is certain that the invasion army numbered close to twenty thousand. Dead reckoning shows there to have been at least nine hundred cavalry.[6]

The men had to embark immediately, because of their numbers, and live on board until departure (Livy XXIX.25.5–6). Crews were also kept aboard, but Cato's duties grew because of this. Even though the task of loading supplies was shifted, the burden was tremendous. Scipio ordered Pomponius, praetor of Sicily, to assume the freightage, but that was a minor relief. Cato was a fleet commander (Livy XXIX.25.10). He had naval duties, including the supervision of hauling and loading on the ships under his command. There would be matters of signalling and stationing and emergency in fog and dark to arrange. Cato had a fourth of the fleet, one hundred ships, to provide for. To make matters worse, crews had to be sent into the mountains to cut and shape the stakes with which the palisade of the first African camp was to be made (Dio XVII.63). Catapults, mangonels, ballistas, and siege machines of Cato's assault team had to be loaded aboard ships (Livy XXIX.35.8). Extra duties were expected of the quartermaster's corps because of the army's living aboard. These tasks were over and above the loading of supplies and so must have been performed by Cato's corps. Scipio ordered food and water for forty-five days, including cooked rations for fifteen days, to provide for life aboard in port and during the voyage. The mind boggles at the numbers of additional men Cato had to draft and the huge, continuous cooking fires he must have had built so as to prepare fifteen days' food for twenty thousand

soldiers besides the ships' crews. No wonder Pomponius was ordered to assume the comparatively light burden of ferrying the
supplies out to the ships. Perhaps Cato acquired much of that cooking lore and knowledge of recipes displayed in his treatise *On Agriculture* (LXXI–XC) during this tour of duty in Sicily.

While all this "kitchen work" progressed, a meeting of the cap-
tains, pilots, and soldiers' representatives from each ship was called
(Livy XXIX.25.7–10). Cato, as a commander of the fleet, must also
have attended that briefing. Reports on each vessel's supplies were
made, and soldiers were told what to do when the fleet got under
way, so as not to interfere with the crew. Signals were arranged, and
each ship's pilot was given his sailing orders. Then the chain of
command was announced: Scipio and his brother Lucius commanded the twenty warships on the right wing of the convoy;
Laelius, technically admiral of the fleet, and Marcus Cato commanded the twenty naval vessels on the left. It is indeed a commentary on Cato's navigational ability that he, who was already far over-
burdened, was also pressed into service as "vice admiral." Cato
must have shown remarkable managerial ability, since Scipio felt he
could assign so many duties to him without sacrificing efficiency.

IV   *The African Campaign: The First Season*

It must have been spectacular. Livy (XXIX.26–27) speaks of the
excited throng that crowded the water's edge to see the great ar-
mada off. When the ships were stationed at assigned intervals, the
convoy must have stretched out of sight over the horizon. At dawn a
flagship herald thundered for silence as a prayer was said and a
victim sacrificed, its entrails flung into the deep in order to assure
good fortune. A trumpet blast gave the signal to cast off, and a fair
wind bore them quickly out of sight of land.

There were tense moments during that voyage, as the wind fell
off and heavy fog settled over the flotilla. Collision was difficult to
avoid, in the throng of 450 ships. The drills and signals that had
been arranged ashore now paid dividends. Most of the journey was
spent in fog, but the breeze blew gently, making it easy to sheer off
before ramming other vessels. It was a short voyage—exactly ninety
miles west by southwest from Lilybaeum to the first headland in
Africa. On the morning of the second day, as the breeze freshened,
dissipating the fog, land was sighted. Scipio decided it was too far
from Carthage and ordered more sail set so as to penetrate farther

into the bay of Tunis. When fog again descended, many must have thought the gods unfavorable. Scipio was muttering prayers to ensure that this first sight of land was an auspicious one. The fleet had to drop anchor so as to avoid ramming or running aground in the fog when night fell. The morning breeze again dispelled the fog, revealing the entire African coast. It was the Cape of the Beautiful One, and Scipio thought the name a good omen (Livy XXIX.27.6–13). The wind had pushed them fifty miles since the previous day, across the mouth of the bay to its western lip. They landed on the promontory of Apollo (The Beautiful One) (Appian VIII.13).

Immediately the Romans sought security. They laid out a camp on the nearest heights, not knowing what their reception might be or what preparations had been made against them (Livy XXIX.28–29). But Carthaginians, admirable wagers of war in foreign lands, now seemed incapable of foresight or planning. They had known for well over a year that there would be an invasion, yet now at the moment of truth, they proved to have taken little thought for the particulars of defense. Scipio was able not only to establish his camp without interference but also to occupy neighboring heights with cavalry pickets. He sent the fleet towards Utica. The amount of activity implied in those few words, particularly for our young quaestor, was formidable. All the remaining supplies, rations for forty days and cooked food for ten, had to be put in the camp *quaestorium* and *forum* under Cato's watchful eye (Polybius VI.27). Further, Scipio sent cavalry around to plunder the countryside. The state share of that plunder became also a part of the quaestor's stores, to be disbursed as needed or sent off to Rome.

The first engagement between Scipio and Carthage, with its rout of enemy cavalry and the consequent occupation of a town, resulted in more work. The spoil and supply now reached such proportions that it had to be loaded on transports and sent off to Sicily. Eight thousand persons, both free and slave, were captured. Doubtless some of these were dispatched to Italy later. Others, especially if they had mechanical skills, were interned in the arsenal. It is likely that Cato used them there for the construction of siege engines—he may have been commander of the assault team, if our former guesses are right (Livy XXIX.29.2, 35.8).

A second engagement between Carthaginians and Scipio, this time with the exiled Numidian King Masinissa aiding the Romans, also ended victoriously for Roman troops. Again, the triumph was

scant comfort to Cato. No sooner had the Sicilian transports returned than they had to be reloaded with new spoil and sent to
Sicily again because of the abundance of supply. It seems this was
entirely a matter of quaestor's business. Yet it was but a beginning:
Scipio continued to lay waste the countryside, bringing in great
numbers of men and cattle and vast amounts of booty. The transports were sent away loaded with plunder a third time (Livy
XXIX.35). Then as though ending the preliminaries, Scipio
mounted a siege of Utica, for he had determined to use it as a base.
Laelius attacked with marines, while Scipio beset the city from hills
overlooking it and Cato with his assault team battered the city walls
(Appian VIII.16).

Forty days, precisely to the beginning of winter, were spent in
the attempt to reduce Utica by assault. But its walls were proof
against the Roman engines. Once again, apparently, Cato was involved in the construction and supervision of *sambucae*. Appian
mentions the use of galleys lashed together by twos as a platform for
a tower from which engines hurled missiles three cubits (forearms:
17–21 inches each) long, together with great stones, at the enemy.
They both inflicted damage and sustained it from the return fire.
Towers and ships were shattered without having done sufficient
damage to the city's defenses. Livy's statement that marines were
used on the seaward side would seem to mean that they worked
with these ship towers. On the landward side, mounds were built as
causeways on which battering rams could advance against the city
walls. But to use these rams effectively, the Romans had to tear off
the hides covering the stones of the walls and blunting the ram's
blows. They had hooks for that purpose.

None of these methods was successful. Utica withstood the assault by turning aside the hooks tearing at hides, by dropping great
beams upon the battering rams crosswise, breaking them, and by
sallying forth against the siege engines with fire when the wind was
favorable. After forty days of this futile effort, the appearance of
large armies under Hasdrubal and Numidian King Syphax to the
rear of Scipio's position forced the latter to lift the siege and fortify a
winter camp a mile away from Utica (Dio XVII.69).

There should have been time enough to take Utica, if the siege
techniques had been adequate. But the shattered Roman naval
siege towers and ships prove Carthaginian return fire was as devastating as that of Archimedes' engines. Accurate missile fire must also

have prevented use of such tactics as sheds and mantlets, under the shelter of which battering rams and other instruments could have been employed more effectively. This technique was familiar, though unsuccessfully used, as early as 218 B.C. in Spain under Scipio's uncle (Livy XXI.61). Cato used sheds and mantlets effectively in Spain in 195 B.C. (XXXIV.17.12). Consul and quaestor obviously knew about this technique, yet they rejected it. One cannot say there was a lack of timber, because that was the main material in the mounds and siege engines. The *vineae*, or *pluteis*, as they were called, could have been built up the *agger* (mound) against the wall. Spanish walls and methods of defense must have been significantly weaker than those of Africa (cp. Caesar, *Bel. Civ.* II.1).

Castra Corneliana, the winter camp, was easily defensible (Caesar, *Bel. Civ.* II.24), a peninsula joined to land by a narrow ridge. There the warships were beached, and the permanent camp occupied the center of the promontory. Winter meant no rest (Livy XXIX.35–36). Cato converted rapidly from the building and maintaining of *sambucae* and heavy artillery to the construction of new granaries. So many food supplies were being sent from anxious Roman commanders elsewhere (XXIX.36, XXX.3) that the granaries could not hold it all. The quartermaster had to build new ones. But the army needed clothing also. Twelve hundred new togas and twelve thousand tunics were sent in from Sardinia and other places. Officials continued to send other supplies also: weapons and other kinds of clothing. Cato's precinct, the *quaestorium* and *forum*, must have been as busy and full of supplies as any such department in the army ever was.

During the elections for the year 203 B.C. further proof of the Roman willingness to stake all on Scipio's African campaign and the possible destruction of Carthage herself was given. Scipio's command was extended, but for an indefinite period not to be limited by a specific date; it was to last until the successful conclusion of the African campaign. A *supplicatio* was decreed for the blessing of Scipio's safe journey to Africa (Livy XXX.1.10–11). Cato and a few others must have been vexed with the unusual nature of these events; the constitutional purists probably demurred. Scipio's career, from the view of such constitutional purists, presented numerous questionable instances. He was elected by the people at the instigation of the senate (Livy XXVI.18–20) to a Spanish procon-

sulship in 210 B.C., having previously held only the military
tribuneship and curule aedileship (XXII.53.1, XXV.2.6); he was the
first *privatus* (private citizen) given proconsular ranking. The year
209 B.C. saw an unusual continuation of that Spanish command
(XXVII.7.17, 22.7) until such time as the senate might choose to
recall him, even though they saw fit to renew the *imperium* the
following year. In 205 B.C. Scipio's *provincia* was extended to include an extraordinary command beyond Sicily, and it occasioned
great conservative wrath and necessitated unusual compromise. Finally, the senate prorogued the African *imperium* in turn until its
successful conclusion in victory.

One might say that the career of this man, Scipio, initiated the
policy of unusual *imperia* and extraordinary commands that have
caused many authorities to speculate that Rome now grew beyond
city-state size and institutions. None can argue the reality of unusal
commands, or for that matter, the necessity for them. If these particulars conspired ultimately to create a feeling of illegality or un-
constitutionality that encouraged habitual winking at the law or
setting aside the constitution, it would be difficult to say that Scipio
or the city-state institutions were at fault. Scipio's rationale for the
African campaign was that of forcing Hannibal to leave Italy—not
that of conquest for the acquisition of land and wealth. Precisely the
same considerations of military necessity urged his Spanish campaign. Having begun the long, ruinous Punic Wars, Rome's extraordinary and technically unconstitutional actions were a foregone
conclusion. Placing the blame for the failure of city-state institutions
is therefore a matter of resolving the causes for the war in the
beginning.

The underlying and immediate causes of the Second Punic War,
if one may briefly digress, are matters for contentious discussion.
The underlying causes customarily asserted seem irrelevant. To say
that there was not room in the western Mediterranean for both
Rome and Carthage, for instance, is tenuous. Rome, as shown above
(p. 35), had contracted that peculiar sickness of successful
militants—insecurity. Her growing capability had encouraged an
increasingly aggressive policy of defense that, by the time of this
war, had bloated to the proportions of "offensive defense" policy.
That rationale, as usual, allowed artificial extensions of the defense
perimeter outside Italy and halfway around the known world—
farther and farther from Rome but always in the name of "home

defense" and "security." Ultimately it would be possible, under this species of insanity, to construe a nasty look or a dirty word from one individual over a thousand miles from Rome as an aggressive act against the city. Invest that potentiality with emotions of pride and honor, and the likelihood of instant confrontation and ensuing war are multiplied a hundredfold. Rome's military success and her defense establishment, always in the name of "security," were behind the war, not the modern concept of *"lebensraum."*

These considerations explain the events of Saguntum and the causes of the Second Punic War. Rome made a treaty with Saguntum that violated a previous accord with Carthage. Hannibal attacked Saguntum legally, by the provisions of the accord, but this activated the secret nonaggression pact Rome had made with that city. Hannibal knew the attack would provoke war because embassies from Rome told him so. But Rome had originally broken its accord, and it was the madness of artificial extension and the fiction of "international security" that had operated to cause her now to speak of an act out of her sphere and halfway around the known world as a deed of wanton aggression against the city of Rome. It is distressing to observe how many moderns exonerate Rome and implicitly approve.

V *The African Campaign: The Second Season*

Spring saw another Roman triumph by trickery. Scipio was enabled to burn the camps of both Syphax and Hasdrubal because they had incautiously made their huts from wood and reeds not covered with any kind of earth. To reconnoiter both camps, Scipio pretended interest in Syphax's pet idea of Roman withdrawal from Africa and Carthaginian withdrawal from Italy, peacefully negotiated (Polybius XIV.1–3; Livy XXX.3.1); observant "envoys" could enter both camps. Similarly, Scipio showed intentions of renewing the siege at Utica, launching his ships with artillery aboard. All was a "show" to divert the attention of Numidians and Carthaginians from his real objective. Since Cato was the person most probably charged with shipboard implements and catapults and since the other commanders, including Scipio himself, were concerned with the attack on the enemy camps, Cato may well have commanded this feint against Utica. It required two thousand men to occupy the hill above the town, as well as ships on station as if to attack from the sea. The ships were important, since the siege was pressed later and they became permanent artillery emplacements, as though they were the *aggeres*, or mounds, Romans ordinarily built on land. The descriptions of Livy make it plain that *sambucae* were built on some of these ships before Utica (XXX.10.1–3). Cato was doubtless the craftsman, once again.

Scipio managed the burning of camps well. Syphax and Hasdrubal lost their armies with great casualties. Livy, with touching concern for the "honor" of this affair, notes that Scipio faithfully terminated the pretense of a negotiated settlement before the fires were set (XXX.4.8). It shows Livy's possession of a moral and ethical sense, though the indifferent application of that sense elsewhere is cause for great concern. The termination is not mentioned by Polybius (XIV.2.10–14), and it is possible that Livy's story is entirely false. If that is true, it would seem that Livy's sense of morality in negotiations was so poignant that it caused him to falsify history. The slaughter of thousands did not elicit such feeling (see also Polybius XIV.4–5; Livy XXX.5–6; Appian VIII.20–23; Dio XVII.72).

When the booty had been transferred to camp, Scipio decided to press once more the siege of Utica. What had formerly been sham now became full-scale siege. But Syphax and Hasdrubal surprised him by collecting another army in short order and threatening the Romans once again, thirty thousand strong. Scipio routed this army too with little difficulty. The battle was won by the Roman and Numidian cavalry, which drove in the wings and outflanked the enemy. The rest was pursuit and slaughter. Afterward, Scipio determined to consolidate his position more firmly: He conquered or terrified the neighboring Carthaginian cities into submission. But in one sense the victories militated against Rome. Carthage decided to send a delegation to Hannibal requesting his immediate return to Africa. Scipio was to be faced by the ultimate enemy, Hannibal. In the meantime Carthage launched her fleet and prepared to harass the besieging fleet at Utica. Scipio had occupied Tunis, expecting to make it his final base before Carthage. He was forced to send the hordes of prisoners and booty he had accumulated to the old camp at Utica and then to follow himself when he discovered that the Carthaginian fleet was sailing toward Utica (Livy XXX.7–9; Polybius XIV.7–11).

Cato's part in all this was doubtless that of remaining with the siege and disposing of the booty sent to the old camp. When Scipio and the army arrived to warn of the impending sea attack and defend the fleet, it was decided to sacrifice freighters rather than dismantle the siege engines and the *sambucae* (Livy XXX. 10–11). Consequently the siege progressed in spite of the ensuing attack by Carthaginian ships. To protect his warships, lying bows-on to the shore, Scipio lashed freighters together four deep to seaward; the Carthaginians attacked them ineffectively with missiles. Finally they used grapnels attached to chains or heavy wooden poles impossible to cut and by means of backing the oars towed sixty Roman freighters off to Carthage, stern foremost. The Carthaginians considered this a great victory, though Livy says they were "clutching at straws" and overestimated its effect (XXX. 10). Appian implies the sacrifice of freighters was deliberate, devised by the man in command at the naval station, but misplaces the location of the encounter and underestimates the losses suffered by Rome (VIII. 25). The fragment of Polybius (XV. 1) says considerable supplies were lost with these vessels, directly contradicting both Livy and Appian. However, the first two agree that Carthage was encouraged greatly by this slight triumph.

Sometime during that summer, 203 B.C., Scipio lifted the siege of Utica and transported the engines to Hippo. He was thenceforth forced to settle for Castra Corneliana, his permanent camp outside Utica, as the primary African depot, since the siege of Hippo was also unsuccessful. Cato again must have had much to do with the maneuvers at Hippo. At the conclusion of this frustrating effort, Scipio had the siege engines burned as useless. This futility, with Cato's earlier lack of constancy during the commission investigations in Sicily, did not endear the quaestor to Scipio. These two seemed destined to abrade each other at every turn. The result was that Scipio, at every opportunity, chose others to crucial command posts—Laelius, Baebius, and so on. But of course Cato had much to do with supplies. Quaestors were not ordinarily commanders in the field (Appian VIII. 30).

The year 203 saw Masinissa, with the help of Laelius, recapture Numidia and then Syphax himself. This was to Rome's advantage because Masinissa and Laelius marched to rejoin Scipio with six thousand Numidian infantry and four thousand horse. Laelius was sent to escort Syphax and other noble prisoners to Rome, as Scipio reoccupied Tunis. There he received the Carthaginian Privy Council, which sued for peace. Sent because of the defeat of Syphax, in whom they had mistakenly placed great hopes, they approached

Scipio in the eastern fashion, prostrating themselves and blaming others. They indicted Hannibal and his supporters rather than themselves. Scipio proposed peace terms and gave three days for decision. The Carthaginians agreed to an armistice on those terms and sent envoys to the senate at Rome, a ploy for time until Hannibal should return (Livy XXX.11–16, 29.4; Appian VIII.26–33; Polybius XV.4.4, 5.11).

Laelius and his prisoners reached Rome and amid great jubilation reported to the senate. Livy has the immaturity to distinguish between the "genteel" manner of "great rejoicing and high hopes" in the senate and the "unbounded delight" the people were unable to suppress but must "express by shouting and such other means as the multitude commonly employs" (XXX.17.1–7). The historian is thus revealed in another kind of bifocalism. Surely commoners would be as hushed in the senate hall and senators as boisterous in the midst of the mob were their stations reversed. Further, men crave a certain intemperance; better they express it shouting in a mob than by rapacity in the provinces, as the senators did. There were far more serious problems that year.

T. Claudius Nero, elected consul for 202, was allowed to draw Africa as a *provincia*, though the people all voted for Scipio to conduct the war in Africa and he had been given command for the duration (Livy XXX.1.10, 23.3). Yet Nero was voted an *imperium* equal to that of Scipio with the title of *imperator*. It was, however, limited to the sea and a navy of fifty quinqueremes and confined to Sicily if Scipio made peace with Carthage (XXX.40.12). Yet in another place Livy says Africa was the province of Nero (XXX.27.1–6) and he had equal *imperium* there with Scipio. Livy has a third version (XXX.23.3–6)—that the senate had voted that authority over the terms of peace be granted through Scipio and that Nero's ambition was frustrated by that decision (XXX.38–39).

It is difficult to know what the situation was, in all this contradiction. Livy's confusion may well reflect differing versions in his own annalistic sources, but even that betokens the annalists' uncertainty about the event. In other words, this seems again to have been a secret compromise of the sort managed by Scipio in 205 to widen his Sicilian *provincia*. This time, however, it was engineered by the opponents of Scipio. The efforts of Q. Caecilius Metellus stopped the proceedings in the senate and forced a referendum to the *comitia tributa*, which voted unanimously for Scipio (Livy XXX.27.2–

4). The compromise then took effect and forced the senate to allot the *provincia* of Africa anyway, under a technicality whereby the rights of citizens were invoked and the senators voted under oath (XXX.40.12). Nevertheless, Nero's *imperium* was limited to the navy and effective in Africa only if peace could not be arranged (cp. Livy XXVI.33.14).

At that point in the "shenanigans," something even more exceptional must have occurred. The senate itself, Livy says in the third version (XXX.38.7), voted authority over the peace terms to Scipio rather than to the consul T. Claudius Nero. If that is so, in spite of the compromise maneuvers of the "anti-Scipions," it means that some pro-Scipionic group took the play completely away from others and decreed that Scipio should arrange the peace terms. This, in turn, would deny the ascendancy of the Servilian-Claudian group that is supposedly reflected by the elections of 203 and 202 and contradict the influence modern authority has imputed to ancient "power blocs" (Scullard, pp. 78–80). The whole consulship of T. Claudius Nero was spent in maudlin "dithering" because of this (Livy XXX.38.7, 39.1–4). Deprived of supervision over the peace terms, he was spiritless and lazy about readying his fleet. When he finally did leave, slovenly management and poor navigation got the flotilla wrecked in a sudden storm. By the time that in turn was repaired, the year was over and Tiberius had to return to Rome, having never been in his *provincia*.

The remarkable thing about all this, in conclusion, is that Scipio himself knew nothing about the final arrangement. Again one reiterates that if vital and influential groups, such as family coalitions or pro- and anti-Scipionic blocs, existed, Scipio would surely have been informed of events. Yet Livy proves he was not by saying that Scipio made peace with Carthage, rather than besiege the city itself after Zama, because of his anxiety that a replacement would assume his command and have the glory of finishing the war after others like himself had won it (XXX.36.11). This fact is repeated again by Livy, driving the point home (XXX.44.3).

Another singular action by the senate was making Laelius a quaestor not by lot but by senatorial decree: *quaestor extra sortem ex senatus consulto* (Livy XXX.33.2–3). No election was involved; one cannot easily assess the significance of this event. It is tempting to read anti-Scipionic overtones into the action because Laelius previously enjoyed the full confidence of Scipio as a prefect of the fleet and a *legatus* in the army (Livy XXX.9, 11, 12, 14.2, XXIX.25.10). Since he was Scipio's right arm, an appointment like this would seem to be a demotion. It may be that a conservative element in the senate wished to place Laelius forcefully on a par with Cato. The *senatus consultum* itself is not mentioned at the time of the creation. It is possible that the quaestorship of Laelius was a part of the compromise arrangement that gave Tiberius Claudius Nero his "*imperium par cum P. Scipione*," though the official designation of each is different: "*senatus consultum*" for Laelius and "*senatus decreverat*" for Tiberius (Livy XXX.27.4). These designations made no difference in Scipio's plans for Laelius. He continued to use the man as a second in command and a line lieutenant, no matter what the decree or intent of the senate.

There were two quaestors in Scipio's command from the beginning of the consular year 202 on. Laelius continued to share specifically in command, posted over the Italic cavalry, but Cato was doubtless trusted in matters of supply and disbursement. Later references in Livy to the quaestors of Scipio prove there were now two rather than one, thereby establishing that Cato was still with Scipio at the battle of Zama (XXX.38.1).

It is not the purpose of this biography to document the end of the Punic War—particularly the issues surrounding location and time of the battle of Zama. Scipio won; Hannibal lost, despite sound planning (Livy XXX.33–36). Livy has preserved a terrible little vignette featuring a personal confrontation between Hannibal and Scipio, calculated to prove the war guilt of Carthage (XXX.30–31). This horridly contrived artificiality was to have taken place before the battle, so that the battle itself could be the final vindication of Roman justice. The pitiful statements of Scipio, as quoted by Livy, lay the blame for Saguntum on Carthage and "arm Rome with the weapons of duty and justice." But even though the historian thinks to set the judgment of destiny, Hannibal's words shine through his inept summary, contrasting with Scipio's callow chauvinism as dark with daylight. The former, through a lifetime of futile militarism and suffering coupled with tearful triumphs, had learned the superior merits of peace. He sought to make Scipio the beneficiary of that experience, but the boy general had sniffed the sweat of Punic fear like a bulldog taught "sic 'em" at Roman hearths. He would not learn to heel until he also gagged on the leash of human inconstancy. Now, however, his illusions reigned; the only sure, honorable way to peace was by defeat of the enemy.

After the triumph of Zama, Scipio plundered the enemy camp and, with a fleet augmented by fifty sail, closed in on Carthage herself. A relieving Numidian army under the son of Syphax was routed, and then thirty councillors, this time in earnest, decided to beseech Rome's mercy once again. Scipio was inclined to make peace rather than besiege Carthage because of Claudius Nero's likely arrival to succeed him in command and because of his sorry experience with siege warfare at Utica and Hippo (Livy XXX.36).

VI *Peace with Carthage: The Terms and Politics*

The terms of peace set by Scipio left Carthage her own territory in North Africa intact, along with internal autonomy. However, her foreign affairs were regulated, Spain was forfeit, all but ten warships must be given up together with all war elephants, and Carthage must pay 10,000 talents war indemnity over the next fifty years. An armistice for the ratification of peace terms by both sides was made contingent upon the return of the ships and crews lost during the previous armistice, or the money equivalent thereof. (During the previous armistice one hundred ships with supplies from Sardinia and two hundred from Sicily had reached Africa, but most of the latter had been scattered by adverse winds and then captured by Carthage in spite of the armistice.) Hannibal, according to Livy, considered these terms so lenient that he dragged an opposing speaker from the public rostrum in outrage lest he sway the assembly of Carthage against the peace (XXX.37)

The armistice being agreed upon, it was up to the quaestors of the Roman general to determine the public loss suffered from wrecked or captured ships by a study of their quaestorial account books. Owners of private property in cargo were to do the same for their reparation. Since Laelius had but recently been made quaestor and then been used as a line officer, this burden of making up the public loss account fell entirely on Cato. Far worse, it was decided to facilitate the peace by accepting one lump sum of twenty-five thousand pounds of silver in lieu of total settlement, after Cato had laboriously summed up a loss account. Adding insult to injury, the weary quaestor had to receive all private claims for personal loss and settle them. Nor was that all. The grain supplies from Sicily and Sardinia had depressed the price of grain in the market so much that merchants used grain rather than specie to pay freightage. That left the quaestors with another headache—the settlement of freight costs and sale of excess grain. The latter could not be managed.

Monstrous amounts of grain were stockpiled there in the African dockyards, to be transshipped to Rome later and sold cheaply to the poor citizens. The facility with which it was handled at that time speaks volumes, once again, for Cato's managerial abilities. Happily, it worked to the betterment of Cato's political image then, for he was a newly elected aedile whose duties included management of the public grain supply (Livy XXX.38, XXXI.4.6, 50.1).

The elections for 201 again hinged on the issue of the province of Africa. This time the tribunes of the plebs pointed out what had happened to T. Claudius Nero who ignored the wishes of the people and came to grief the previous year (Livy XXX.40.9). Scipio's command in Africa was continued with the armies he already possessed, and the consul for the year was given Nero's former naval *imperium* with a fleet of fifty ships (XXX.41.1). The consul, Cn. Cornelius Lentulus, attempted to continue the war so that he might have the honor of ending it (XXX.40.7, 43.1). He stopped the peace negotiations by the rare expedient of a consular veto. Thereupon the tribunes of the plebs once again brought the matter before the people who voted unanimously that peace should be made, that Scipio should negotiate it and bring back the army (XXX.43.4). The senate then decreed that Scipio, on the advice of ten envoys, should make peace with Carthage on such terms as he saw fit. The fetial priests, who supervised the making of peace and war, were dispatched to Africa for that purpose, with their flint knives for the sacrifice and the sacred herbs from the Capitoline hill to solemnize the peace proceedings (Livy XXX.43.4–10; Polybius XIX.2).

Peace was made on the basis of the terms stated before the armistice. The entire Carthaginian fleet was surrendered and burned at sea—five hundred vessels, it was estimated. The war elephants were turned over to the Romans, along with Roman deserters, runaway slaves, and four thousand captives, including one senator. The fleet was ordered to Rome, and the ten envoys were to carry the agreed terms to the Roman senate and the Roman people for confirmation (Livy XXX.43.11–13). Finally, the army was transported back to Lilybaeum (XXX.45.1–7). Most were then transshipped to Rome, but some provided an escort for Scipio who travelled to Rome by land, greeted as a savior and lionized as a hero all the way. He entered Rome in the most distinguished of all triumphs and deposited 123,000 pounds weight of silver in the public treasury, having already distributed 400 *asses* worth to each of the soldiers. This last act Cato would have disapproved, had he been with the army during the triumph and demobilization. It would have been an official disapproval, not a personal one, as Cato made the same sort of donative in his consulship (Plutarch X.4). More strenuous would have been his disagreement with the final and later act of the senate with respect to Scipio's soldiers.

At the very end of the year 201 B.C., just before the elections, a distribution of lands in Samnium and Apulia was made by an appointed decemvirate (board of ten men) for the veterans who fought under Scipio (Livy XXXI.4.1–4, 49.5). Seemingly, the reason may have been the volunteer status of many veterans who had served Scipio. Apparently Scipio had seen fit to promise land to those who enlisted for the African campaign. Necessary as this may have been from the view of military expediency, it was the first precedent for that combination of factors that later created the professional army of Marius with all of its attendant failings.

Cato, according to Nepos' tradition (I.4), was not in the triumphal procession because he went to Sardinia upon leaving Africa. It was part of his duty as quartermaster to return surplus imperishable supplies that had been sent to Africa by Sardinian businessmen and to settle accounts for the supplies that had been lost when a fleet foundered with its cargo on the way to Africa during the armistice of 203 B.C. The quaestors had to handle and settle claims by private merchants for their property lost in that event, it will be remembered (Livy XXIX.36.1–2, XXX.19.5, 24.5–10, 38.1–2). Sicilian claims were doubtless settled by quaestor Laelius and perhaps Scipio himself. The poet Ennius returned with Cato from Sardinia to Rome. Ennius had been on duty as a centurion on the island, and his tour must have been over. Roman troops in Sardinia had apparently seen long service. Two years later Cato, as governor (praetor) of that island, was required to recruit new troops so that he could send home over two thousand veterans (Livy XXXII.8.8). Nepos (I.4) affects to see more benefit to Rome in Ennius' return than all the possible victories in Sardinia.

Whatever the benefit to Rome, it is likely that Cato himself profited from this association with Ennius. He probably learned Greek at this time, tutored by the poet during the remainder of 201, through 200, and in whatever spare time his aedileship of 199 B.C. allowed. Ennius, though an "inferior" allied citizen, must have been readily accepted at Rome. He came from Rudiae in Calabria, which had been a part of Magna Graecia, and therefore he knew Greek as well as Latin. Perhaps he studied at Tarentum. In the final analysis, no enduring friendship was developed as a result of the tutelage. Yet Cato, by the evidence of Plutarch, did know Greek just ten years later, and there is no other time he could have learned it. Ennius became the friend of Scipio, however, rather than of Cato. His liberal ideas were irritants to the conservative mind (Plutarch XII.4).

Cato must have spent a welcome year at home, perhaps even working in the fields with his domestics as he used to do. There was not much time for that, however. The following years show Cato had a lot to do with the revival of a conservative group of senators who formerly considered themselves followers of Fabius Maximus. At the time of his discharge from service in Africa and through the year 200, Cato could only have been planning the pursuit of curule magistracy so that he could join the ranks of the senate and exercise most influence. The patronage of Publius Valerius assured him of attaining that end, as did the friendship of Lucius the son. Future political battles beckoned, to be sure. The death of Fabius in 203 had left the hard-core conservatives without leadership. They merged, in the last years of the century, into a generalized anti-Scipionic coalition dominated by the Servilian and Claudian clans, though there is great danger in overasserting the coalition's influence (Scullard, chap. 6). The obvious reasons for saying Servilians and Claudians dominated is that they and their friends were more frequently elected to high office in those years. Yet, as shown above, the group proved incapable of asserting its policy in the senate and, more crucially, in the assembly. Scipio got his way in both, even though he was absent from the city. Since the whole idea of the political bloc in this period depends upon the extent of its influence through familial connections in the senate and through clientage in the assembly so that it could deliver votes and implement policy, it is obvious that no conservative bloc worthy of that definition existed. Cato, then, was not so much anxious to lead a political bloc as he was to ensure a conservative hearing or voice in the Roman senate. He was capable of ingratiating himself with Claudians.

One of the Claudians, Gaius Claudius Nero, had been Cato's commander at the battle of Metaurus River in 207. It will be remembered that Cato is said to have won high praise at that battle, probably as military tribune. Scullard hazards a close tie (p. 58) and agreement between Marcellus and Fabius that involved gentile patronage for Marcellus in the years 217 to 213 B.C. and beyond. The Claudii, particularly Gaius, served under Marcellus extensively and, until the period after the death of Fabius, were a part of the anti-Scipionic group. Cato fits into that configuration because the Valerii were tied familially to the Fabians (Scullard, p. 111, n.4). Cato's Valerian affiliation continued to be vitally important to his political plans. He now ran for the aedileship while Lucius Valerius was a successful candidate for the praetorship in Sicily. Moreover, they were colleagues for the consulship in 195 (Livy XXXI.49.12, XXXII.7.13, XXXIII.42.7).

VII *Effects of the Punic Wars on Rome*

This year, in which Cato prepared to run for the aedileship, studied Greek, worked on the farm, and practiced law in Roman tribunals, was crucial in Roman history. It was a year that saw Rome weigh the issue of intervention in the East and continued militarism against peace and her own exhausted state. The decision was crucial for the future of the Republic as for the East. The Punic Wars had practically assured the fall of the Roman Republic; the decision to campaign in the East sealed her doom. The eastern involvement lasted for the remainder of Cato's life, so that the events of this year affected the orientation of his entire existence.

The fate of the Roman Republic was sealed by the Punic Wars, though that is a statement to be made only in retrospect—the Romans were not aware of it—and in knowledge of the factors that ultimately caused the fall of the Republic. This statement is not one of historical determinism; it recognizes only that Rome might have averted a fall if she had known one was coming.

Part of the consequence of these wars was the weakening of the constitutional provisions governing the *imperium* and the magisterial or *curule* offices of the administration. There can be no doubt of the necessity for such redefinitions as were temporarily made in the course of war emergency or for reasons of imperial expansion; the problem was failure to recognize that necessity by permanent alteration of the constitution. The alterations should then have been provided with adequate legal safeguards to prevent violations of the sort that became common in the last century of the Republic. What happened instead was a reassertion of the old customary definition of the magistracy and its *imperium*, first by electoral consensus and then by the *Lex Villia Annalis*. Though Rome had grown to an empire, she was singularly unwilling to recognize that fact by reform of her constitution. As a matter of fact, Rome was at first uninterested in territorial acquisition, and some of the decisions she was to make during the eastern involvement show her complete lack of desire for such expansion.

Other consequences of the Punic Wars were fully as devastating. They virtually eliminated the vital liberal element that had created the democratic republic—the plebeian class (defining "democratic" as the principle of self-determination implicit in a "one-man-one-vote," legally equalitarian electorate). They also decimated the ranks of the senate, which had learned, by cooperation with that class, to respect the plebeians and accord them the privilege of self-expression. Both were casualties to the victories of Hannibal and the destruction of entire, successive consular armies. Perhaps the element that suffered most was the rural group of rugged small farmers that formed the backbone of the Roman citizen militia. This portion, by reason of its effectual isolation from the sophistication of the city, was, like Cato himself, the more intensely and traditionally "Roman" element in the Republic. With its loss, and considering the alienism and the Hellenization of the urban population, the "Latin Romanism" Cato struggled to resurrect disappeared. Consequently, appeals to the past, to the tradition of conservative democracy or republicanism, fell on deaf ears. Rome presented the spectacle of enforcing anachronistic constitutonalism on people who had not fought for it and had little appreciation of its meaning.

The rural population could not be replaced, and a comprehensive program of land repatriation and agricultural revitalization was entirely too late in coming. Over the years after 200, hardy farmers in the army were gradually replaced by men whose main motive was personal gain rather than patriotism. These felt little sense of belonging and were not morally responsible citizens whose army was a militia of proud individuals. The latter, as law-abiding Romans, would have refused to march with Marius or Sulla or Caesar against their own fatherland. Now the army became increasingly self-sustaining, independent, professional, and non-Roman.

The difficulties of returning to the farm after the Second Punic War were well-nigh insuperable. Many had been burned out by the sixteen years of "scorched earth" Fabian warfare. If farmers were now to borrow money, it would be at a high rate of interest, and a large sum would be needed to rebuild homes and make the land productive. They were deprived of annual cash crops in cereal grains because they would need reasonable market prices in order to pay interest on their loans and exist through the year, but even those prices were automatically depressed by the cheap grain coming in from Sardinia, Sicily, and North Africa each harvest season. Those areas seem to have enjoyed superior fertility, better organization of labor in the form of slave gangs and the like, and cheap transportation by sea to Roman ports. The only alternative for Italians was diversified production or a different cash crop. Each required capital and time before it could be effective. It seems that most who tried farming gave up in disgust and gravitated to Rome.

Former veterans and farmers, these men who came to the city lacked a definition of function and a means of livelihood. They had a sense of resentment and hopelessness together with a physical need of subsistence that combined with their assertion of having served their country to make them demanding and "righteous" beggars. But this condition of their lives degraded them of course, and they soon became undignified clamorers with no sense of personal pride. Coupled with pauperized aliens who migrated to Rome from every corner of the Mediterranean, they swelled the ranks of the Roman mob with all of the consequences attendant on that status. The most consequential for Roman politics was their possession of votes and their undignified willingness to sell their votes for money with which to buy the necessities of life. The price of successful candidacy for office was immensely raised by that fact, as was the necessity of currying favor with the mob while holding positions construed as "public service" offices. The aedileship especially was to become a post open to abuse because aediles had charge of the supervision of games and festivals as well as overseeing the grain supply for the people of the city.

These considerations about the Roman electorate vitally affected the posture of the aristocracy. Many, no doubt, would still continue to vote for candidates on the basis of merit or demonstrated ability. But delivering the actual number of votes needed to win in elections required the financial means to buy the votes from the mob. Aspiring senators simply did not have that kind of money. They had to borrow it from a new middle class, later to be known as "equestrians," which emerged from the wars with money. Since the interest on such loans was prohibitive, as the farmers had also discovered, the patricians could not run for office unless means were found with which to recoup the losses from campaigning. The means were found in provincial gubernatorial corruption and the profits of a successful military campaign to enlarge purses.

Though territorial empire was not a Roman ambition at the time of the decisions of 200 B.C., it had become a prime consideration by the time of the Third Macedonian War. The patricians and senate had begun to realize that their political control depended upon imperial exploitation. They could not afford the price of political popularity and campaigning, so they adopted attitudes of imperialism that would ensure continued dominion over the city. For a century after this, the only honest governors of Spain, for example, were Cato and Gracchus. All the rest practiced corruption on a massive scale. This situation made provincials ripe for rebellion.

Another group that developed vested interest in empire was the new middle class, mentioned above. These equestrians had acquired riches by profiteering during the Punic Wars, especially the Second. They were wealthy plebeians to begin with who speculated in the sale of products to the government and increased their capital. They were the men who shipped hundreds of boatloads of supplies to Scipio in Africa (Livy XXX.38.2, 5). Speculation was so profitable that Cato, according to Plutarch (XXI.6), indulged in it later in life, whereon his farming became something of an affectation. The equestrians, however, fed on various other kinds of state contracts as well. Yet this middle class was a poor substitute for the former plebeian class. Commercially oriented, its motives and interests were very different.

Tax farming was the really profitable endeavor after the Second Punic War. This was the process of buying contracts to collect taxes in behalf of the state. Equestrians would incorporate, pool their capital, and buy contracts they could not afford individually. They had to outbid others, including provincials who might try to buy their own tax contract. They would then collect enough over the required tax to profit from the venture. Like the senatorial governors, they corrupted this procedure by collecting as much as the traffic would bear. In bad years, they became bankers, loaning needy provincials the amount of the tax at exorbitant rates of interest. Tax collectors were known by the term *publicani*, and one can judge the extent of provincial prejudice against them by remembering the Biblical usage of that word in the New Testament: publicans and sinners. This abuse had become so serious already by 198 B.C. that Cato thought it necessary to expel bankers—people who lent at interest—from Sardinia (Livy XXXII.27.3).

This middle class posed a serious threat to senatorial control of politics. It had money and therefore could not lightly be put off. As a matter of fact, the class was often the creditor of many senators. Adherents did not want membership in the senate, for senators were curtailed by the *Lex Claudia* from engaging in overseas commerce or taking state contracts. Equestrians required a political voice to protect their commercial interests and guarantee legislation favorable to business. This was the group that replaced the plebeians as contestant with senators for political control of Rome. Their advent in politics was ominous for the future of the city. All too soon they became cold, calculating machines to whom people were mere ciphers. Morality, to them, was to become pure expediency. People and, ultimately, the state itself were expendable if they interfered with the "computer-integrity" of this class (cp. Scullard, *A History*, p. 309).

A final group vitally affected by the wars, and exercising great effect on the Roman Republic therefore, was that of Latin and Italian allies. In a real sense they had won the war. Her legions shattered by Hannibal, Rome could field new armies only by drawing heavily on allied cities. The allies felt, with full justification, that they had a right to share in the fruits of victory. They soon began to demand full Roman citizenship so they could enjoy the benefits of empire like everyone else. They did so with a sense of true vindication, since they had fought and died in great numbers for the city of Rome.

These domestic problems show clearly that Rome could ill afford to concentrate on foreign affairs in 200 B.C. Her internal disarray, caused by protracted warfare, urgently required attention. The impoverished and depressed condition of the electorate and the senatorial response of accelerating interest in empire for the sake of exploitation and political dominance needed reform and regulation. Rampant "equestrian" capitalism would soon contort politics to suit its own best interests. Rome's continuing conquest of the Mediterranean would be performed by an army increasingly professional, non-Roman, and threatening to freedom and self-determination. This was the world of Cato, after the Second Punic War. He showed little sign of being any more perceptive than other Romans. Cato was not, as will be shown, an isolationist. Even if he had been, it would likely have been for the wrong reasons, not because he perceived a genuine necessity for the state to aid her depressed masses and remove the milieu for political corruption. His solution would have been that of some simplistic moderns: "Fight poverty—go to work!"

Having looked at the Mediterranean world in retrospect so as to place Cato in historical perspective, it is essential once again to refocus to the Roman view, lest Cato be seen completely out of proportion to the political realities as his contemporaries saw them. One cannot impute "global vision" to the Romans without serious error. To say, as some do, that Rome's historic mission lay in the western Mediterranean, where she was both civilizer and political organizer, and that therefore she was ill-advised to turn now to the East, where her mission was only political, is pointless. Rome had no sense of "mission" in either direction. Her decisions were made on other bases. It is equally fruitless to think with Polybius in terms of "Roman Imperial Destiny." The Greek historian wrote after the Romans had become deliberate imperialists for the reasons mentioned above.

The only reality Rome heeded in 200 B.C. was security. Her increasing capability had operated insidiously to convert this understandable need to a virtual imperialism. "Home defense," in the name of ever-widening spheres of "security," had created an unwitting empire. As she began to experience the tensions and needs of empire, Rome would improvise continuous foreign policies along basically "party" lines; but the Rome of 200 B.C. cannot be criticized for deliberately contriving an imperialistic foreign policy. It only answered the needs of the moment—threats that could be construed as endangering security. The surprising lethargy of Scipio after his return; Rome's withdrawal from Greece after the Peace of Phoenice in 205; her rejection of intervention against Philip V in 202; the assembly's initial refusal of war in 200; Rome's piecemeal involvement in the north and west only when necessary, but her immediate interest in Cisalpine Gaul—all substantiate Rome's security orientation. So, too, does her refusal to hold any Carthaginian territory after Zama, although maintaining her governance of Sicily as a buffer.

The declaration of war against Macedonia in two hundred was

preceded by interesting political maneuvering. It has been called variously a change of senatorial attitude, a lack of agreement between the people and senate, and a following change of heart on the part of the Roman electorate represented in the *comitia centuriata*. P. Sulpicius Galba, consul-elect for the year, had been allotted the *provincia* of Macedonia in anticipation of war (Livy XXXI.5.9, 6.1). When he put the question to the assembly, it totally refused. (XXXI 6.3–4). That would seem to be impossible. The *centuriae* (voting centuries) were dominated by the senate, unlike the *comitia tributa*. The vote against war in the *centuriata* means a majority of the senate (not necessarily including the leadership) was against war. Surely, there were not yet enough wealthy plebeian "equestrians" ranked in the centuries by census qualification to influence its vote radically—the only other way to account for such rebellion and lack of agreement.

The centuriate vote in 200 is the first real indication of a schism in the nobility, aside from the incipient occurrence of 205 B.C., when it was articulated by Fabius Maximus through negative means of coercion. It will be recalled that at that time the senior statesman formulated opposition to Scipio's "African amendment"—the widening of imperium to include North Africa—by rallying the minor nobility to vote with him "because of fear or else to curry favor." True, Livy does not call them "minor nobility," but as he differentiates them from "the leading senators," the inference is plain. Further, they were a majority even then; Livy shows this group included "all the rest (but the leading senators)." The recurrence of that split here is associated also with the defiance of the people, as can be seen from the statements of the tribune Baebius. Perhaps the same disaffection is to be inferred from the confusion over awarded *imperia*. Those of Nero and Lentulus in 202 and 201 are particularly pertinent. Both men thought their commands included North Africa and some share in the glorious defeat of Carthage, but neither was allowed.

These incidents indicate that *provinciae* could be awarded or modified without the knowledge of the recipients or, for that matter, of significant minorities in the senate. It seems to have happened again in two hundred, as the *provincia* of Macedonia was awarded by lot apparently without any expression of senatorial consensus in favor of the war. Livy nowhere indicates that a majority of the senate was actually in favor of the declaration of war or of a

Macedonian *provincia*. The language he uses in describing senatorial reaction to the vote of the *comitia centuriata* coincides with that which is so deceiving in the case of Scipio's alleged misbehavior in Sicily and the affair of Pleminius. One assumes that most of the senators disapproved of Scipio's conduct. Such was not the case, as he later shows that many of the senators failed to speak out, through fear or favor (Livy XXXI.6).

The action of the *centuriata* was taken, says Livy, by men worn out by a long war of great severity, weary of hardship and peril (XXXI.6.3–6, 8.1). Further, Quintus Baebius, tribune of the plebs, tauted them with sowing the seeds of war upon war so that the common people might never enjoy peace. That substantiates the contention that this decision was not made by the people, but rather by centuries dominated by the aristocrats. It must have been the leadership of the senate, not the majority, that was incensed at this setback, assailing the tribune with abuse and urging the consul to reconvene the *centuriata* and upbraid its voters for their supineness. Unfortunately for the future of the republic, they succeeded. Once again, the leaders of the state prevailed—the *centuriata* reversed its vote, and the Romans went off to war and to ruin.

Sulpicius, in urging the war before the reconvened centuries, sounds painfully modern. "Remember Saguntum," he said in essence, "and observe that unless Romans attack Philip in Greece, he will attack Rome in Italy. Athens has been attacked, and it is another Saguntum. If we hestitate to act, he will invade Italy. Philip is only five days from Italy by boat, while Hannibal was five months from Italy in Spain. Do not allow him, like a second Pyrrhus, to invade and despoil our native land!" (Livy XXXI.7). Finally—again like a ghostly echo of the modern world—the religious "clincher": "The immortal gods favor war," said Sulpicius, "For I have sacrificed and the omens are all propitious." (In other words, "God is on our side.")

The twin arguments from bogus security and godliness, as always, proved irresistible. The argument put forth by many, that Rome changed her mind for war because of knowledge of the secret treaty between Philip V and the Seleucid king Antiochus III "The Great," is not borne out by Livy. He says nothing of that knowledge either in the considerations for the senate or the deliberations by the *comitia centuriata*. A minority of that body, its leadership, succeeded in stampeding it to war despite majority opposition.[7]

It was among circumstances like these that Cato sought to align himself with influential people so as to run for office at the end of the year. Nothing very significant took place in the military campaigns in Greece, but it was a show of force sufficient that Aetolia decided to join Rome, as did a number of other states. Sulpicius was shortly replaced by the consul for 199, Publius Villius Tappulus. He in turn, according to all but one source (V. Antias), accomplished nothing (Livy XXXI.27, 33–34, XXXII.3.1–6.4).

VIII *Cato's Aedileship*

Cato's aedileship was not particularly eventful because of the efficiency of the former aediles. Rome, like many another political democracy, assumed from the first that it was the duty of the state to see that the people were supplied with grain at a reasonable price. This was no problem in 199 because two generous distributions of grain had been made in two hundred, both from the African grain stores left by Cato as function of his quaestorship under Scipio. At the beginning of two hundred (Livy XXXI.4.6) grain was sold to people at 4 asses per peck (*modius*) and at the end of two hundred at 2 (Livy XXXI.50.1; the as [*aes*] was about .02 cent then). Tangential to grain distributions was the aediles' supervision of the market place. They had an obligation especially to oversee the weights and measures of merchants there. This duty amounted to a minor jurisdiction. For violations of the regulations the aediles levied fines, the proceeds going to separate plebeian and curule fund chests out of which the cost of Roman and Plebeian Games, also supervised by the aediles, were in part defrayed. Cato and his colleague, the other plebeian aedile, as well as the curule aediles, four in all, inherited a well-regulated market from the previous aediles.[8] Livy says (XXXI.50.2) aediles the year before gained so much from fines charged in "aediles' court" that they cast five bronze statues as well as giving magnificent Plebeian and Roman Games. Yet there was something amiss—something to be desired in more space or more markets—and Cato seems to have discovered that during this year. His later censorship saw the construction of new markets (Livy XXXIX.44.7). The young aedile received other impressions of need as well.

Aediles were supervisors of the water supply. The two aqueducts to be kept in repair and cleaned at this time in the Republic were the *Aquae Appia* and the *Anio Vetus*. One can visualize Cato and his colleagues on lengthy trips out into the country, along either the eleven-mile length of the former or the forty-three miles of the *Anio Vetus*. Most of the extent of both was underground, cut in soft rock. These fellows had to shinny down through the manholes and vertical shafts placed periodically along the length of the water channels to allow inspection and cleaning. If any flaws were discovered, they had to be reported immediately to the censors, who contracted for repairs. Especially touchy would be the inverted siphon of the *Anio*, which carried the water across the valley at Ponte Lupo. That must be kept airtight because of its working principle. Service of this engineering masterpiece would remind Cato of his boyhood hero. The *Anio* was built by Manius Curius Dentatus in 272 B.C., just two years before his death. It was a remarkable aqueduct for that early period because of the use of the inverted siphon principle, its forty-three-mile length, and the fact that it had a capacity of forty million gallons in twenty-four hours as estimated by a later Roman expert (Frontinus, *De Aquis*).[9]

It was from service of the water supply that Cato learned the abuses of that utility practiced by the wealthy. The aqueducts ended in main large reservoirs whence water was piped to city fountains and baths. To get water, one had to carry it from the fountain or reservoir. Wealthy persons attempted to avoid that by piping water to their homes either by piercing the aqueducts outright or by piping any overflow from the reservoirs and fountains through private lead pipes to their own property. The lowly aedile could do nothing about this abuse, but he filed it away mentally for future reference. Then he forcibly corrected the abuse during his censorship (Livy XXIX.44.4).

There is no indication that unusual repairs had to be made to the public buildings or streets that year, though Cato must have found flaws in existing public works. He spent a good deal of time in his later censorship correcting abuses and effecting repairs that must then have come to his attention. Fully as important, for the year 199, were the public occassions and festivals at which the aediles had to keep order and for which they were fully responsible.

At the very beginning of the year, the Latin Festival had to be repeated (Livy XXXII.1.9) because of error. The aediles had to furnish the proper order in the city and the means with which to renew it. They also had to keep order in the city during the potentially dangerous entry of Lucius Manlius Acidinus with his train from Spain. He had been in command there and, in consequence of a successful governorship in crisis, had been granted the right by the senate to enter the city in ovation (Livy XXXII.7.4). The grant had been vetoed by a tribune of the people. Lucius had to enter as a mere private person—always a potentially dangerous situation because of possible friends and sympathizers among the viewers of the processional. It went off without incident because of the vigilance of Cato and his colleagues.

Censors were elected after the year began, one of whom was Scipio. They were enjoined by necessity to let contracts for new taxes to be collected in Italy—in Capua, Puteoli, and Castra—again without incident, despite the explosive potential of both tax contract bidding and collecting. That lack of incident is further tribute to the aediles (Livy XXXII.7.3).

CHAPTER 4

Sardinian Governor, Sumptuary Legislator, and General in Spain

CATO attained the praetorship in 198 B.C., after repeating the Plebeian games and hosting a banquet to Jupiter in cooperation with his aedile colleague, Gaius Helvius (Livy XXXII.7.13). The games did not necessarily cause election. Other games and banquets were more magnificent. Those the previous year and two years before had been especially memorable. Yet Cato's patron, Lucius Valerius Flaccus, had been a praetor in Sicily the previous year (Livy XXXII.1). Election was managed by Cato himself, and it is probable that such events as games would be necessary for purposes of image. But perhaps this plebeian had a prior patronizing acquaintance with others in the Servilian-Claudian group who could now help him or a working knowledge of the liberal Fabians formerly partial to Marcellus but now affiliated with Flaminus, who was elected to a consulship in Macedonia that same year. Such an acquaintance would of itself account for Cato's election, as Flamininus became the man of the hour, concluding the Macedonian War by defeating Philip V (Scullard, pp. 93, 98). Servilian-Claudians and moderate Fabians were the most influential coalitions at the turn of the century. Cato himself surfaced as a leader of revived conservatives of the Fabian group just two years later, proving that he had a good deal of political knowledge and influence of his own. Possibly he knew how to manage a campaign without any help at all.

I *Cato's Unique Image as an Honest Administrator in Sardinia*

Cato's *provincia* in 198 was the island of Sardinia. He was allotted two thousand new infantry and two hundred cavalry, to be raised by the consuls from Italian allies and Latin confederates (Livy XXXII.8.5–7). A magistrate with *imperium*, Cato now had the *ius auspicium* and had to take auspices for the success of his command while still at Rome. New recruits were being sent to relieve veterans who had been in Sardinia since approximately 207 B.C. (Livy XXXI.8.9–10, XXX.2.4, XXVIII.10.14). They sailed together: therefore the familiar direction of boarding and transport was once again Cato's portion. This task was not difficult, compared with the massive operations he had supervised under Scipio's command, both in Italy, Sicily, and North Africa. Yet it marked Cato's first autonomous command and *curule* magistracy. One may imagine the burst of pride and skilled efficiency with which he began his official senatorial career. Very soon affairs in Sardinia took on the stamp of Cato's personality (Plutarch VI).

The first detail Cato faced upon arriving in Sardinia and receiving the *imperium* from Lucius Villius Tappulus was to arrange transport back to Italy for the five thousand retiring Sardinian legionaries (Livy XXX.41.2, XXXI.8.9). The task of organizing the garrison of Sardinia with half that many troops was also important. They had to be quartered strategically, for maximum effect, at the chief centers of Carales, on the southern end of the island, and Olbia, in the north (Livy XXVII.6.13). Such interior rendezvous and rallying points as the city of Cornus must be guarded (Livy XXIII.40–41.7; Dio XII.48). They would serve as outposts against the hazards of the rugged, cave-marked interior with its heavily forested mountains. That part of the island had never really been subdued, and it was a historic sanctuary of revolutionaries, *pellitos Sardos* ("skin-clad" Sardinians; Livy XXIII.40.3).[1]

Sardinia had a history of rebellion and was considered explosive until the end of the second century B.C. Originally occupied in 238 B.C. on claim of piracy against Roman shipping, Sardinia was assigned a praetor in 234 B.C. and was governed continuously by praetors from perhaps 231 B.C. onward. Between 235 and 231 the Romans had to fight five major campaigns to pacify the island, each a consular command. As recently as 215 B.C. there had been a disastrous insurrection partially inspired by Carthage that had required twenty-two thousand infantry and twelve hundred cavalry to suppress it. There was relative calm after 207, and the island had even begun to furnish vitally needed supplies to Scipio's North African campaign, though previous gubernatorial requests for Italian money and grain for the Roman forces in the island suggest Roman control included only the coastland, not the fertile interior.[2]

Cato had now to hold this potentially troublesome island with two thousand soldiers and two hundred cavalry. Perhaps his task was facilitated by conciliatory measures. Cato's limitation of gubernatorial expense must have been a remarkable contrast to the opulence of former governors. They had thrown lavish banquets in luxurious pavilions, equipped splendidly and attended by swarms of servants and friends. Cato required but 3 Attic *medimnoi* of wheat (1.4 bushels each) a month for himself and his entire retinue, and less than 1.5 *medimnoi* of barley a day for his beasts of burden. As in the days of his youth, Cato was to be seen walking the administrative circuit of the cities on foot, followed by a single attendant (Plutarch VI).

The object of this tour was the judicial duty of hearing cases in each city. Marcus had ample experience to see that firm justice was done. He became the incorruptible judge who masterfully executed the law and the edicts of Roman government. The solitary walking figure acquired more respect and dignity than others who had ridden in splendor. The provincials, taught by aristocratic example to associate authority with luxury, now learned that that combination was a human weakness. Henceforth they would regard it with proper disdain. Similarly, they experienced the fear accompanying all administrative decisions that are impersonally objective. The singular success of these attitudes in Cato's praetorship inspired other effects.

The curule aspect of the praetorship allowed Cato to sponsor legislation affecting provincial administration. The *Lex Porcia de sumptu provinciali* (Dessau, *ILS* p. 38; Scullard, p. 112) is exemplary. It was the first attempt to impose his own standards of official behavior on others by law. There is little indication that this law forced rapacious Roman governors to limit their exorbitant demands for luxurious upkeep in the provinces. Yet the actuality of the law and Plutarch's description of other governors suggest that the imperial attitude of vested interest was a crucial problem already by 198 B.C. Such considerations may ultimately force reassessment of the causes for the Second Macedonian War.

Cato's policy of imperial exploitation was made more palatable by his own ideal of provincial administration as conveyed in his example and his laws. That same policy advocated by others who practiced massive corruption was utterly repugnant. Yet it was Cato's behavior that was anachronistic, not that of his contemporaries.

There was no necessity for him to practice corruption because of his frugal tastes and his ability to be elected to office on the basis of merit. Few senators possessed Marcus' taste, will power, or electoral profile. Most of his contemporaries merely wished to maintain the life-styles to which they were now becoming accustomed. The entire patrician class, to continue its political control of Rome, had to find means to retire debts incurred during aedileship and in general campaigning for office. Given the realities of an enfranchised mob, the anachronistic constitution, conflict with equestrians, and the existence of empire, the invitation to political and provincial corruption was irresistible, as far as most senators were concerned. Only a Cato could avoid it.

The management of men Cato had learned in Sicily became valuable for his personal career in Sardinia. Rigorous discipline had been limited officially by Cato's own *Lex Porcia de provocatione* and a *Lex Porcia* passed by a plebeian tribune the previous year. Both curtailed the prohibitive powers of provincial governors: The latter allowed Roman citizens to appeal governors' decisions on death penalties or heavy fines, while the former extended that right of appeal to include scourging. Though this legislation affected only Latins and Italians who were Roman citizens, it probably made military discipline more difficult to achieve. Cato was a hard taskmaster, drilling his men often, to judge from later habit (p. 111). Holding the restless Sardinians with two thousand men would necessitate tight security, in the eyes of such a man. That strictness, coupled with his native thrift, would naturally make soldiers resentful of his leadership. An added burden was the unhealthy climate. Two previous governors and a significant number of men had fallen deathly ill from the humid heat and bad water. One governor had died of it; the other suffered a lingering malady. One may say Cato's Sicilian experience became invaluable, as conditions in Sardinia resembled those during the plague at Syracuse, and Marcus had learned how to handle men in that environment.[3]

History does not record changes that may have been made by Cato in the administration of the province of Sardinia. Even as he sponsored laws that affected future provincial affairs, so he probably governed by edicts that brought considerable change in the lives of the provincials. One of these is known, and its effect must have been profound. Livy says Cato expelled usurers from the island and was considered harsh for it (Livy XXXII.27.3–5). Perhaps there were many such changes that inhibited dissatisfaction and revolution. At any rate, Cato's praetorship was undisturbed by rebellion or any other disorder. He was peacefully replaced, at year's end, by Lucius Atilius. Marcus returned to Rome, to become a powerful politician and a candidate for the consulship in 195 (Livy XXXII.27.7, 28.2, 11).

II Cato's Election to the Consulship

Cato and Lucius Valerius Flaccus must have forged something of a conservative faction in the years 197 and 196 if, as some believe, Cato led the fight against Scipio's African policy in 196 (Scullard, p. 114). It would have been composed of people formerly favorable to the policies of Fabius Maximus. It caused the exile of Hannibal from Carthage and marked the beginning of open enmity between Cato and Scipio. Ironically, but typical of human affairs, Scipio now championed Hannibal by arguing against Roman involvement in Carthaginian affairs. The latter had been elected *sufete* (*"praetor"* in Livy XXXIII.47 and *"rex"* in Nepos, *Hannibal* XXIII.7.4, the title originated in Semitic *"shophet,"* which the Bible translates "judge") and had made necessary liberalizing and economic reforms that pleased the masses but antagonized the leaders who attempted to undermine Hannibal's position by deceiving the Roman senate. They felt Roman interference would eliminate Hannibal. Accordingly, they sent letters to their peers and friends at Rome (Livy XXXIII.45.6), falsely alleging that Hannibal was intriguing with Antiochus the Great, monarch of the Seleucid Kingdom in the East. This could be construed as a threat to Roman security and would allow the "war senators" to urge that same loaded argument from defensive fear. At the same time, Scipio knew the true state of affairs, and so he must have been in communication with Hannibal or his adherents. He urged that Rome should not become involved in what was actually a matter of internal Carthaginian politics, and he was not fooled by the argument from security this time, according to Livy (XXXIII.46, 47).

One is led to believe by all this that Roman and Carthaginian leaders enjoyed a good deal of social intercourse. Livy says Carthaginian leaders wrote—each to his own friends at Rome—while Scipio, as shown above, may have been in touch with Hannibal himself. Yet the decisions relative to Carthage were made as if Rome knew nothing of the realities in that city. An investigating embassy sent by the senate to Carthage claimed it was there to stop trouble with Numidian King Masinissa! The embassy left in 195, the year of Cato's consulship, and thus Marcus had little to do with final implementation of the entire affair. But his participation in its beginning and continuation against Scipio marked both Cato and his colleague as well as the conservative Fabians whom they now began to lead.

There is little doubt that Cato received correspondence from certain acquaintances in Carthage. While he was quaestor there, he may well have learned to know more people than many a higher commander could cultivate. A lot of them, like Cato himself, may have risen to high office. It must be assumed he knew what the real cause of trouble in Carthage was, just as Scipio did, perhaps even more so. Yet he chose to instigate proceedings on the surface charge of intrigue with Antiochus. One might almost say this was a crucial psychological point in Marcus Cato's life, except that practicing a minor deceit to gain political prominence was completely predictable. His entire career to this point, all of the command decisions made in the military, most of the questionable items in provincial jurisdiction and *imperium*—all had been based on simple expediency. One can see in the background of this man a psychological id that merged a bloody wolfskin cap with patriotism at Casilinum; equated might with right in Sicilian atrocities; saw a godlike Fabius Maximus play the hypocrite at Tarentum; and suffered the disdain of a Scipio at moral criticism before Carthage. Cato's own first sally in the political arena was but a page taken from the leaders who had been his schoolmasters. "Good" was definable and recognizable only in terms of measurable gain.

Cato's fight against the interests of Scipio at this juncture gained him a political power-base. But in another sense, it was a disastrous mistake. Conservatives were committed to an African policy of interference or supervision and virtually identified with an imperialist orientation in spite of their individual wishes. This fight with Scipio, in other words, reduced the options of the conservative Fabians to almost nothing internationally and to opposing Scipio on domestic issues—a limited range of choices for a "party"! These were to be widened by artificial interpretations and expedients until the death of Africanus (Scullard, p. 113).[4]

Porcius Cato won the consulship for 195, with his good friend and patron Lucius Valerius Flaccus. Inaugurated on the Ides of March, they laid the question of provincial assignments before the senate. The senate decided that Spain, because of the conflict raging there, should be made a consular command and that the other command should be Italy. Whichever consul received Spain in the casting of lots should take two legions and fifteen thousand of the Latin confederates as well as eight hundred cavalry and twenty warships for that command. The other should recruit two legions specifically for the defense against Gaul. Cato was fortunate enough to cast for Spain, and Valerius drew Italy. Publius Manlius (Vulso?), a praetor, was duly elected governor of Nearer Spain for the year 195, with an additional legion, two thousand new infantry, and two hundred cavalry. The entire complement was to be enlisted by the consul, of course, as well as additional troops for other fields of action such as Etruria, Macedonia, and Farther Spain. As soon as the commissions had been received, Cato dispatched his military tribunes to enroll the armies and set a place in which they should muster for departure. The port of Luna in northernmost Etruria was chosen. There was a natural bay there, and it was far enough north that the troops would be well on the way to Spain should Cato be delayed by political details (Livy XXXIV.8.4–5). Luna was two hundred miles north of Rome (Appian VI.8.39; Plutarch X.1; Nepos II.1; Livy XXXIII.42–3).

This proved to be admirable foresight, as Cato was indeed detained in Rome. First, there was the matter of a religious ceremony of the "sacred spring" (*ver sacrum*) that had been vowed to the gods in 217 B.C., twenty-one years before. All animals born within a designated period were dedicated to the gods as expiation or in return for specific acts. There was some defect in this observance, because the ceremony had to be repeated the following year by the decree of the *pontifex maximus* and under the supervision of the college of pontiffs. A month was set aside for that purpose, March to May (Livy XXXIII.44.1–4, XXXIV.44.3).

A second item was sending the commission to investigate affairs in Carthage. That was the logical culmination of the fight led by Cato and his conservative cohorts against Scipio's African policy, representing quite a triumph for the former, politically, but limiting his choices in future (Livy XXXIII.45–9; Dio XIX [Zonaras 9.18]). Ironic that this deterred Cato from leaving for his command as soon as he wished! Since the whole point of the commission was that of security against Hannibal, the venture was a disastrous failure.

Hannibal escaped and fled to Antiochus, dramatically increasing that danger (Nepos, *Hannibal* XXIII.7.4; Appian XI.1.4).

III *Cato's Antifeminism and the Repeal of the Oppian Law*

Finally, the repeal of the Oppian Law was proposed to the assembly, and implications of that event drew Cato in spite of himself. It furnished a possibility of extending an austerity begun in wartime, the kind of thing Cato fervently wished to support. Passed in the heat of the Second Punic War, the Oppian Law had provided that no woman should possess more than half an ounce of gold, wear a multicolored garment (particularly one trimmed in purple), or ride in a carriage within a mile of the city of Rome. Now that the emergency was over, Roman matrons, as well as distinguished men, wished to repeal the law. The tribunes Marcus and Publius Iunius Brutus supported the law, while two other tribunes of the people opposed it. Feeling ran high over this issue because of its many implications. Livy himself echoes a later prejudice that must have operated at the time: "The matrons could not be kept at home by advice or modesty or their husbands' orders," he says, "but blocked all the streets and approaches to the forum, begging the men as they came down to the forum that, in the prosperous condition of the state, when the private fortunes of all men were daily increasing, they should allow the women too to have their former distinctions restored." Affairs became so intolerable, he continues, that soon the women dared even to approach the consuls, the praetors, and the other officials. But Cato, Livy says, stood firmly against them, opposing the repeal of the Oppian Law (XXXIV.1). It is obvious that Livy agrees with him.

Cato's early training and the orientation of his youth had now culminated in this: He advocated a return to the ancient, austere ethics of the fathers and believed in the power of legislation to effect it. Prescribed virtues and adherence to set standards of behavior had long been Cato's habit. He did not care that others wished to change the standards. It was better for them to begin practicing self-denial. The problem was that behavior might be affected by law but attitudes were not. One could impose all manner of sanctions while never changing opinion or the wish to live in a way other than that allowed by law. If it is true that law emanates from social conscience, then anachronistic regulations invite violation. They do not arise from conviction or rational assent and are virtually unenforceable. Cato never really grasped the meaning of that axiom; indeed, he denied it. This factor tragically affected his influence and his career.

Cato delivered an oration against the repeal of the Oppian Law. Most experts agree that Livy's summary of the speech is false. It does not have any traces of the man's style and contains anachronisms, they say. Yet these same experts assert that the speech caused party antagonism and affected politics. The two opinions seem contradictory, since there is no copy of the speech other than Livy's and no way of knowing either speech or effect apart from Livy. One may assume, therefore, that modern authorities do agree that Livy has the tone and trend of the speech correct. If that much is true, it surely is possible to proceed as though Livy's quotation is an adequate paraphrase of the speech.[5]

Cato's argument, apart from the obvious male prejudice both he and Livy display, is that laws are born from the human passions that make them necessary. First comes extravagance, then the necessity to curb it legally. The determining factor, according to Cato, is the greatest good for the greatest number. If the desires or luxuries of one person operate to the detriment of the majority, they must be legally curbed. "No law is entirely convenient for everyone," says Cato, " . . . [but] if every law which harms someone is to be repealed, what good will it do to pass laws? Those at whom they are aimed will instantly annul them!" If women, to paraphrase Cato yet further, were already practicing seemly propriety, they would not be agitating for repeal. They wished only to practice ostentation and so fought for the repeal of the law (Livy XXXIV.4).

Lucius Valerius Tappo, a tribune calling for repeal, rose to speak against Cato. In terms of legal theory and the derivation of laws, he contended that there were two different kinds of laws: One has to do with institutions and ought not to be repealed because of its enduring benefit to people and state, but the other is more temporal and transitory in nature, suited to time and circumstance, and change often renders it out of date. The Oppian Law, he said, was of the last sort, since it was passed in the heat of emergency during wartime, not after calm reflection as constitutional statutes are. Since that was true, it ought to be repealed because all the sanctions that had curbed the extravagance of men during the war had been removed and the law had thus become grossly discriminatory. Further, he asserted, the repeal of the law would not create a kind of sudden opulence in women, but would only allow it if they chose, so that they enjoyed an equal freedom with men (Livy XXIV.5–7).

Cato's prejudice against women in this debate is extravagant. He denies them the right to say anything about the laws. "Not even at home," says Marcus, "if modesty would keep matrons within limits of their proper rights, did it become them to concern themselves with the question of what laws should be adopted in this place or repealed." He goes on to point out that the Latin ancestors permitted no woman to conduct even personal business without a guardian to intervene in her behalf; Latin women used to be under the control of fathers, brothers, and husbands. "If each of us, citizens, had determined to assert his rights and dignity as a husband with respect to his own spouse, we should have less trouble with the sex as a whole," says the consul. "As it is, our liberty, destroyed at home by female violence, even here in the forum is crushed underfoot because we have not kept them under control . . . Give loose rein to their license . . . and this is the least of the things . . . to which they will submit with a feeling of injustice. It is complete liberty, or rather . . . complete license they desire" (Livy XXXIV.2–3).

These monstrous views of the human female would be mystifying unless one remembered Cato's doctrine of the laws and his standards for human behavior. Human extravagance that might harm others necessitates laws. The trouble was that his personal austerity would cause him to define extravagance differently from others, and his ideal was that laws must be retained so as to preserve old standards of simplicity, not changed to accord with modern, sophisticated personal apparel and refinement. Cato was not alone in that. Polybius (IX.10) felt Rome's ancient simplicity imparted the strength of conquest. Livy (XXVI.21.1, XXV.40.1) agrees, as does Plutarch (*Marcellus* XXI–XXII). All speak of modernized ostentation and luxury as responsible for degradation of character. Many Romans concurred (Tacitus, *Germania;* Sallust, preface to *The Conspiracy of Catiline*).

Cato's argument failed. In the absence of other evidence, it becomes necessary to suppose that Lucius Valerius' statement about different kinds of law and the adaptable nature of some won the day because it carried more conviction. If we may digress briefly, despite Lucius' contention that repeal of the law would not create opulence in women, the demonstrable result was an increasing taste for luxury thereafter. Therefore, arguments centering on the essential morality of repealing the Oppian Law must consider not as much the matter of legal theory as whether the resultant trend to luxury indeed corroded Roman morality and enervated Roman society in a way that was detrimental to her foreign and domestic aspirations. If conquest is an adequate measure of Rome's sense of her own function, the answer would seem to be in the negative—she concerned herself with little else for the ensuing half-century and subdued the entire known world. Similarly, one would have to decide whether the demand for refinements forbidden by the law was a reasonable desire or not. There can be little doubt that prosperity resulting in large part from imperialist expansion furnished the means to become ostentatious. The agonies suffered in throes of warfare no doubt caused some expectation of prizes and rewards to be enjoyed thereafter. National luxurious refinement, then, can be seen as a logical adjunct to continuous and excruciating war, not necessarily to individual passion.

Cato's views on women were contradictory and archaic. He said, for instance, that if women were allowed equality with the men, they would become unendurable and, at that moment, would be superior to men, according to the paraphrase in Livy. He cried that female violence threatened "our liberty," both in the home and in the forum, if Livy is correct (XXXIV.2–3), while cautioning that men should keep their women individually under control at home. This forceful pacification of Roman females is to be contrasted with Plutarch's pronouncement: Cato felt that a man who struck his wife laid violent hands on the holiest of things, he believed that a good husband was more worthy of praise than a great senator, and he admired only one thing in Socrates of Athens—that he was kind and gentle with a shrewish wife and stupid sons (XX.2)!

The archaic aspect of Cato's ideals about women is in his work *On Agriculture* (CXLIII), where the wives are required to stand in awe of the men, refrain from extravagance, visit the neighboring ladies and others seldom, and not have them in the house. They must not go out to meals or be gadabouts. They must not engage in religious worship, for that is the prerogative of the father of the household. Wives must be neat and keep the farmstead clean, tidy the hearth every night, hang garlands over the hearth on the first, ninth, and fifteenth of the month as well as on holy days, and pray to the household gods as opportunity offers. Finally, they must keep a supply of cooked food on hand for husband and servants.

IV   *Cato's Arrival in Spain and the History of Spain until that Time*

No sooner was the Oppian Law abrogated than Cato at once set out for Luna harbor with his allotted twenty warships plus five from the allies. He issued orders along the coast to collect ships of every kind for the transport of supplies, just as he had seen Scipio do in Sicily for the African campaign. Here the former training of Cato was useful not only for the method of transport, but also for navigation. From Luna he immediately set sail for Pyrenaeus, on the southern lip of the Gulf of Lyons, called the Gallic Gulf by Livy (XXXIV.8.4–6), leaving orders for the fleet of transports to follow. Cato's quaestor must have been responsible for that detail of operations, since the praetor, Publius Manlius, operated independently in a way that actually invites criticism (Livy XXXIV.17.1–2). It is certain that Cato's entire force was marshalled at Pyrenaeus, whence, he said, he would proceed against the enemy with all the fleet. It required precise timing, since Cato set a certain day for the arrival of warships and transports at Pyrenaeus, and that date was met. The distance was four hundred miles, provided both fleets sailed across the Gulfs of Genoa and Lyons rather than staying within sight of land. Under the best of conditions and with the best of vessels, that trip would have taken approximately two days for the warships, three days for the transports (reckoning 7½ knots for the former, 5 for the latter; cp. P. Harvey, *Oxford Companion*). If one doubles this to allow for adverse conditions, the voyage would take four days for the warships and six for transports.

Once the entire fleet of warships and transports had been gathered at Pyrenaeus, Cato ordered it around the Pyrenaeum Promontory against the fortress of Rhoda, a distance of barely ten miles. There was only a small Spanish guard in the fort, and it was ejected forcibly. After the maintenance of Rhoda was assured, they proceeded against Emporiae, across the bay. It was about fifteen miles from Rhoda, demonstrating that the recapture of Rhoda had been a strategic necessity. All the forces except the allied fleet were landed at Emporiae. The two posts Rhoda and Emporiae, it seems, dominated the coastal road between Spain and Gaul. They were located on the coastal plain in the shadow of the Pyrenees Mountains. The people in Emporiae were Spanish and Greek, each in different, walled-off portions of the city. The Greeks were of Phocaean descent, as were many of the Greeks in Spain. Marseilles

(Massilia), on the opposite shore of the Bay of Lyons, had also been colonized by Phocaea. The Spaniards in Emporiae, on the other hand, displayed a "fierce and warlike" nature to the Romans, according to Livy. One may hazard that they were probably no more barbaric in their hostility than the Greeks of Syracuse had been. No people ever willingly open their homes to infamous, conquering pillagers (Livy XXXIV.8.6–9.10). The natives in that immediate area of Spain may well have been more civilized than the Romans themselves. They were descended from the Iberians, an immigrant people thought to have come from Africa to Spain in the Neolithic age (6000–3000 B.C.) with well-developed Anatolian affinities. Their so-called Almerian culture centered in Tartessus on the Baetis River. Settled in a fertile, temperate area and mingling with migrating Phoenicians and Greeks, the Iberians flourished more than the rest of Spain. They spread up the east coast and north to the Tagus River basin. The east and south coasts of the peninsula were walled off from the interior by high coastal ranges; the inland folk were naturally suspicious and secretive. Also, the people of the interior were disturbed by invasion between the sixth century and the time Cato brought his armies to the coast. That invasion carried the Celts to Spain, who later mingled with the southern Andalusian Iberians. The resulting Celtiberians became the most warlike people in Spain, resisting Rome the longest and fighting the hardest. The Iberians proper manufactured bronze with the aid of "tin-stone" from the north before Greeks, Phoenicians, Carthaginians, or Romans arrived in Spain. Their art, as witness the lions of Corduba and the "Lady of Elche," shows refinement and sophistication. This so-called Tartessian empire was destroyed by Carthage before 508 B.C., and Carthage in turn was defeated by Rome in the person of Scipio Africanus by 206 B.C.[6]

Scipio Africanus' settlement was based on the idea that Spanish administration was primarily a military problem. The territory was composed of two natural divisions. In 206 B.C., Scipio had put each of these under the command of a general, each of whom was given successive grants of proconsular *imperium* by the senate. After 200 B.C. proconsular commands in both of the provinces were granted by plebiscite through the assembly. Two praetors were added to the annually elected number in 197 B.C., and these replaced the proconsular governors in Spain. Their territories were the lower Ebro valley with the eastern coast, known as Hispania

Citerior (Nearer Spain), and the valley of the Baetis River with the southern coast, known as Hispania Ulterior (Farther Spain). Citerior was four hundred miles long, stretching from the Pyrenees Mountains to a point just north of Baria. It included the coastal plain and its flanking ranges, going inland as much as 115 or as little as 15 miles. This was Cato's first theatre of operations. Hispania Ulterior ran 350 coastal miles beyond Citerior. The extent alone demonstrates Scipio's wisdom in creating two administrative districts.

It was obvious to Africanus that a Roman army of occupation could not be scattered throughout the length of this subject territory. He therefore designated certain garrison centers that became the key tactical fortresses and focuses for military government. Those in Hither Spain were Tarraco and Carthago Nova. That in Farther Spain was Italica.

The present action seemed focused in Citerior, where Sempronius Tuditanus had died of wounds received in battle and Minucius Thermus claimed a victory over Budares and Baesdines, Spanish leaders, with twelve thousand enemy casualities, at the end of 196 B.C. (Livy XXXIII.25.9). Turda, the mythical town where the battle took place, is thought by some to indicate the territory of the Turdetanians. If that be so, it may mean that the problem of Ulterior was temporarily slaked by the defeat of minor chieftains. More urgent for the moment was Hispania Citerior, which Cato, according to Livy, said had been lost to the Roman empire this side of the Ebro River (Livy XXXIV.13.8; *CAH* VIII, pp. 312–13).

The strategic situation was that Spaniards between the Pyrenees and Tarraco had severed communication and supply between Rome and Spain by their rebellion. That much is obvious from the geographic details and from the fact that M. Helvius, en route from Farther Spain to Rome, passed through the camp of Cato. There seem to have been no other communication routes (Livy XXXIV.10.1). The rebellion had to be settled, or it would amputate most of Hither and all of Farther Spain from Rome. Cato's first tactical problem was thus confined to the area of rebellion in Catalonia—inland to Osca in the north (about seventy miles) and south 140 miles to Tarraco (about seventy-five miles wide). Seven Spanish tribes inhabited parts of that area, but only the friendly Ilergetes are mentioned by Livy. Most of the rest must have formed Cato's opposition. They were the Indigetes, Ceretani, Laietani, and Cessetani. The Lacetani are specifically excluded by later events, and the Ausetani are mentioned by Livy as rebelling afterward. Livy's designation of opposing "states" in the plural implies more than just one or two of these were the enemy. He refers to the rebels as "allies" in another place. Appian says that the Spaniards assembled against Cato numbered forty thousand from all quarters. Surely most of these tribes were involved (Livy XXXIV. 11. 1, 16. 9, 20. 1, 3; Appian VI. 8. 40; Shepherd, *Atlas*, p. 38).

The reason for this united resistance by a relatively advanced group of Spaniards was probably oppressive Roman corruption (Livy XXXI. 49. 7). There had been a rebellion as recently as two hundred B.C., and in 199 Gades (Cadiz) in Farther Spain protested the impositions of a certain Roman *praefectus* (Livy XXXII. 2. 5). The war of two hundred was in *Ager Sedetanus*, just fifty miles south of Cato's battleground in 196–95, and the Gades affair was no doubt activated by the Turdetanians, who had been the middlemen for Carthaginian commerce in Spain and now resented Roman rule, which estranged them from their lucrative position. The Turdetanians were of that haughty Celtiberian group in the Andalusian south of Spain that was later extensively recruited by Romans. The administrative fault lay with Roman abuse of the system of appointing *praefecti* as governing assistants, ostensibly to supervise various town and city institutions, but actually to line their own pockets. So flagrant did this practice become that the prefectures had to be terminated in 171 B.C. This demonstrates that the affair of Gades was caused as much, at least, by Roman corruption as by Turdetanian intransigence. The actual monetary extent of private Roman larceny in Spain is impossible to determine, of course. One cannot seriously doubt that it played a large part in Spanish discontent (Livy XXXIV. 17. 4, XLIII. 2).[7]

Official exactions in Spain, on the other hand, given by Livy for 196–95 B.C., are appalling. Cornelius Blasio in 196 brought back to Rome 1015 pounds of gold bullion and 20,000 pounds of silver bullion, as well as 34,500 coined silver *denarii*. His province was Hither Spain, and he had been in authority there for two years. Lucius Stertinius, returning at the same time from a two-year tenure in Farther Spain, deposited 50,000 pounds of silver bullion in the treasury and erected two arches in the Forum Boarium with gilded statues on them but requested no triumph, meaning the exactions were regular taxes. The following year Marcus Helvius returned to Rome with 14,732 pounds of silver bullion, 17,023 *de-*

narii stamped with the two-horse chariot, and 119,449 Spanish silver *denarii* of Osca. All this, brought to Rome, is to be considered aside from the expenses of army and administration, which would add considerably to the total. Cato was the only Spanish governor in this period of history considered honest. It follows that there must have been abundant gubernatorial exaction above legitimate costs. The wonder is that Roman rapacity did not cause the Spaniards to fight Rome more consistently. Yet there were sporadic localized revolutions in all but three of the ten years after Cato's governorship. Indeed, it is likely that Cato started the long, disastrous wars with the Celtiberians centered in Numantia. Only 191, 188 and 187 were peaceful years, and in 181 there was another widespread revolt.[8]

Without doubt the holding of Spain was at first accidental. When Scipio appointed generals over two divisions of it and established fortresses, it was with the constant threat of Carthage in mind. She was still very much alive at that time. After Zama, if our speculations about Rome's motivation in international policy are right, there was less reason to hold Spain. The only motives for doing so would be those of psychotic fear lest Carthage rise again, asserting the old argument from security. None of the sources imply anything about the matter. There was concern about the rebellion of 197 B.C. but no question whether Spain ought to be released. There is no way to reconcile this imperialism with the evacuation of Greece after the Second Macedonian War, synchronized with Cato's return to Rome after the Spanish campaign. Surely Carthage was less to be feared at that time than Philip and Macedonia. Probably the Romans had indeed become attached to the sight of monies pouring in from Spain. That is a damaging indictment, for those same resources cost untold thousands of Spanish lives and many Roman casualties as well. Only the calloused would consider it a fair exchange (Livy XXXIII.26).

Partial vindication for the idea that greed, as well as security, was responsible for the provincialization of Spain exists in demonstrable policies and trends there. The vast majority of the Spanish communities were tenant municipalities (*civitates stipendiariae*). They were compelled to pay tribute (*stipendum*) in money and in kind. They also had to furnish *auxilia* for service in the Roman army and, to some extent, observe Roman law. The *stipendum* was a fixed sum assessed by a census of the ratable value of buildings, land, and produce, rather than a percentage that varied with earnings (*decuma*). Spanish *tributum*, unlike that of other provinces, was a direct tax and the provincial quaestors were responsible for collecting it. It is possible that the *stipendum* was dual: part on property (*tributum soli*) and part on persons (*tributum capitis*). The "fixed-sum" tax and its direct collection encouraged payment in specie rather than in kind and stimulated the establishment of provincial mints (note above the coined *denarii* brought to Rome from Spain already in 196–95 B.C.). This, in turn, facilitated commerce in the province and enlarged the flow of money to Rome (n. 6).

Exploitation of Spain proceeded in other areas as well. Not only did the Turdetanians of Andalusia lose their profitable middleman status when Carthage left Spain, but they were increasingly replaced by Romans and Latins. That was true both in commerce and industry and, worst of all, in the mining industry. This was a most lucrative endeavor, and it was monopolized by Romans.

Provincial Spain gradually became an established fact rather than a negotiable point of policy. When annual praetors replaced generals with proconsular *imperium* in 197 B.C., that plateau had been reached. Simultaneously came the rebellion that brought Cato to Spain. There was at that time no question of releasing the province. It was only a matter of keeping what Rome by now considered as much a part of her as many areas of Italy itself. Cato refers to it as "the Roman Empire," and that reality is to be seen in the disposition of non-Roman cities and towns in Spain.[9]

Theoretically Rome held conquered lands as an extension of the possessions of the state—the corporate people of Rome. Most of provincial Spain was therefore "public land" (*ager publicus*), a classification applied also to much of Italy. This was of course the justification for arbitrarily classifying natives of Spain as "tenant dwellers" on land now belonging by right of conquest to Rome. That was the reason they had to pay tribute. Though Rome would have wished to use some of the Phoenicio-Carthaginian and Greek trading towns that dotted the coast to facilitate administration, it was not possible in any directly functional way. Some cities were, to be sure, made exceptions to the *ager publicus* classification and therefore exempted from the usual taxes. Doubtless the reason for such exception was that of promoting stability by awarding privilege to potentially troublesome or particularly sophisticated and exemplary cities. Thus the Phoenician city of Gades became an "*ager privatus ex iure peregrino"* (private land under [Roman] international law). That status would permit the citizens of Gades to become either *"civitates liberae"* (free citizens), with autonomy and their own code of laws in all internal matters but subject to the *ius peregrinus* in external affairs or any transactions with Romans, or *"civitates liberae et foederatae"* ("confederate" or "allied" free citizens), if their freedom depended on a formal treaty with Rome. According to some experts, such classifications were rare, particularly in the case of Spanish cities (n. 6).

Greek cities may have been in a category all by themselves. Doubtless they would have become culture dispersion centers, except that theirs was not Roman culture. Romanization might be called the business of cities after it had been decided that Spain should be kept. That was the only way to achieve real stability. Greek and other foreign trading towns did not possess any extended *"territorium"* and so could not become centers for the acculturation of surrounding Spaniards. That function was assumed by the fortress cities of Scipio and by the later Roman colonies settled in Spain.

Doubtless Livy means to convey the status *foederatae* for the Greeks in Emporiae when he applies "under the shelter of Roman friendship" *(sub umbra Romanae amicitiae)* to them (Livy XXXIV.9.2, 10, 11). They received Cato's army with courtesy and kindness, and the Romans lingered in the city a few days so as to orient themselves and reconnoitre. Emporiae had been used in the same way by the Scipios in 218 B.C.; it must have been an ally before then (Livy XXI.60.2). Cato and his men shortly moved out to encamp a little distance from the city and began encountering the enemy. Obviously, then, the city did not offer adequate security. Livy hints at this when he describes the short city wall of Greek Emporia and talks about the Greeks' habit of constant vigilance against Spanish Emporiae.

Commander and army were not idle, even during the days they billeted in Emporiae. The entire time was spent in drilling so as to avoid indolence and to learn maneuvers. These were inexperienced troops, and the more hours they spent in training before a serious campaign, the better. Cato began sharpening them for combat by burning and laying waste the fields of the enemy around Emporiae. This served the purpose also of supply, since these conditioning forays happened to be synchronized with the harvest—Spaniards had the grain on their threshing floors. Thus fate seemed to play hand in hand with Cato's good fortune. He was able to send the grain contractors back to Rome, saying that the war would support itself. The plundered grain supply would be sufficient. This seems contradictory, when combined with other particulars (Livy XXXIV. 9. 11, 13.3; Appian VI. 8. 40).

The Roman calendar began on the first day of March. All the days Cato had spent in Rome after election on that date and time consumed getting from Rome to Spain could not possibly have totalled more than two months, perhaps only one. Thus it was still wintery when the consul and army arrived, though in Catalonia the winter temperatures average only fifty degrees Farenheit. The weather was sufficiently chilly that Cato ordered a winter camp built three miles from Emporiae as the campaigning season approached. Contradiction appears with the simultaneous mention of the burning of harvest fields and grain on the threshing floors (Livy XXXIV. 9. 12). Spaniards of Catalonia must have altered their growing season to suit the climate. That area of the peninsula is the hottest and driest in summer, averaging eighty degrees Farenheit with but fourteen inches of rainfall annually, most of it in winter. The withering, scorching *solano* that blows over the coastal plain for as much as two weeks at a time in summer probably burned crops seeded in spring. Irrigation methods that now make Catalonia and the Ebro valley productive were first introduced by the Moors after eight hundred A.D. Cato's adversaries must have planted their fields in January or February, or in the fall, harvesting them in April or May, whichever is the more likely date of this peninsular confrontation (Livy XXXIV. 9. 13). Word of the winter crop had not been reported by the Scipios—contractors accompanied Cato as if to buy grain from storehouses.

V   *The Campaign in Hither Spain*

One of the first decisions Cato had to make was unpleasant (Livy XXXIV. 11). The only friendly tribe of Spaniards, the Ilergetes, was under attack. Their ambassadors' entreaties for help were difficult to refuse. The important mint at Osca, whose coins paid tribute (Livy XXXIV. 10), lay in their territory. If exploitation were now a consideration, it must be said that the Ilergetes may have had a Roman treaty. Indeed, the ambassadors speak of "breaking pledges" in Livy (XXXIV. 11. 7). Cato had to decide whether it was more politic to aid and thus directly reward a friend or to avoid dividing his command in the interest of military safety. As the consul weighed choices, psychology came to his aid as a hand from the past. Lessons learned from Italy and Sicily demonstrated that the illusion of reinforcement often serves the same purpose as actual troops. So he sent word that help was on the way, keeping the chief's son as hostage for the good behavior of the Ilergetes should they learn of his perfidy.

The ambassadors did not leave until they saw soldiers marching on board ship—one-third of each cohort was thus ordered—and their rations were being prepared for departure on the third day. Since the country of the Ilergetes was over a hundred miles up the Ebro River, the Roman seagoing vessels must have been able to sail up the Ebro a certain distance. Livy specifically implies they were to sail. Cato, who had determined not to split his command beforehand, ordered the boarding to cease when the envoys had departed and prepared to meet the enemy. The ruse worked, apparently. Livy speaks of the envoys' filling friend and foe alike with the news of approaching Roman aid (Livy XXXIV. 12).

Having thus provided for every contingency, Cato moved against the enemy. Scouts had reconnoitred their situation so that he could choose the advantageous strategic position by arriving early. The auspices were taken, and the army embarked after midnight. After they had landed, Cato led them beyond the camp of the enemy to force the Romans to fight as though their retreat were cut off. It is perhaps this act, with the boarding of ships, that caused Appian (VI.8.40) to record that Cato had sent the fleet away so that the soldiers had no choice but to fight. Livy gives the truth of it (XXXIV.13.5–14.4, 16.1) but then says the positioning of the army was praiseworthy because it left the men no recourse but their own courage. Indeed, he quotes Cato to that effect in his harangue before the battle. One might well question the extent to which an artificial affair of strategic position could be called real courage or how much one should admire a commander relying on such methods.

The battle itself was a near thing. Cato must have been outnumbered. It is well known he had two full legions, 15,000 Latin allies, and 800 cavalry—28,200 men (Livy XXXIII.43.3). Appian counts the Spaniards at 40,000 (VI.8.40). The cavalry onset was a disaster for the Romans. It was offset by the dispatch of two cohorts to harass the Spanish rear, but Cato himself had to stop the precipitate flight of Roman infantrymen from the right wing (Livy XXXIV.14). The day was saved by reserves from a second line attacking in wedge formation. Yet the entire second legion was in reserve, for it led the attack against the camp of the Spaniards. Hence the battle was won by a single legion with allied forces. Appian's documentation of the embrace of affection tendered Cato by his soldiers upon return is perhaps of a piece with that historian's confusion over the entire Spanish campaign. Plutarch also seems puzzled over the narrative of events. Both have confounded this campaign in Hither Spain with that later waged in Farther Spain and the central highlands, as though there were only one. That is the reason for an assumption that the Celtiberians were involved. Plutarch even misquotes Polybius by mentioning forts all the way to the river Baetis in Farther Spain, extending almost by misunderstanding the theatre of operations in this initial confrontation (X. 1–3).

Beginning with this battle, Cato reduced all hostility on the nearer side of the Ebro by force. Many states, as Livy calls them (Livy XXXIV. 16. 4), were persuaded to submit by the victory. Now, as though in realization of psychological values, Marcus began a series of rapid moves and shifts of bases of operation. Wherever he went, he received envoys surrendering to Rome, and he hosted them with wine, food, and kindness, sending them back home satisfied. This was a thinly disguised parade in force through the entire district of Catalonia. By the time he had reached Tarraco, at the other end of the area, the "empire this side of the Ebro" had been pacified. Yet all was but a sham, as was shown by a vagrant rumor.

The story was circulated that Cato meant to lead his army into Turdetania, that is, Farther Spain. This prospect of military absence encouraged further revolts among the mountaineers in the outlying districts of Catalonia. Seven forts rose as at a signal. They were easily subdued but rebelled once again before Cato had left Tarraco. The prospect of continual threat caused the consul to capture and enslave all these so-called Bergistani. Yet he feared the example of these independents and so sent forth the order that all Spaniards should be disarmed. This they took so hard that some began to commit suicide. Livy says they were such high-spirited people that life without arms was useless to them (Livy XXXIV. 16. 8–10). Cato called senators of all the states together and harangued them to the effect that it was in their own best interest that they not rebel; that always cost the Spaniards more than the Romans. Disarmament was, to his mind, the only way to effect submission with least trouble. But he offered to alter his method if they could suggest other alternatives (in other words, resistance to rape was more painful than rape itself). No suggestions were made (Livy XXXIV.17.5–12), and after thought, Cato toughened the directive by demanding that all the city walls be torn down as well. Towns that refused were attacked promptly. Only Segestica resisted, and they captured it with sheds and mantlets (*vineis ac pluteis*).

Appian devotes more time to this particular than other historians (VI.8.40–41). He is certain that the technique used by Cato was that of simultaneous command. Cato had so timed the delivery of sealed orders regarding the town walls that all were opened on the same day. None of the cities was given time to consult with others. They were told that they must dismantle their walls or suffer immediate enslavement. All therefore complied rather than run the risk of perishing alone. Appian limits this act to the territory along the Ebro River. Plutarch (X.3) quotes Polybius to the effect that it included all towns to the Baetis River. Livy (XXXIV.17.12) confirms Appian in limiting the territory to Spain "this side of the Ebro." Dio (Zonaras 9.17) agrees with them, calling the river "the Iberus." Plutarch's statement is ridiculous on its face, the Baetis valley being some 650 miles to the south of the Ebro, in the midst of Farther Spain. This would be one of the few times Polybius must be wrong, unless Plutarch has misquoted the historian.[10]

One might interject at this point evaluating criteria that indicate the direction of Cato's military and political career. The sardonic cynicism with which the consul treated Spanish subjects, bidding them hold still while being victimized by Roman avarice, was to be an indication of his later senatorial ideology. Though Livy exonerates Cato himself, speaking of his frugality, vigilance, and exertion, the historian does say (XXXIV.18) Cato had a more difficult task in subduing Spain than others. The earlier Romans had freed the Spaniards from the burden of Carthage. Then came the disillusionment of Roman administration. They freed themselves by rebellion. Now Cato had the task, in Livy's words, of renewing Roman lordship over Spanish slaves after they had tasted freedom. Perhaps one can see in the action of the man some wish to moderate when faced with the hysteria of disarmament suicide. But his solution was to ask for alternatives guaranteeing no rebellion, which meant resignation to greed once again—so the Spanish senators were silent.

VI   *The Campaign in Farther Spain*

The march to Farther Spain and subsequent events are not well covered by any of the sources, even though the rebellion had begun in Turdetania (Livy XXXIII.21.6–9). Governors there had been M. Helvius in 197, Q. Fabius Buteo, and then Appius Claudius Nero in 196–95. Those in Hither Spain had been C. Sempronius Tuditanus, then Q. Minucius Thermus and P. Manlius Vulso (Livy XXXII.27–28), also during 196–95. Livy is confusing in this because he omits Buteo and then treats Minucius as the successor of Helvius and Manlius as succeeding to Minucius' command (Livy XXXIII.24, 26, 43, XXXIV.10.5–6, 17.1–2). Livy seems to think that Manlius and Cato shared the command of Spain between them, Claudius being a sort of supernumary. That was hardly the case. Claudius had furnished a guard of six thousand men for Helvius on his leaving Farther Spain, and that guard was returned once Helvius had reached the camp of Cato in 195. Yet Livy persists, saying that Manlius took over the armies both of Minucius, whom he succeeded, and of Appius Claudius Nero from Farther Spain and with these as his new troops set out for Turdetania. Something is wrong in all this. Publius Manlius was specifically assigned to the two thousand troops and two hundred cavalry that had been mustered when he was named praetor to Hither Spain. In addition, he received the legion that Minucius had commanded. Cato, on the other hand, was given two legions plus fifteen thousand allies and eight hundred cavalry. That would number close to twenty-eight thousand troops. These must be the true dispositions for 195.

On the other hand, Claudius in Farther Spain must have had forces similar to those received by Manlius; the designation of Livy indicates it. This combination of commands is unusual. Claudius in Farther Spain had trouble with the Turdetanians who had started the war. There must have been cooperation between the two praetors because Livy says that Manlius with his own command and the veteran troops of Claudius from Farther Spain set out for Turdetania and then attacked the natives of that district, easily overcoming them. Yet the war was not ended because the Turduli, apparently part of the Turdetani, hired ten thousand Celtiberians and prepared to carry on hostilities, causing Manlius to summon Cato (Livy XXXIV.19.1–2). There was no question of authority involved. The extraordinary command of Cato was a consular *im-*

perium superior to that of the governors. Confirming that fact is Manlius's designation as *audiutor consuli* (XXXIII.43.6). Cato's authority overrode that of Manlius. There is little warrant for the assumption that the praetors of Spain had proconsular rank. The epigraphical evidence can all be read and understood as either "*pr[aetor]*" or "*pr[opraetor]*"; it is not necessary to read "*pr[oconsul]*." On the other hand, it is significant that the explicit reading and abbreviations are present (i.e., "*procos.*") for Cato and Flaccus, who actually were proconsuls according to the evidence. Surely then, there was no question of jurisdiction or seniority in these commands.[11]

When Cato reached Farther Spain, he began to skirmish with the forces of the combined Turdetani. These no trouble—he was at once successful against them (Livy XXXIV.19.1–10). The Celtiberi were offered three alternatives. First, they might change sides for twice the pay they were receiving from the Turdetani for their services. Second, they might march away with no harm done and no threat of further action from Rome. Finally, they had the option of naming a time and place for an armed settlement with Cato, if they were in honor obligated to do battle. The first of these became the most fabulous historically. Plutarch's version of it shows that even Cato's officers thought the amount, 200 talents, excessive (X.2–3). Conversely, Cato felt it was justified because victory would in the final analysis pay for itself, whereas potential defeat would be costly. Again, cynicism was Cato's attitude. It is possible, though not mentioned by any of the historians, that an officers' council, of the type Cato participated in as a tribune, was called. Livy says that some of the military tribunes were sent to bring the alternatives to the Celtiberians, and Plutarch's mention of staff differing with Cato as to the amount indicates organized discussion. It is interesting that Cato, unlike his former commanders, refused to listen to the will of his officers. He acted as he personally was inclined.

Plutarch is invaluable here, for he shows what history does to an act like that of Cato. He says that a host of barbarians fell upon Cato and his army and threatened to drive them out of the province. Cato therefore begged neighboring Celtiberians to become his allies, offering them two hundred talents for that service. Whatever the action of Cato, the result was neutralization of the Celtiberians— they did not fight. Practical results vindicated his deed. Yet gossip and rumor contrived to fabricate a Celtiberian "payoff" from Cato's doings, which would surely be repugnant to the consul. Dio combines all these options given the Celtiberians into a single event and says the result was so confusing to the Spaniards that they refused to fight (Zonaras 9.17).

Livy seems objective when he cites the three choices given the Celtiberi and their subsequent refusal to fight. It is curious that Livy never does say the Celtiberians accepted money for neutrality. That is the impression given us by Plutarch. Cato's actions seem to indicate uncertainty. As he tried to draw them into a battle by one means or another, he discovered that the Celtiberians would not fight. This, together with subsequent events, means that the Celtiberians adopted temporary neutrality but did not choose any of the Roman options officially. There was no exchange of pledges or assurance as to future status between Celtiberians and Romans. If there were, Cato would never have attacked the fields and belongings of the Celtiberians, as he later did for strategic reasons.

The do-nothing policy may have been the most effective defense to use against a commander of Cato's talents. The Celtiberians got word of his exploits in Hither Spain, and their realization that Cato must leave at year's end led them to adopt the waiting policy. According to Livy, Cato paid the entire Roman army including the troops of Manlius, left all of it but seven cohorts in Manlius' camp, and went back to the Ebro (XXXIV.19.10). Knowing the contemporary army, Cato must have returned with but forty-two hundred troops. It has been shown before that Marcus was notoriously unwilling to divide his command. That he now did so reflects appreciation of the seriousness of the brewing crisis in Farther Spain and his tacit recognition that the campaign there had accomplished nothing. It is also final proof of his uncertainty as to the status of the Celtiberians.

VII   *Rousing the Celtiberians and Return to Hither Spain*

The events of Cato's return to the Ebro, particularly his attack on Saguntia, are well-nigh incomprehensible. Mounting a siege against that central bastion of the Celtiberians with only forty-two hundred men must have seemed the height of folly. It proves there was no agreement between these two. Livy mentions the attack, though he implies that it was part of Cato's earlier attempt to draw the Celtiberians into battle, inferring therefore that the full army was with him at the time. But that would necessitate a separate campaign, since Saguntia was three hundred miles upland from the Turdetanian

territory, on the very inner border of the Celtiberian country: the
Meseta, or central plateau, of Spain. It seems conclusive that the
siege was part of the march back to the Ebro. Archaeology proves
that two Roman camps were built there in the time of Cato within
striking distance of Saguntia, at Aguilar and Alpanseque (thirteen
and sixteen miles from Saguntia, respectively). Archaeology also
shows that a Roman camp was built four miles east of Numantia, the
main Celtiberian base, in the time of Cato. The camp was at Gran
Atalaya and the remains of all three camps substantiate Livy's inference that the siege was unsuccessful; indeed, it was not even a
serious attempt (cp. Schulten, *Numantia*, iv, 37, 191, 196).

The aggressive acts of Cato's return to the Ebro make it certain
that no agreement or treaty had been made with the Celtiberians.
But they are mystifying in view of the number of men Cato used.
The interpretation that seems to fit all the facts is that of diversion.
No doubt Cato undertook a siege because the Celtiberian menfolk
were with the army in Turdetania. He knew that nothing had been
accomplished there, leaving most of his army with Manlius in recognition of that fact. Conceiving the strategy of an attack on their
homes in order to force the hasty return of the Celtiberian army and
thus relieve the pressure on Manlius and the Roman army in
Farther Spain would be a masterpiece of planning, accounting at
once for the use of so small a force to mimic a siege and putting the
risk at naught because the Celtiberian men were absent. It would
further explain why the camps were built so far from each city (four,
thirteen, and sixteen miles). Two cities under attack would force the
return of the entire army, and the whole scheme, in this explanation, is thoroughly worthy of Cato's known ingenuity. The usual
assumption that there was a treaty with the Celtiberi and that Cato
besieged these cities in earnest on the way back to the Ebro, on the
other hand, would imply he was a dishonorable idiot.

Conversely, the facts seem to indicate that Numantia and Saguntia could not have been attacked on Cato's initial march to Farther
Spain rather than on the way back. His first approach to the Celtiberians in Farther Spain was that of negotiation and attempted conciliation, even to the point of offering a donative. It is highly unlikely
that such an approach would have been possible if the Celtiberians
had already known Cato as an attacker of their two main cities—an
unsuccessful one at that. The whole atmosphere of first confrontation in Farther Spain would have been different. Finally, Cato must

have known something of the capabilities of the Celtiberians. That is
shown by his caution in dealing with them. He did not offer any
other people money to lure them into the Roman camp. It would
have been foolish, on the eve of an uncertain campaign answering
the appeal of Manlius, to risk arousing the anger of the Celtiberians
by attacking their cities (Livy XXXIV.19.3–6).

To be sure, the policy of forcing the Celtiberian army to rush
home by the feint of a siege proved to be hazardous. It aroused
them and it marked the beginning of the Roman-Celtiberian wars
that raged for a century and a half thereafter, as these finest fighters
in Spain failed to surrender as others had done. The ultimate cost of
this strategy, then, was appalling. To that extent, Cato stands indicted as instigator. Perhaps, had it not been for his action, central
Spain would never have been added to Rome, and the Celtiberi
might have become peaceful allies.

Once Cato returned to the Ebro, he found it necessary to subdue
another rebellious tribe—the Lacetanians. In the course of doing
so, he captured several other towns. The Sedetani, Ausetani, and
Suessetani joined the Roman alliance. The latter were particularly
bitter at having been attacked by the Lacetanians while Cato and
the Romans were away in the south. That is difficult to understand
because they were not themselves a part of the alliance at the time
Cato left. Livy specifically says that these three peoples now for the
first time "came over" (*defecere*) to the Romans (XXXIV.20). The
young men of the allied peoples were enraged at the Lacetani, and
Cato was inclined to allow their wrath full expression. He led picked
cohorts of Romans with a great body of the allied Spanish youth
against the Lacetanians. Then he ordered the youths to show in
force before the citadel of the Lacetani, and when the latter, holding
other Spanish youth in contempt, pursued them, Cato led his con-
cealed Romans into the town from the opposite direction. When the
Lacetanians returned, they discovered their own gates shut against
them and the Romans in control. They shortly surrendered.

The consul captured the fort of Bergium soon after that. Though
this district and the people, the Bergistani, cannot be located, they
must not have been far from the district of the Lacetanians. Both
seem to have been mountaineers of Catalonia. Livy says Cato
marched to Bergium "quickly" (XXXIV.21; p. 000–00). The Bergistani, it will be remembered, were the people who rebelled when

they heard Cato had left for southern Spain, forcing a separate march against them. They had risen again shortly thereafter, bringing Cato to his infamous decision to disarm the people and dismantle their walls. Since the Lacetanians certainly, and ostensibly the Bergistanians, were mountaineers of Catalonia ("remote and forest dwelling" in Livy XXXIV.20.2), controlling the Catalonian iron and silver area, there was good cause for alarm. But the taking of their fort is an issue.

A leader of the Bergistani reported that their town had been taken over by robbers who were using it as a base for raids on peaceful communities. Cato then proposed that the Bergistani act as a "fifth column" in their native city and when the Romans appeared, occupy the citadel as the robbers concentrated on defense against the army. This was effective (Livy XXXIV.21.1–5). As Romans attacked the wall, robbers could not defend for fear of the missiles poured upon them from the citadel in their rear. All this reminds one of a major discrepancy. The walls of the Bergistani, which were to have been torn down after the consul's campaign in Hither Spain together with those of numerous other rebelling towns, had not in fact been torn down. After all, the rebellion of the Bergistani had been the cause for the harsh dismantling of walls (pp. 114–15). Either the mandate to tear down walls was but loosely enforced— hardly likely seeing the character of Cato—or the Bergistani had already rebuilt them. If the latter, Spanish walls were but flimsy affairs. Further, the Bergistani would have been among those people disarmed by Cato; yet now they have missiles enough to use against the robbers from their citadel. If they could rearm that readily, what mattered the original disarmament, and why were there suicides of despair over it? Livy must exaggerate the original events somewhat.

The motive and trend of all this provincialism is shown by Livy subsequently (XXXIV.21.6–8) when he says that Cato restored order in the province and arranged for large revenue collections from the iron and silver mines, and that as a result of the regulations made at that time, the wealth of the province increased every day. Five hundred forty thousand Oscan *denarii* were carried in his triumph (XXXIV.46.2). There is supreme irony in the concluding sentence: "By reason of these achievements in Spain the Fathers decreed a thanksgiving for three days." Roman divinities had indeed acquired materialistic attributes! Economic imperialism had

now followed the Roman standards into Spain for reasons of "security."

According to Plutarch and other authorities Cato completed this
campaign against the Lacetanians and the Bergistanians after his
term of office had concluded, so that he was in effect a proconsul
with prorogued *imperium* at the time. Plutarch says that he was on
the way home and accomplished the feat with but five cohorts and
five hundred horsemen (XI.1–2). He also records a tradition that
Cato was succeeded in Spain by Scipio Africanus, who was anxious
to minimize the prestige and influence of Cato. None of that is to be
found in Livy, and in fact it is commonly discarded by modern
authorities (Scullard, p. 118, n.1; Livy XXXIV.46.1), who retain
only the dates and the idea of proconsulship, strange to tell! The
entire justification for a proconsulship is the combination of factors
found in Plutarch—continuation or termination of an action begun
in the *imperium* (Livy XXXIV.43.3–4). They discard the justification
and retain only the effect—proconsulship. Nepos has the version
that Scipio tried but failed to succeed Cato in Spain (II.2). In fact, a
Publius Cornelius Scipio (Nasica) was elected praetor to Spain after
Cato, accounting for confusion over the name; a namesake of Africanus actually did succeed Cato. The tradition recorded by
Plutarch and Nepos may well mark an attempt by Africanus to
enforce the system of annual commands, so that Nasica would immediately supersede Cato and deprive the latter of the privilege of
finishing his campaigns. Though Plutarch reports failure, Cato later
had to defend his Spanish conduct in court, probably over just such
a technicality as this: the cessation of his *imperium* and therefore the
questionable legality of his final *acta*. The evidence of a proconsulship would seem to exonerate Cato of this charge.

Livy shows by his sequence (XXXIV.42.1–2) that Cato was not
overlong in his province. The three days of thanksgiving decreed by
the senate fell just at the end of 195, not in 194 as would otherwise
have been the case (XXXIV.43.1–3). Further, the dispositions of the
provinces were made as if the war in Spain were over, additional
proof the senate was fully aware of Cato's Spanish actions. It was,
finally, just at the beginning of 194 that Cato returned to celebrate a
triumph over Spain (XXXIV.46.2). His booty was the largest so far,
in spite of the fact that he prided himself on frugality and honesty
and is so commended by Plutarch and Livy (XXXIV.18.1–5). In the
triumphal procession of Cato over the Spaniards, twenty-five

thousand pounds of silver bullion, one hundred and twenty-three thousand silver *denarii*, five hundred and forty thousand silver coins of Osca (probably of the size of *denarii*, as in former triumphs), and one thousand four hundred pounds of gold were carried. In addition to all this, he gave to each foot soldier 270 asses and thrice that amount to the troopers. This distribution is emphasized by Plutarch, but it serves to show hypocrisy (X.4; Livy XXXIV.46.3). Blind ego! The man indicted everyone else for giving donatives but himself obviously found them a necessary fact of life. Yet Cato continued to insist that other commanders and women exercise an exemplary thrift and frugality.

CHAPTER 5

Factional Politics and Relations with Greece

I Conservative and Moderate-Conservative Politics in the Prelude to War with Antiochus the Great

NOW that the struggle for "survival" was concluded and Rome could look forward to a predictable future with reasonable assurance, political factions may have begun to display coherence on the basis of sustained foreign policies that had undeniable domestic implications. Certainly, the main difference between Cato and Scipio after two hundred B.C. was that of foreign policy with the domestic overtones of Hellenization it involved. Though that is a generalization, it will do for the present. Cato now returned to the political arena as a commander with battle laurels. Though he could not contend with the likes of Scipio Africanus in that dimension, he certainly had enhanced his political profile. Since the issue between these two was to be that of foreign policy primarily, albeit more notoriety attached to its corollary, domestic Hellenization, it is perhaps fortunate that Cato had acquired the military capabilities popularly mistaken for acumen in foreign affairs.

The year 194 B.C. was the date of Scipio's return to affairs in active politics, as it was the year of Cato's triumph over Spain. The ascendancy of Scipio was painfully obvious, for he secured control of powerful offices in Rome during that year. Cato's conservative faction had to scramble to compete. Including Africanus, five Cornelii were elected (Livy XXXIV.42.3–4). Scipio was consul, three other Cornelii were praetors, and one was a censor. The second consul is reckoned a Scipionic friend by those who compute such things, because his father and namesake, Tiberius Sempronius Longus, was a colleague of Scipio's father (Scullard, p. 115). One praetor was an allied naval officer (*socius navalis*) under Scipio before New Carthage, Spain, in 209 B.C. He had been awarded a mural crown (*corona muralis*) as first to the top of the wall when the city was stormed, a signal honor. His name was Sextus Digitius, and he probably received Roman citizenship at that time. Another praetor, Cn. Domitius Ahenobarbus, was considered friendly as well, though that is wishful thinking since Africanus preferred Laelius to him for the consulship in 192 B.C. Perhaps the point at this juncture is just that the idea of all these men agreeing with Scipio to the point of party affinity is somewhat tenuous. Yet there can be little question that now for the first time continuous policies transcended individualism (cp. F. Münzer, *Römische Adelsparteien*, pp. 92 ff.).

Plutarch alone states that Cato served Sempronius, consul-elect for 194, as an ambassador in Thrace and on the Danube River, subduing the natives as consular representative (XII.1.). Most importantly, the territory was not a part of Sempronius' *provincia*. He had been given the command over Italy and had campaigned in Cispadane Gaul and Liguria. Thrace and Danube territory bordered on the *provincia* of T. Quinctius Flamininus in Greece, but even he had no authority that far north. It is true that Flamininus had need of ambassadors that year as he left Greece with his army (Livy XXXIV.48.2–52.3), but it is unlikely Cato was one or that he was sent on a mission outside Flamininus' theatre of operations. To be sure, there was cause for concern in that area, especially as more attention was given to Antiochus the Great of the Seleucid Empire and the possibility of his invading Europe. But sources agree that the consul most concerned with that problem was Scipio, and it seems unrealistic that he would have sent Cato on a legate's task. It is more likely that Plutarch confuses this with the year 191 B.C., when both Cato and Sempronius served as legates under M. Acilius Glabrio in that same area against Antiochus. Both were sent as ambassadors to various towns in Greece in order to secure their friendship to Rome.

It will be remembered that Cato shared the control of the old conservative bloc, the Fabians, with Flamininus. Yet he dominated only the "old guard" of that faction. Flamininus had more influence with young moderates (Scullard, pp. 116–18). Cato's following was very respectable; he could count on old nationalists and the conservative ideology held by all aristocrats, new or old, to gain a hearing on all occasions. It is agreed that Cato had the leading part in Roman interference in Carthage in 196, which caused the expulsion of Hannibal from that city (pp. 99–100). The flight of Hannibal to Antiochus was the cause of the political reaction ensuing in the election of so many Cornelians in 194. Since Romans received the news of Hannibal's residence with the Seleucids just before the elections, it was seemly that they choose as consul one who had experience against that enemy.

Cato and Flamininus did not sit on their hands after the Cornelian victory at the polls. Flamininus celebrated a magnificent triumph over Macedonia (Livy XXXIV.46.2, 52.4–12). Cato had never brooded over errors. After he also celebrated a splendid triumph over Spain, Marcus regaled the people with a speech on his Spanish exploits *in contione*, that is, at a convened meeting of the people. Called the *De triumpho ad populum*, the speech was popular (Meyer, p. 25; Scullard, pp. 119, 257). Conservatives were in temporary eclipse because Cato's policy had forced Hannibal to become a lieutenant of Antiochus, and as long as that matter seemed to affect foreign affairs, the conservatives were doomed to a secondary position. Yet there were things to be done, and Cato was busy.

Much is made of the comparative claims of Africanus and Flamininus to the philhellene Greek policy pursued by Rome after her victory over Philip V and the Macedonians at Cynoscephalae, ending the Second Macedonian War in 197 B.C. It is said that an immature man like Flamininus could not have conceived of, nor persevered in, a program requiring the influence and prestige necessary to this Greek policy. That is as absurd as to claim Scipio himself could not have innovated Spanish administrative policy at a similar age. Scipio's letter to Heraclea-by-Latmos in 190 proves that he was a philhellene in 190. By no means does it show he held philhellene ideals in 196 or that he educated Flamininus in those principles before 196. Yet authorities eagerly impute Greek policy to Scipio and deny it to Flamininus. In the issue at hand, Scipio seems to have favored continued occupation of Greece while Flamininus did not. Seemingly, Scipio feared Hannibal, particularly because of his liaison with the Great Antiochus. One hears that Scipio knew the measure of Hannibal's hatred of Rome and sensed that Roman instigation of Hannibal's expulsion from Carthage in 196 would inflame him to attack a vacant Greece and then perhaps Italy herself. But Livy specifically shows (XXXIV.43.3–9) that Scipio's policy was defeated in the senate in 194, at a time when he was consul and had every advantage. The senate explicitly approved the policy of Flamininus over that of and in spite of Africanus. It is sophomoric to insist in the face of this evidence that Roman posture in Greece was either "Scipionic" or required the power and influence of Africanus. No more is it certain even that Scipio founded maritime colonies at unprotected seaports in southern Italy to provide against sea attack. Sempronius, the other consul, is credited by Livy (XXXIV. 45. 1–5) with the establishment of five of the eight colonies; one may question that Scipio had anything to do with them. One cannot prove, or assume, that Sempronius was a mere errand boy.[1]

Aside from all this, 194 was uneventful. Little was accomplished by the great Scipio. Hence the main tradition that Plutarch records—Cato accomplished much in his consulship, but Scipio was relatively inactive—is true, though Plutarch has the details wrong (XI.2). Perhaps it is symptomatic that Scipio resorted to such petty triumphs as that of declaring that Cato and Flaccus had performed the "sacred spring" ritual wrong and redoing it (Livy XXXIV. 44. 1–3; Scullard, p. 118). The jurisdiction was that of the *pontifex maximus*, Licinius Crassus, who was a friend of Scipio's. The Licinii were supposedly aligned with the Scipionic faction, therefore begetting the assumption that this event was mere politicking and not a *bona fide* issue. Scipio was guilty of even worse petty haughteur. He it was who suggested that the seats of senators be separated from those of plebs (commons) at the Roman games. It caused such a public fuss at the end of the year that it became a political liability as bad as the "Hannibalian slip" of Cato. This, it should be remembered, happened at a time when some modern authorities wish to install Scipio as the prestigious developer of Roman eastern policy (Livy XXXIV. 44.5, 54.8).

It is important, for future formulation of eastern policy, that Scipio was unable to establish his ideal: the continuous occupation of Greece. The great philhellene would not in the future dominate considerations of international affairs as he had in the past. It is possible that the Fabians were capable of more, at least in foreign policy, than is often supposed. They must have had something to do with Scipio's significant rebuff. The attitude of nonoccupation was to become characteristic of the conservatives in the future; these may be formative years for Cato's partisans. In retrospect, Scipio's policy would have been a tragic mistake for the welfare of the Greeks themselves. Imagine, for instance, a Greece prostrate to the tender mercies of governors such as those who dominated Spain.

Scipio's faction dominated the elections for 193, nevertheless (Scullard, p. 120; Livy XXXIV.54.1–4). Scipio presided; the consuls, a Cornelius and a Minucius, were friendly. Two of the praetors, the brother of Africanus and C. Flaminius, were reliable; and the two curule aediles, Aemilians both, were of an allied clan. But the expectations of the people were again disappointed. Conservatives accomplished more than the elected Scipios (Livy XXXIV.57.1–6); a commission led by Flamininus negotiated satisfactorily, though inconclusively, with Antiochid ambassadors. Simultaneously, an intrigue begun at Carthage by an agent of Hannibal so frightened Rome that she reverted to neo-isolationism in the West (Nepos, *Hannibal* 33.8; Livy XXXIV.61.1).

II *Roman Negotiations with the Seleucids: Questions of Honor and Politics*

Flamininus' commission was empowered to hear the eastern ambassadors and to reply in a manner consistent with the dignity and interests of Rome. The envoys were at Rome, so this delegation of authority was considerable. Usually the senate heard such embassies. Surely, it is a tacit recognition that Flamininus was the formulator of eastern policy. Because the negotiations mark a shift in policy, it is important to emphasize that Flamininus and the conservatives were responsible.[2] Lamentably, expediency rather than altruism marked the policy change, as will be shown. Quinctius Flamininus began a highly idealistic program when he defeated Philip, returned the Greeks' freedom to them, and then vacated Greece. That liberal image gave Flamininus a surprising diplomatic edge over almost any maneuver the astute Seleucid attachés made.

The eastern ambassadors insisted that the discussions were between friendly equals and that therefore the particulars were to be negotiated, not imposed by Rome. Flamininus answered with a proposal of spheres of influence. He said that friendship was out of the question unless Antiochus would either give up his claims to territory in Thrace (Europe) or permit Roman interference in Asia (Greek cities on the shore of Turkey). In other words, if the Seleucids would stay out of Europe, the Romans would stay out of Asia (Livy XXXIV.57.6–58.4).

This was the change in direction and policy with respect to Greece, as it is the point on which Cato would also have differed with Scipio. He would have enjoyed such a prospect of cheap security. The Roman pledge of freedom to the Greeks had included autonomous Greek cities in Asia Minor. Now these were to be forfeited to secure Greece (Livy XXXIV.58.1–3, 59.5–6). We have this from the very lips of the man who articulated "philhellene" ideals everyone erroneously attributes to Scipio. Further, Flamininus, in this year after the final negotiations, showed beyond a doubt that what he meant by "freedom" was quite another thing than what the Greeks imagined.[3] Roman "freedom" was local autonomy; all foreign affairs were to be negotiated by the Roman senate, and Rome reserved the right to order Greek external affairs without the prior consent of Greeks. As Flamininus gives no indication he realized the discrepancy, he and the senate must have implicitly understood that "Greek freedom" was to be like that of the "*liberae et foederatae*" status of the Spaniards—locally autonomous but subject to the *ius peregrinus* internationally. This is that "more realistic Greek policy" so many wish to canonize Scipio for, saying, "The influence of Africanus" may have been at work on Flamininus (Scullard, p. 120; cp. Livy XXXV.46.4–13). But they were of opposing parties.

"Spheres of influence" are a more blatant form of exploitation than Scipio's military presence. They are much like Cato's utilitarian expediency in Spain and Sicily, and he, far more than Scipio, is apt to have been the creator. They did not require a continuous military presence any more than the Roman-Carthaginian accommodation over the Ebro River before the Second Punic War. Finally, Cato and Flamininus were in continuous communication because their cooperation resulted in a sweeping victory for conservatives at the polls in 192 (Livy XXXV.10; Scullard amusingly says little of the 192 elections; he grudgingly hopes consul Domitius was "friendly" to Scipio, p. 123, a strange assumption, as Scipio campaigned for Laelius). If Flamininus conceived this Spartan concept of freedom and so applied it in his famous speech at Corinth, he is the most cynical of men (Livy XXXIII.32).

The negotiations reached an impasse because of the concept of honor. The eastern diplomats of Antiochus insisted that they had a right to the provinces of both Asia and Thrace, as conquests and treaties long antedating Roman contact in the East had conveyed that right. Conversely, the Roman presence in the East was of recent origin. Antiochus could not honorably accept limitations from a power having no viable rights in the East, from conquest, inheritance, or treaty. Flamininus responded by making the point of honor his Greek policy allowed. He who had "freed the Greeks" when he could so easily have claimed the rights of conquest pointed out that dominion of the Seleucid sort meant virtual slavery for the cities involved. Was this either honorable or noble? The envoys, failing to realize the deceitful "expendable Asiatic Greeks" aspect of the spheres of influence proposal, were embarrassed by this issue of honor. Nor had they taken care to examine Roman dominion in Italy or Spain, so they could indicate that indeed Rome's "protection and freedom" there amounted to something much like Antiochid "slavery." Of course, it goes without saying that the reason for their discomfit was the presence of the envoys from Greek cities. If the Seleucid answer to Flamininus' dramatic question were either "yes" or "no," they were equally condemned. Further, an answer of "no" was more than their function as ambassadors empowered them to give. They could not, in honor, say that Seleucid dominion of cities was ignoble (Livy XXXIV.58.7–13). Implicit here is a feeling that the entire Flamininian Greek policy was at issue.

The negotiations failed to accomplish any treaty of agreement because of this issue. The eastern ambassadors had no authority to make treaties that would limit the power of Antiochus. The Romans would not admit his claim to both Thrace and Asiatic cities. A Roman commission of three was sent to wait on Antiochus' decision whether to treat on that basis or not. Yet it was one of the envoys of Antiochus who begged both sides to observe caution and exercise moderation lest the world be thrown into confusion before one side or the other had time to make concessions. As the Romans had assumed the palm of honor and peacemaker in the name of freedom, they should have made this plea automatically. But representatives from new republics seldom do. They have such an overwhelming conviction of rightness that no concession other than their condescension to be present is felt necessary (Livy XXXIV.59.3,6).

No sooner had the hearings adjourned and each returned to his respective countries than word came from Carthage that Antiochus was surely preparing for war with the aid of Hannibal. The presence of an agent of Hannibal at Carthage seemed further to argue for the possibility of a Third Punic War with Carthage. Such fears were very real to Rome; she still lived in the shadow of Carthage's handiwork in Italy, and the results of Fabian policies against Hannibal were much in evidence over the ruined lands. Cato, if not others, retained at least a folk memory of what pre-Punic Rome had been like, and his very presence was a reminder of what had been lost. Further, the city of Carthage itself had never been razed or besieged. Theoretically working from this base, Hannibal could harrass Italy once again. Livy has capsulated Hannibal's thought: The war ought to be fought in Italy so that dissension might be encouraged among the Italian allies. If Rome were allowed to draw on the total resource of Italy, no enemy could stand against her. Livy says that Hannibal requested a hundred warships, ten thousand infantry, and a thousand cavalry from the eastern king. With that force he would first visit Africa, where he hoped to encourage rebellion among the Carthaginians. If they hesitated, he would land in some part of Italy and arouse a war against Rome among her Italian allies. The king, meanwhile, should cross to Europe and hold a large army in readiness in Greece, which would start the rumor of war in Italy and waken the hopes of disgruntled allies. Some modern authorities doubt that either Antiochus or Hannibal seriously contemplated this action (Livy XXXIV.60–61; cp. *CAH* VIII, p. 203).

A commission was appointed to travel to Africa, ostensibly to settle a boundary and jurisdictional dispute between Numidian Masinissa and Carthage, but perhaps more to discover the truth of the matter of Hannibal's agent and assess the feelings at Carthage with a view to probable war with that city. The committee was composed of Africanus and two of his friends. They left the border dispute undecided, for which Livy rightly castigates Africanus. Some scholars hold the theory that when the commission returned, Africanus went to the East and that he became an *ex-officio* member of the commission that had been sent to wait on the decision of the Seleucid king Antiochus: Sulpicius, Villius, and Publius Aelius. This tradition is substantiated by Cassius Dio, Appian, and Livy in citation of Claudius, who in turn cites the Greek historian Acilius. Appian and Livy tell identical anecdotes of a meeting between Scipio and Hannibal, making it likely that they depend on the same source. Perhaps the fact that this same anecdote is contained in two of Plutarch's biographies strengthens the idea of Polybius as a basis for the tradition. At any rate, Scipio's travelling to the East can hardly be discarded in the face of these authorities. Epigraphical evidence also agrees.[4]

Historians use the fact of Scipio's journey to the East and his visit with Hannibal to account for Africanus' knowledge of the intentions of Hannibal. They say that if he did not go to the East and confer with Hannibal, he would have had to assess the great Carthaginian's actions in another way. But these same scholars have stated that Scipio knew Hannibal's intentions in 194 and 193 B.C. and that is the reason he insisted on a realistic Greek policy. Apparently events in 193 saw something of a reverse in the visions of "Africanus the prophet." Conversely, it was time he did something of the sort. The two years of his faction's ascendancy had accomplished nothing toward the solution of problems it had been elected to solve. It may be that Africanus undertook the diplomatic journey to Asia to give the appearance of doing something, at least, for the eyes of the critical and the less perceptive. If that be true, Scipio succeeded in converting a commission inspired by Flamininus of the moderate conservatives and headed by Sulpicius to reflect credit on himself. But Dio, Livy, and Appian show that the visits between these two served quite another purpose (n. 4).[5]

Antiochus became suspicious of Hannibal because of his interchange with the Romans, and that alone was an accomplishment. He refused to support the projected expedition to Carthage and to Greece and tried to de-emphasize the influence and prestige of Hannibal in his army and his country out of jealousy and fear. Thus the potential of the African general was neutralized by a shrewd diplomatic blow at the pride of Antiochus. Livy alone gives credit for this to a member of Flamininus' commission: Publius Villius Tappulus. He says (XXXV.14, 19) Tappulus deliberately sought out Hannibal at Ephesus for the purpose of frequent meetings so as to assess his sentiments and dispel Hannibal's fear that he had anything to apprehend from the Romans. It followed automatically from the number of these conferences, as well as from personal pique, that Antiochus reconsidered his war plans, and that had the effect mentioned above. It is a matter of considerable importance which of the two men is to be given credit for all this. Seemingly, if Africanus had been able to report firsthand knowledge of the intentions of Hannibal to the senate, it should have made a considerable difference in that body's policy. On the other hand, if Tappulus returned to report his findings, it would not only make the same difference but also reflect political glory on himself and the party of Flamininus and Cato. There is no way to decide the truth of the matter except to indicate that the political result was an overwhelming victory for Flamininus' conservatives at the polls in 192.

The commission of Sculpicius itself accomplished little. It had to return to Rome uncertain of anything. At least, the worm had turned on the moral argument. The representative of Antiochus showed by his opening remarks that this argument had not gone unnoticed. He immediately drew the parallel between the mainland Greeks whom Rome had freed and the Greeks in Italy who were under their hegemony and paying tribute to Rome. Then he outlined the similarities between the latter and the Asiatic cities of Greeks which Antiochus claimed. Mentioned also were the Greeks of the island of Sicily. Finally, he asked for equity, not war. Sulpicius denied the validity of the argument as far as the Italian Greeks were concerned, because he insisted that they were still under their original treaties with Rome. These Greeks, he said, had enjoyed one unbroken continuity of right under one sustained sovereignty. The Asiatic Greeks had seen several changes of hegemony and gone from a free status to dominance and then to freedom again. And as the Seleucids were now holding the Asiatic Greeks in slavery after they had tasted freedom, the moral argument obtained (i.e., one must taste freedom to assess slavery). As for the Italian Greeks, it was as if they had never known any other state than that which they now had—dominance by Rome—and they were in no worse case than they had ever been. On the other hand, Rome had returned to the mainland Greeks the freedom that they had once loved. As a manifest, the ambassadors from the Asiatic cities were brought forward to testify to their wishes and their desires. They were loud in condemnation of Antiochus, but also in their demands for this and that, so the meeting was turned into a wrangle and nothing was gained (Livy XXXV.16.1–17.2).

The argument of Sulpicius defeats itself, of course. It simply asserts that if one has established *possessio* of subject cities in such a way that they have not reestablished independence or challenged that subjection, then one has a right to them. *Possessio*, as of subjects, in other words, was the unchallenged occupancy of property for a period of time. That was sufficient to establish good title. Therefore, it was enough to argue that the Greeks of Italy and Sicily had become possessions of the Roman people—they had never challenged their original Roman agreements or treaties. The Romans obviously wished to argue that continuous occupancy was title of possessions and put people in an altogether different category than those who had seen changes of *possessio*. The Antiochids, conversely, refused to recognize that Roman legal definition, preferring to argue from a similarity of rights among all Greeks or, indeed, among all mankind. But of course that side of the argument did not interest them. They were intent to establish, not that the Greeks were free, but that Roman domination of Greeks in Italy and Sicily gave them a similar right to conquer Greeks elsewhere. Rome could not allow that, of course. Not only would it admit that others also had a right to conquer, but it endangered her Greek settlement. Macedonia would then have a right to reconquer the Greeks when she was able. Finally, both sides insisted upon trying to prove that their previously nonnegotiable positions were morally and logically superior to the other. Since the previous meetings had already shown that morality and logic made no difference, the ultimate decisions being made on entirely selfish definitions of principle, this was the ultimate *reductio ad absurdum*. It is almost a truism of diplomacy that principles are nonnegotiable, as they are also invariably relative to the best interests of the nation involved. Hence meetings beginning from a position of equality that set out merely to persuade others of one's own rightness are automatically pointless. There seems always to be a hope that the "other side" will compromise.

The vaccilation of policy, nonaccomplishment in the East, and perhaps some mixture of Roman hesitation to become involved there again caused the triumph of the conservatives and particularly the moderate wing of that party in the elections for 192. There was rather a sharp contest between Flamininus and Scipio particularly over the issue of foreign affairs and the comparative merits of the brothers of each, who were running for the consulship. Livy says (XXXV. 10) canvassing was more spirited than usual. Flamininus was preferred, says the same source, because his brother could argue unity of the two in command during the recent wars with Philip V in Macedonia. It is not likely that was the reason; more was at stake and more was implied than simply the reputations of the two brothers of the candidates. Livy further insists that the election of the plebeian consul Cnaeus Domitius Ahenobarbus shows Africanus' complete lack of influence, though modern Cornelian apologists call Domitius "friendly" to the Cornelians in summing up the elections of 194 (Scullard, p. 123). But Scipio worked for Gaius Laelius. If Ahenobarbus was a partisan of Scipio before 192, perhaps he was no longer so after that year. The results of the election seem to indicate that Rome endorsed the Flamininian Greek policy while rejecting that of Scipio.

The Romans were cautious, for they designated one consul, Domitius, to lead the legions wherever the senate decided (Livy XXXV.20). If Antiochus chose that year for the invasion of Greece, as everyone seemed to expect, at least some precaution would have been taken. The elections show also that Romans wanted defense at home, not in Greece. Actually, the popular policy of keeping the main defensive force in Italy was realistic because of the presence of Philip and Macedonia. As long as Rome was unsure of Philip's intentions, she could not commit her entire force to the East lest Macedonia outflank it and threaten invasion of Italy from the rear. Even when Macedonia declared for Rome, Antiochus could use limited forces supplemented by his Aetolian allies to neutralize Philip, while maintaining a large force to threaten invasion of Italy. This gave the Romans chills, as suggested by Hannibal at that time. The proposals of Hannibal along this line, set forth in the thirty-sixth book of Livy (7), show he was still the strategic genius of the age. But since Roman victories were won by men, determination, and perseverance rather than by strategy and tactics, it is questionable how much difference his presence in strategy sessions would have made. One thing is sure: Talk of ultimate foreign policy in Greece was superfluous because of the lack of knowledge concerning what Macedonia would do. There is no way policy makers could have known that. Cato's orientation in this was that of favoring "spheres of influence"—dominating Greece but staying out of it, the whole point of such a policy. Yet in this case, his wish to moderate the exploitative imperialism he so obviously approved in Spain and Africa was caused only by what he considered the corrupting influences of the Greeks. Calculating as that may have been in theory, it would have left Greece open to the eastern Seleucids and in the end helped Greece. There is little reason to speculate whether the Seleucids' military men could have brought it off or not. The Roman alternative ultimately destroyed Greece, and that is all we need to know. Cato's policy therefore, no matter what the reasons he suggested it were, was the right one for the future of Greece. Few recognize that fact.

The change of Flamininus to an "either-or" foreign policy of spheres of influence actually doomed Greece, for it led Romans again to contemplate military presence there. So Africanus' idea won in the end—to the detriment of the very Greeks he affected to esteem. Hannibal managed to reconcile himself to Antiochus before the end of 192, according to Livy. That meant that the ultimate result of all the eastern negotiations was nothing, as far as stopping the threat of war was concerned. The Roman attempt to construct an artificial parity on the basis of Asiatic versus continental Greeks failed. Since they had negotiated on that point alone, leaving themselves no other option, war was imminent (Livy XXXV.19).

III   The Beginnings of War: Aetolian Defiance

The Aetolians, who had been instrumental in the rupture between Rome and the East, acted first. Their ambassador to Antiochus, Thoas, returned breathing the flames of war and bringing with him Menippus as an ambassador from the king. Together they spread abroad all the rumor of the power of the naval and land forces of the king, the number of cavalry he mustered, and the huge quantity of elephants requisitioned from India. Finally, they swayed the minds of the people with details of the wealth of gold being brought—so much that even the Romans might be persuaded to join the king (Livy XXXV.12.6, 23.5, 31.1–6, 32–33.11). It is a truism that Greek resistance to gold had always been weak, and the assurance that protection would be furnished by others made them less than usually constant. All the members of the Aetolian League became triumphantly confident and openly advocated breaking the alliance with Rome. A commission headed by Flamininus himself was sent to Greece to oppose Aetolian influence and attempt to rally the Greek communities against the eastern king. He travelled to Athens, to Chalcis, to Thessaly, where he addressed the full council, and then to the city of Demetrias. The commission seemed successful. It accomplished the reminder of Roman alliance and fear wherever it went, with, however, disturbing signs and one exception (Polybius XXI.31).

The alarming signals were everywhere. Greeks were disenchanted with the Romans. Nearly all symptoms were those of a healthy people wishing for the determination of their own international affairs. Rome held out the alliance arrangements and expected stability on the basis of the status quo. The two seemed inimical. As was said in the presence of Flamininus himself, "Demetrias is free in appearance, but in reality everything is done at the

Romans' nod" (Livy XXXV.31.12). This tactlessness brought banishment to the Magnetarch who spoke (XXXV.32.1, 34.6), but people both there and everywhere showed it was the common feeling (XXXV.31.13, 32–34) by their actions and those of many of their leaders, as was evidenced at Aetolia. There the oratory reached unprecedented heights. Menippus, envoy of Antiochus, sounded the keynote by speaking of the possibility of a new freedom that might stand by itself rather than depend on others (Livy XXXV.32). Athenians were there by the specific request of the Roman commission—Livy says Flamininus "begged (*petit*)" them to be present—and they dared to remind the Aetolians of their alliance with Rome and urge caution before spoiling the good elements of that relationship (Livy XXXV.32–33, 46.4). They suggested that the commission headed by Flamininus be invited so that all matters could be settled. Though the majority opposed this, the elders secured them an audience before the council. The councillors agreed to go because Flamininus believed that a presence would show the world the Romans wished peace.

Before the council Flamininus reviewed the history of the Aetolian-Roman alliance and reminded everyone how often they had broken the terms of the agreement. About the allied cities, if there were disagreement, it would be better to settle that amicably by sending ambassadors to Rome than for the entire Roman and Seleucid peoples, with Aetolians as "*lanistae* (gladiator trainers)," to go to war. Further, he added, those who had caused the war would be the first to experience its calamities (Livy XXXV.33.4–8; precisely that lack of foreign autonomy Greeks hated). These remarks inflamed the Aetolians. Impetuously, without waiting for an adjournment, the council passed a decree by which Antiochus was invited to liberate Greece and to arbitrate between Rome and Aetolia.

What a bitter irony that must have seemed to Flamininus, the commission, and the Romans! Antiochus had now succeeded in confounding Rome with her own *fait accompli*. Rome was herself cast in the role of villian while orientals became "The Champions of Greek Freedom," magnanimously offering to mediate between "the enemy" (Rome) and the Greeks. So abruptly had the situation reversed that Flamininus seems to have been taken aback. He had little to say by way of rejoinder to the remarks of the Aetolian party, its leader, or the chairman of the council, ingeniously called a *praetor* by Livy. He was personally affronted in a direct way; when he asked for a copy of the decree, the chairman, Damocritus, airily replied that he had more pressing business to attend to—he would deliver a copy of the answer and the decree presently, when his military camp was pitched on the banks of the Tiber. Livy resents that insolence (Livy XXXV.33.7–11), saying Damocritus showed no respect for Flamininus' high position. But the "high position" Livy mentions was that of legate from Rome to Greece. It bore no *imperium* and was not empowered to commit Rome in foreign affairs. Livy means to say, no doubt, that a lowly Greek had no right to ignore a specific request from a senator of the Romans. But if a Greek had presumed to ask for copies of a senatorial decree, one imagines what the answer might have been!

Greek defiance of Rome was based heavily on momentary expectation of a king from Asia. They had, however, to show enthusiasm for his advent. Aetolia cast about for means of fomenting revolution and enthusiasm for Antiochus. It was taken for granted that the common people in all the Greek cities sympathized with Aetolia and resented Roman interference in Greek affairs but that the leaders and the officials in all those cities wished for the status quo and Roman guidance. For that reason Aetolian leaders planned a treacherous uprising in Chalcis, Lacedaemon, and Demetrias. The last of these was taken successfully by stealth rather than by strength. Lacedaemon proved to be different. There the crafty Aetolians were slaughtered after they had slain the tyrant Nabis. But the power vacuum resulted in occupation of Sparta and annexation of that city by the Achaean League. There was potential danger in that, as the Achaeans were already under the leadership of Philopoemen, who was dangerously proud, assertive, and nationalistic. Chalcis forced the Aetolian plot to a complete standstill and gave the spies little to do but return to their homes. Yet Demetrias was quite a prize to offer Antiochus as a base of operations. It presented that leader with a problem (Livy XXXV.34.3–39.8).

Antiochus could ill afford to invade Greece at this time. There was rebellion among the Asiatic Greeks (Livy XXXV.42.2), the Attalids were agitating against him (XXXV.17.1–2), and he had not prepared a sufficient force to face the Romans. He, like Rome, had hoped to carry Greece diplomatically and force concessions from Rome in that way rather than by trial of arms. Yet he could ill afford, now that the die was cast, to ignore the pleas of the Aetolians and sacrifice all the enthusiasm his promises had encouraged. He planned to invade with just an advance token force, since Rome had no army in Greece as yet. That proved to be a mistake, just as the Aetolian pledges to Antiochus had been mistakes. Both had hoped for infinitely more from the other than they received (Livy XXXV.43.1–6, 44.1–7).

The Aetolians had promised that there would be embassies flocking in to join the standard of the Seleucids. None appeared. The Greeks, on the other hand, expected to see armies, navies, and elephants without number. The tiny force of ten thousand infantry, five hundred cavalry, and six elephants, though billed as an advance token force, was disappointing to Greeks who had expected an oriental horde. To be sure, that was not the case in Demetrias and in Lamia, where the Aetolian council met him (Livy XXXV.43). In both there was enthusiasm, but these Greeks were predisposed to look on all Antiochus did with favor. Others were to be more critical (XXXV.46.4–13). Yet the initial enthusiasm for one who offered "freedom" was so intense that many, as Plutarch admits, wavered in their loyalty to Rome (XII.2), in spite of the fact that Plutarch himself impugns the theme that Antiochus would bring freedom to Greece. He feels that the Greeks already had their freedom as a gift from the Romans who liberated Greece from Philip and the Macedonians. However, the inconstant states were brought back by the action of Flamininus and by such legates as Cato, who now buried the hatchet in his country's emergency and volunteered for action under Manius Acilius Glabrio, consul-elect for the year, assigned the *provincia* in Greece (Livy XXXV.48–50, XXXVI.1–3).

IV *Cato's Contributions to the Roman Effort in Greece*

The service of Cato is treated as something of a triumph by Plutarch (XI.3–XII). Others had given themselves to ease and enjoyment, but Cato girt his loins anew, ever ready to serve friends and fellow citizens in forum or field. It was not time for the young plebeian to begin asserting himself. He had followed the lead of Flamininus, despite differences of opinion, for the good of the conservative bloc. That policy had led to war in Greece, and winning it was the prime consideration. As the war became imminent, the Scipionic faction had again won the early elections for that year, and opposing senators took service as best they might. There was no opprobrium attached to serving as tribune or legate, if there were need. The much worse error would be not to serve at all. Cato made the most of every opportunity and covered himself with glory from a subordinate position.

There is some difference among the sources as to the actual office held by Cato in this year 191. Livy calls him a lieutenant of consular rank, but all other available sources say he was a legionary tribune appointed by Manius. Whatever the office, his was a signal service (Dio, Zonaras 9.19; Livy XXXVI.17.1; Cicero, *Cato* X.32; Plutarch XII.1; Appian XI.18).

The career of Cato as a legate to cities that wavered in their allegiance to Rome is documented by Plutarch (XII). He visited three that were very prominent in the configuration and plans of the Achaean League and that should have been constant, if the presence of Flamininus meant anything. One was Corinth, which Flamininus had used virtually as a base of operations for his own embassies to other places (Livy XXXV.39.1, 8). Aegium, which was to be used as the diplomatic seat of the Achaean League in their councils entertaining the representations of the Aetolians, was another. A third was Patrae, which had been used as a headquarters for military movements by Philopoemen in his conflict with the Spartan tyrant Nabis. Finally, there was Athens, where he went not as an official legate, but rather on his own, as Plutarch implies.

The diplomatic mission seems to deny Cato's famous prejudice. He had learned Greek, probably in studies with the poet Ennius. Now that ability bore fruit in diplomatic negotiations for his country. Doubtless part of the reason Cato was selected to travel to these cities was his Greek-speaking ability. The simple fact that he was able to persuade the Greeks to back Rome rather than Antiochus implies that Cato was fluent in the use of their language. Plutarch explicitly says as much, while also showing that at Athens Cato preferred to seem ignorant of Greek. He used an interpreter to deliver a speech that astonished the Athenians. Athenian Ionic Greek was by reputation brief, pungent, and pointed in its expression. Therefore Cato took pride in the fact that his Latin delivery required many more words to translate into Athenian Greek and, even then, gave the translator difficulty compressing his few words into those many. While he affected to despise Greeks, he was not above a fatuous acceptance of their praise. Lamentably, though he could have spoken to the Athenians in their own language, as

Plutarch says, Cato preferred to cling to a show of narrow Latinity and mock those who admired things Greek.

This kind of shallow nationalism lay behind much of the later Roman treatment not only of the Greeks but also of other peoples, such as the Spaniards. The "native ways" to which the man clung were presumably archaic Latin folkways. Their superiority or advisability consisted only in this—that Cato had been born to that heritage and its power had been magnified by a successful militarism parading under the guise of security. Surely, that was less to be admired than the cultural and intellectual attainments of the Greeks. Whether those in turn were enervating to the Roman folkways is another issue altogether.

Sophisticated civilization seems always to corrode the militaristic enclaves of naïve primitives whose energy is focused on physical survival, muscular courage, and mechanical security. It naturally generates other concerns and depends upon an assumed personal integrity that has little to do with the competition of bulls for the procreative cows that represent pride and identity in cave and jungle. Primitive nationalism is little more than a graduation from the caveman ethics of clubs and muscles, to the status symbols of wealth and material possessions, the sacred cows of advancing technology. Such was the "native way" of those like Cato; but those Greeks— and there were many—who tilted with him merely descended to his level.

Some small triumphs were vouchsafed Antiochus in Greece, but his entire operation there seemed less that of a man who had reconquered all the Seleucid domains than of some beginner in the art of war. He had undertaken a major invasion with inferior force and allowed himself to be cajoled into abandoning his planned diversion with Hannibal at Carthage (Livy XXXV.42). That left him as a guest in the land of others, dependent on their promises for armies and supplies. The history of the Aetolians should have warned him of the folly that policy actuated (Livy XXXV.43.6; Appian XI.12). In addition, Hannibal had warned him how dangerous it would be to invade Greece without taking provision for enlisting or neutralizing Philip (Livy XXXVI.7.16–21; cp. XXXIV.60–61). He had done neither, jealous of the reputation of the Carthaginian. Further, he did not listen to the urgings of Hannibal that Italy be invaded or all else was in vain (Appian XI.14). Sought out later on, Hannibal reiterated all these points, adding the emphasis on military dependence. That, as a matter of fact, was the only advice Antiochus was able or cared then to take. He sent to Asia for the imperial army (Livy XXXVI.8.1). In the meantime, Manius Acilius Glabrio entered Greece with an army of twenty thousand foot soldiers, two thousand cavalry, and fifteen elephants (Appian XI.15; Livy XXXV.20.11, 41.4, XXXVI.1.6, 14.1).

The Romans had taken a long time to prepare, but there were reasons for that. They had anticipated attacks in several places throughout the Mediterranean because of Hannibal's connection with Antiochus. The great king and the great general caused the Romans to take every precaution. The invading army would probably have been larger but for the uncertainty about Philip. Antiochus took care of that unknown himself by attacking Thessaly and seeing to the burial of all the corpses left at Cynoscephalae by Philip after his loss to Flamininus and the Romans there in 196. He dared to draw the parallel between himself and Philip in the way they cared for the dead and presumably, therefore, for the living. Philip then joined the Romans and remained true to his treaty of alliance signed after Cynoscephalae (Appian XI.16; Livy XXXVI.8.3–6).

The Battle of Thermopylae was an historic one, in the sense that Antiochus, like the Spartans under Leonidas almost three hundred years before, occupied an impenetrable position in the pass. He had no other choice because he discovered to his sorrow that Hannibal was right and the Greeks were unreliable broken reeds to lean upon in time of need (Livy XXXVI.7.2; Appian XI.14). Fiercely advocating war when they thought Asiatics would do the battling, they now meekly counselled caution and could muster at best four thousand fighting men of the Aetolian League. These in turn were almost worthless so far as holding a position was concerned. (Appian XI.17; Livy XXXVI.15.3). Antiochus was worried lest his position at Thermopylae be outflanked and turned, as was that of Leonidas in the same place, by a force going around him to the rear via a mountain pass. Therefore he stationed two thousand of the Aetolians on the heights.

Antiochus' situation in the pass of Thermopylae was secure. The Romans attacked it to their own cost and discomfit. The pass was blocked by a double wall and ditch and here and there a stone rampart. Slingers, archers, and javelin men were massed on the heights to the right of the Romans, while the elephants were grouped on the left with the cavalry. Two assaults were necessary to take the first line under a veritable hail of missiles from the right. Then under pressure the Asiatics withdrew to the walls and there stood at a great advantage over the Romans attempting to attack them from below. As Livy says (XXXVI.17–19), the Romans would have withdrawn, their task unaccomplished, or more would have perished had not Marcus Porcius dislodged the Aetolians and shown his standards on the heights behind the enemy (Plutarch XIII–XIV; Appian XI.19–20). At first, the enemy thought the Romans were Aetolians, but as Cato's column drew near and they recognized the Roman standards, they panicked and threw away their weapons as they fled. Only five hundred remained with their king, and with that token force he made his way back to Asia. The consul, with his army, consolidated the Greek cities and then demanded that Aetolia surrender Heraclea. She refused, so war with Aetolia continued (Livy XXXVI.22.1–4).

This was Cato's finest hour! With an inferior force he dislodged the enemy and performed a maneuver so strategically necessary that it meant victory and the saving of certain Roman defeat at Thermopylae. Plutarch (XIII–XIV) adds the personal touch, describing Cato's precipitous and precarious wandering about the heights on a dark, moonless night and then, by near accident, blundering into the Aetolian camp they sought and ascertaining it by sending men of Firmum to capture an enemy and discover the truth from him (Appian XI.18–19; Livy XXXVI.18; Polybius XX.8.6). These men of Firmum were from near Cato's home district, and Plutarch says they were always trusty and zealous in their neighbor's service. It is another instance of Cato's surprising popularity with the men he commanded, popularity won by the mixture of strictness and leniency he displayed in Spain and elsewhere, by the tolerance in fundamentalism that alone makes rigid conservatism palatable.

The rewards of that strategic triumph were great. Cato was able to sound his triumphant note in Rome and thus counterbalance the deeds and tutelary leadership of Flamininus. His own extravagant praise of his action does not endear him to modern generations of men who suffer the trauma of performing mighty deeds in silence and then endure the gnawing doubt of mock humility, waiting for others to hymn their praise. It did serve the purpose of allowing Cato to contest leadership of the conservatives with Flamininus and proved to be the stepping-stone for his career of leadership there.

He was able to say, without exaggeration, that those who saw him pursuing the Aetolians and hewing them down saw in him the vengeance of Rome—Rome owed more to Cato than he to Rome (Plutarch XIV.2–4).

Consul M. Acilius Glabrio, stout partisan of Scipio that he was, embraced Cato in the flush of victory, crying out that neither he nor Rome could fittingly reward Cato for his deed. He did not, however, forget to send one of his own party with the news of victory to Rome before publicly awarding that boon to Cato. Cato, not to be outdone, and with perhaps some inkling of the truth, traversed the entire distance from the field of triumph to Rome with great speed—in five days' time—and arrived there at night. Not sparing a moment, he went to the praetor Marcus Junius and had the senate summoned at daybreak. He was before that body, giving his report, when the secret messenger of Manius arrived, found with dismay that he was after Cato, and entered the senate while Cato's report was in progress (Livy XXXVI.21.4–10). The senate, temporizing between the two men, ordered both to make their report to the assembly of the people. But Cato had again seized opportunity by acting with dispatch. The message was plain for everyone to see, and the triumph of Cato was complete.

V *Footnotes to the Victory*

There is a sordid and tragic little footnote to the victory that is always overlooked. It comes in two parts, one given in the exhortation of Glabrio to his men and the other in the following war between Rome and the Aetolians. The speech of Glabrio pictures the Roman attitude to all enemies. It describes the enemy as Syrians and Greeks, the most worthless peoples among mankind and born for slavery. The king himself was worse, because he had during the winter and for the sake of love alone married a girl of obscure and common family (Livy XXXVI.17.2–16, 11.1–6).

This exercise in bigotry was capped by the hortatory propaganda commonly used by generals for spurring naïve soldiery to selfless bravery in doubtful military encounters. "Remember men," he said in effect, "you are fighting for the liberty of Greece—to set free a people from the Aetolians and Antiochus. Besides, you will get all the fabulous wealth from the camp of Antiochus and fall heir to the riches of the East." Cynically, one doubts the soldiers knew or cared about the Greek heritage of freedom; but the gold of Antiochus! That was another thing altogether.

War mottoes are like that! Some time has been spent here showing that the only reason Rome permitted war in the East was that of security for Italy. In the field that argument was ridiculous before men who would be called on to fight and die. There, other egotistical and psychological reasoning had to be used as inspiration. They must feel morally superior, righteously outraged, and motivated by greed. All the mottoes had to be ambiguous, so they would sound like the glory of mankind but also lend themselves to immediate personal interpretation. The more of glory and self in the "principles" of a nation at war, the greater its success. Thus personal motives lie behind the specious reasoning of all foreign conflict parading as "good" or "right." Hardly ever are the trumpeted moralistic, altruistic slogans a true indication of the thought of the people, who do their fighting for personal reasons or motives that can be personally interpreted.

After a successful siege and storming of Heraclea, the sordid detail in the war with Actolia is that of Glabrio's demand for unconditional surrender. To be sure, that demand was based on his own misunderstanding of the Greek expression of committing oneself to the faith of a victor. By that phrase the Greek meant he came as a suppliant and was due that kind of consideration, but would also be free to break off relations if the opportunity presented itself. The Roman, however, understood by that same phrase that the vanquished had surrendered unconditionally. Therefore Glabrio thought he had won (Livy XXXVI.22.7–24.12, 27.1–28.8; Polybius XX.9.1–10.12) when Heraclean envoys used the expression. The protesting legates were claimed to demonstrate their real status. Only then did these Aetolian ambassadors realize their true estate before the Roman general, but they still had to refuse his terms until they had time to call the assembly of the Aetolians that alone could negotiate such agreements as were demanded by Glabrio.

The concessions he asked were in some cases virtually impossible to fulfill, and the Aetolians called them neither just nor Greek. Glabrio angrily retorted that they had no right to speak of what was proper according to the customs of the Greeks since they had just surrendered unconditionally. Yet when the Aetolians had been assembled in council they became so incensed at the terms of surren-

der that they were tempted to continue the war (Livy
XXXVI.28.9–29.11), particularly because Thoas had successfully
petitioned Antiochus to send them money for the continuance of
hostilities. It would serve the king by holding the Romans in Greece
until he was ready (Polybius XX.10.13–11.10).

Meanwhile Glabrio had begun the siege of Naupactus, the armistice for making peace having terminated with no official peace
signed. This continued for two months, while Philip, the ally of
Rome, consolidated a number of cities in his control with Glabrio's
blessing. Many of these surrendered to him rather than submit to
the mercies of Glabrio, having heard of the way he treated Aetolian
suppliants. Therefore Philip was regaining his control in Greece
under the shield of Rome—hardly a fortuitous state of affairs. A
second friend of Rome, the Achaean League, used her presence and
success at Thermopylae to enlarge the league. All of this strenuously
tested the Roman settlement in Greece—the ideal was, after all,
freedom rather than renewed domination by Macedonians,
Achaeans, or whatever (Livy XXXVI.30.1–35.14).

At this juncture Flamininus, still in Greece with his commission,
took action. He personally brought the commander of the Achaean
League to book and then moved to Naupactus to talk sense with
Manius. This he did by pointing out to that individual exactly what
Roman policy was, in Greece and the East, and where he fit in that
picture. The man had not seen it before. Then Flamininus, by the
force of his personality and popularity alone, got the Aetolians in
Naupactus to accept an armistice during which they should appeal
to the senate in Rome. Thus did the whole war in Greece with
Antiochus and the Aetolian League come to an end. But that end
was as much the gift of Flamininus as of Glabrio.

One must indicate in all fairness that the prejudice moderns display against this man Flamininus in contrast to Scipio ought to be
re-examined. The way he persuaded Achaeans and Aetolians by the
sheer force of his personality, as well as their obvious affection for
him, attests that here is a charismatic figure as underrated as any in
history. The manner in which both Flamininus and the Greeks
blithely assume that he, rather than Scipio, was the author of Greek
freedom speaks volumes. In the crucible of eastern deeds,
Flamininus alone survived. If, as modern advocates of Scipio say, he
indeed authored that Greek policy without, one recalls, ever having
been in Greece, they must account for the tremendous power of

Flamininus' personality in Greece. They must also explain how an old pro-Scipionic campaigner like Glabrio meekly agreed with Flamininus when the latter spelled out the A-B-C's of foreign policy to him. After all, Scipio's party was supposed to have invented that policy!

CHAPTER 6

Cato's Middle Years:
Private Life and Public Service

I   Cato's Social Marriage and the Birth of Licinianus

THE triumph of Thermopylae and Cato's breathless race to Rome were followed by an event probably as important to Cato, though less sensational in historical terms: Cato married Licinia, a lady of gentle birth, in the middle of the year 191 B.C. Forty-three was rather a late age for marriage, as Roman custom went, but it may be that Cato had determined to remain single until his consular rank and senatorial membership were well established. He could then hope to marry better in terms of social rank, and his issue would be assured of higher political connections. The late marriage by no means symbolized unusual continence. Between his first and second marriage, when Cato was well advanced in age, according to Plutarch, he was prone to indulge his sexual appetite by taking solace in a slave girl who secretly visited his bed. Some such arrangement was probably true of the years before his first marriage.[1]

The match seems to have been a happy one. Licinia fulfilled Cato's expectations in that she had a horror of what was disgraceful and therefore was obedient to her husband, though there is every indication she also had a mind of her own (Plutarch XX.1). Cato was disturbed by her garrulousness. Though his On Agriculture (CXLIII) said that a wife should visit neighboring and other women seldom and not have them visiting in her house, Cato was unable to impose that ideal on his own wife. Plutarch says (IX.6) one of the few times Cato repented of anything in his life was when he had entrusted a secret to Licinia. That would be cause for regret only if she found it difficult to keep secrets, and the occasions of such "gossiping" would be the socializing functions Cato frowned on.

Similarly, also according to Plutarch, Licinia meddled in Cato's politics more than she was supposed to. It will be recalled that Cato forbade women to say anthing about politics or the laws, even at home. "If modesty would keep matrons within limits of their proper rights," he says, "they would not concern themselves with the question of what laws should be adopted or repealed." Cato also exhorted Roman husbands to keep their wives "individually under control." Ironically, he was incapable of doing that himself. Plutarch says (VIII) Licinia acted as transmitter of requests for young Marcus and was rather insistent—so much so that Cato petulantly retorted, ". . . you rule me. . . ." More important still, the episode was in a political setting: "Wife, the Athenians rule the Hellenes, I rule the Athenians, you rule me, and your son you. Therefore let him make sparing use of that authority which makes him, child though he is, the most powerful of the Hellenes." It is clear from this that Licinia did not maintain silence meekly at home, even in affairs political. She insisted—Plutarch adds that Cato found himself "much under his son's orders through the lad's mother."

Cato seems to have been as undemonstrative in public as he was hesitant to divulge personal details at all times. His speech against the Oppian Law testifies that he could scarcely conceal the blushes as he made his way through a crowd of women to the forum. That confrontation was entirely verbal, however, as he follows it by saying that the women blocked the roads and spoke to the husbands of other women in behalf of the repeal of the law. He styles such behavior immodest and undignified (Livy XXXIV.2), a very strict interpretation of verbal confrontation, though Cato blushed at it! The man must have been something of a shrinking violet with the ladies. He did not embrace his wife in public, says Plutarch, unless some catastrophe such as loud thunder frightened her (XVII.7). The bashful bravado of a shy man caused Cato to add that he was happy when it thundered. Political circumstance allowed him to identify his own timidity with propriety and enforce it on others. As censor, Cato expelled a senator who embraced his wife not only in public, but also, and even worse, before their daughter. Apparently this was "indecent behavior for a senator." Yet Marcus is known to have said it was more praiseworthy to be a good husband than a good senator. Imagine this human study in contradictions surreptitiously pecking his wife on the cheek at farewells or arrivals in public! He who had held a hundred enemies at bay and single-handed stemmed the tide of battle turned to blushing jelly at a wife's fond glance. Loud champion of a husband's sway, "The Censor" had only subdued reverence for his own wife.

Marcus and Licinia lived in the same unpretentious dwellings that Marcus affected when he was a bachelor. Small and simple, Plutarch calls them "cottages," and Cato bragged that none was plastered. The central house was so little that it did not afford adequate privacy. When his son Marcus had married Tertia, after the death of Licinia, the house was too small and simple to shield the comings and goings of Cato's concubine. The newlyweds were embarrassed, especially as the slave had a tendency to show off. Yet from Cato's boasting he could afford a commodious home. So too with the food Cato and Licinia ate. Plutarch says that Cato continued to esteem and eat turnips as a delectable dish, while his wife was kneading bread. Still, Cato later set a sumptuous table for convivial gatherings in the country, and they never lacked for domestics. Surely, Licinia did not have to knead bread (Plutarch IV.4, XXI.5–8, XXIV.2, XXV.1–3, Comparison, IV.4–5).

Marcus Licinianus was born in 190 B.C. (n. 1). Though Cato stood for the censorship in the following year and involved himself fully in public affairs, he was almost always present when Licinia bathed and bundled the child. Cato would forego all but state business to be home at that time. Not only did Licinia nurse the child, as was customary, but since it was an ancient belief that mother's milk had a psychologically binding effect on others, Licinia gave suck to the infants of her slaves, says Plutarch (XX.3), so that they might cherish a brotherly affection for little Marcus. Plutarch himself, in his essay On Liberal Education, advised mothers to nurse their own children because of the feeling of warmth and security it brought to the child. Ancient people were aware of psychological factors.

II The Seleucid War and Triumph of Lucius Scipio

The years 191 and 190 were totally dominated by the Scipionic faction. It was something of a triumph for them that Glabrio, the commander at Thermopylae, was able to chase Antiochus out of Greece, even though Cato stole the show in that particular engagement. Simultaneously, the other consul had soundly whipped the Boii in north Italy (Livy XXXVI.38–40), helping to open that area for settlement and colonization and also freeing the Romans from a nagging fear of the Gauls. He was Scipio Nasica, and judging from his military exploits, he may rank with the best of the Cornelian generals. The elections for 190 returned Lucius Cornelius Scipio and Gaius Laelius for consuls; as Livy says: "*Africanum intuentibus cunctis*" ("all looking toward Africanus")—favoring Africanus through his brother Lucius (XXXVI. 45. 9). The senate expected Africanus to command through his brother as seen by the later allocation of *provinciae*, when the senate appointed Lucius to Greece, against Antiochus, after Africanus said he would go along as *legatus* (XXXVII. 1. 7–10).

Many assume that the Roman decision to pursue Antiochus into Asia was that of Africanus. The proof is Africanus' pursuit of Hannibal into Africa in 205 through 202 B.C., from which it is inferred that he now persuaded the senate to apply the policy of conquest for security to Antiochus and the Seleucids. The personal opinions of Scipio can only be surmised; there is evidence he used influence to cause the people's assembly to vote a declaration of war against Antiochus. This need not imply that the war was Scipio's idea. Indeed, the senate had initiated the proposal. The original declaration of war, in 191, had been "against Antiochus and those under his authority." Hence there was no alteration of policy involved in the actions of 190. The battles of 191 with the Aetolians in Greece were merely a prelude to the main engagement with King Antiochus— separate war with Aetolia was never declared.[2]

The renewal of war in 190 was also directed by the senate. After receiving favorable omens from all shrines, it asked that the question be proposed to the assembly whether they wished and ordered war to be entered upon with King Antiochus and those who had followed his path. If this motion should be adopted, the consuls could lay the whole question before the senate. Scipio was delegated to carry the motion in the assembly. The senate seems to have been the impetus behind the question of war in Asia. Finally, the 191 delaration of war was the basis for two clarifications of *provinciae*: those of Lucius Scipio in 190 and Cn. Manlius Vulso in 189. The former stated that when Lucius arrived in the *provincia*, if the public interest seemed to demand it, he should lead the army over into Asia. That of Vulso caused the senate to stipulate that his army should be used against Galatia merely because Gauls had fought in the ranks of King Antiochus (n. 2).

It is, if I may digress, this hazardous clarification of *provincia* that may have caused all the confusion about successive *provinciae* ear-

lier. If the senate had the right to interpret a magistrate's *provincia*
at the time it authorized troop levies, often days later than the actual
decision on the *provincia*, simply "appending" (*adicio/adiectum;*
Livy XXXVII.2.3) grave qualifications to it, there would indeed be
confusion as to the scope of his command. This could have caused
Fabius Maximus to misunderstand Scipio's North African jurisdiction. Fabius may have been absent for the troop allocation and its
qualifying *adicio*. Needless to say, this interpretive power must
have been open to abuse. All foreign policy might be altered by a
mere quorum of the senate, if dissenting individuals were absent,
when the troop levy was made. Indeed, decrees of the senate were
sometimes passed by stealth at poorly attended meetings
(XXXVIII.44.3, XXXIX.4.8–9).

The actions of the navy under C. Livius Salinator before the
elections of 190 continued to press the war in the Aegean to Asia,
thus committing Rome to further war with Antiochus, as was
pointed out by Hannibal (Livy XXXVI.41–45). It might be reiterated that Scipio the Great had little to do with the senate's determination to carry the war to Asia. Livius acted as though that were the
intent all along—as inferred by the 191 declaration of war. And, as a
matter of fact, the war with the Seleucids was won without significant help from Africanus. If anything, his presence was negative
because his son was captured (Appian XI.6.29; Polybius XXI.15.2;
Livy XXXVII.34.4). Antiochus was honorable, but Scipio's loyalties
were divided; circumstance placed him in a position that encouraged consorting with the enemy (Livy XXXVII.36.3, 37.8).

Philip remained friendly, escorting Scipio's army through Thrace
(Livy XXXVII.7.15), but an attack by fifteen thousand Thracians put
Philip's ability into question (XXXVIII.41.12). The Battle of Magnesia was Lucius' triumph, since Africanus was ill (XXXVII.23, 37).
The latter had conducted negotiations privately, trying to control
the time of battle. He was probably put in charge of army fiscal
matters at this time because of his rear-echelon activities and back-
door acquaintance with Antiochus. In that capacity he assisted the
quaestor, C. Furius Aculeo, and became more closely associated
with A. Hostilius Cato, who was, like himself, *legatus* under Lucius.
Therefore, Publius was a logical mediator between Antiochus and
his victorious brother, Lucius (XXXVII.45.5).

Historians have sullied the name of Lucius Scipio to enhance that
of Africanus. They agree that credit for the victory was due a

lacklustre figure, C. Domitius Ahenobarbus. He was city praetor in
194 and consul against peaceful Boii in 192 B.C. Nothing in his
career hints of strategic or tactical ingenuity—he had never commanded in battle. Lucius, on the other hand, had been with Africanus in commanding the "expeditionary force" to North Africa.
He directed a part of the fleet. He was at Zama, observing the
tactical maneuvers there. But Appian says Scipio Africanus left
Domitius as counsellor to Lucius in his absence, so many hasten to
infer that Domitius must have been a military expert—"Thus spake
Africanus." Lucius probably was not a "great general," but Appian is
the only tenuous voice asserting that Domitius was. One of the
commanders at Magnesia, Eumenes of Pergamum, in his later dep-
utation to Rome makes Lucius supreme commander. He speaks of
Lucius' assigning the various wings of the Roman formation to the
three commanders and then begs for recognition of the way in
which he carefully obeyed the commands given him by Lucius.
Antiochus' own deputies acknowledged Lucius the supreme commander in their negotiations with Rome afterward. The Romans
themselves styled Lucius "Asiaticus" after the battle in recognition
of his triumph over Antiochus. Finally, T. Sempronius Gracchus, in
a later defense of Africanus, called Lucius the commander who was
"willing to admit his brother (Africanus) to a share of the glory" of
having defeated Antiochus.[3]

III   *Peace Negotiations*

Peace was negotiated in phases. Since the "eastern policy," along
with the earlier settlements in Greece, is said to articulate factional
political blocs in Rome and to distinguish isolationist from imperialist, it will be necessary to analyze developments in the eastern
settlement closely.

Scipio is usually called the protagonist of the imperialists. Their
Greek policy of a Roman military presence rather than complete
evacuation has been debated above (p. 127). Authorities say Scipio
championed a similar idea in the East and base some of their as-
sumptions on negotiations before the battle of Magnesia (Polybius
XXI.14; Appian XI.29; Livy XXXVII.35). These are supposed to
represent the views of Scipio. But Appian is again the broken reed
on which it rests. Even he says that the pre-Magnesian peace "feel-
ers" were those of the Scipios jointly rather than Africanus alone.
Polybius and Livy agree that this stratum of the settlement was

conducted by the army council rather than Scipio. The policy expressed, therefore, would be that of a conciliar agreement. Polybius denies even that Publius was spokesman, saying the council decided that the consul should answer the spokesman of Antiochus. Polybius consequently destroys the theory that these conversations display Africanus' ideals.

The terms set forth in negotiations were simple: Antiochus offered to withdraw from cities in Thrace and those in Asia that had sided with Rome and to pay half the cost of the war incurred by Rome. The army council demanded he withdraw from all Asia as far as the Taurus mountains (all of western Turkey as far as the Halys River) and pay the whole cost of the war. The Seleucid offer was realistic, the Roman proposal ruinous. Further, the Roman stipulations would create a mid-Asian hinterland for the protection of Greek cities and Roman interests on the western, southern, and northern seashores. This "buffer zone" would absorb future irritations along a borderline and encourage peace in Asia Minor. It is impossible to say at this time whether the council foresaw an ensuing power balance in the East between Macedonians and Seleucids screened by intervening client states sponsored by Rome (Scullard, pp. 130–31). It would deny a "Scipionic Greek policy" transferred here, as it would not require military presence: Smaller states, backed by Rome, would become guarantors of the status quo. However, one cannot prove that policies of military presence anywhere except in Spain were Scipio's ideal. One can only show his fear of Hannibal and consequent wish to pursue the war with Antiochus (Livy XXXIV.60–62; Appian XI.9).

The second phase of negotiations was that immediately following the Battle of Magnesia. Livy (XXXVII.45.10) and Polybius (XXI.16.10–17) say terms had been arranged by the army council, which now asked Scipio to convey them to Antiochus' envoys. It is clear that Africanus was not the architect of any part of the eastern *acta*. He did not draft preliminary or secondary truce terms. Therefore, one must conclude that no agency other than the council or any technique other than consensus politics guided the conditions of armistice in the East. If it be asserted, however whimsically, that policy advanced the concept of a delicate power balance between Macedonians and Seleucids to be maintained by Roman client states, it was the creation of the army council.

It is not strange, ultimately, that a group rather than an individual could articulate sophisticated policies such as the armistice terms and the concepts behind the eastern settlement. One may see the army council as a miniature Roman senate here, deliberating foreign affairs with an "on the scene" expertness. There is no necessity to impute these negotiations to an ingenious individual, as most seem inclined to do. In fact, the whole operating principle of a democratic republic like Rome was that "the people" were capable of intelligent planning and action. That principle is embodied in the recurring inscription *"senatus populusque Romanus,"* loosely translated as "[The corporate will of] the senate and the Roman people," a rather grand concept proposing that superior intelligence and common weal reside in the corporate folk, which justify its deeds and clothe its leaders with authority but also endow its councils with responsible wisdom. Political theorists, grasping the magnificence of this ideal, perpetuated the Roman heritage: Rousseau's "Common Will" and Thomas Jefferson's "We the People."

Conditions of the armistice at Sardes drafted by Lucius Scipio and the council seemed lenient (Livy XXXVII.45.4; Polybius XXI.17.1; Appian XI.38). Antiochus had to withdraw from Europe and Asia as far as the Taurus Mountains. He had to pay for the war (fifteen thousand Euboean talents—five hundred at once and twenty-five hundred upon ratification of the peace. The remainder had to be paid in twelve yearly installments of one thousand talents each). The king had to pay the four hundred talents owing to Eumenes, king of Pergamum, and the balance of the grain due his father. Hannibal was to be given up to the Romans, as was Thoas the Aetolian, Mnasilochus the Acarnanian, and Philo and Eubulidas of Chalcis. As security, Antiochus was to give twenty hostages (Livy XXXVII.55.2, XXXVIII.45.1, and Polybius XXI.40.8 emphasize Lucius' leadership; Dio, Zonaras 9.20, that of both brothers).

The senate ratified these terms, dispatching a commission of ten legates to settle all particular problems. However, general disposition of the lands provided for in the terms was made by the senate: one-third of Asia Minor, south of the Maeander River, was given to Rhodes (she had helped with the naval victory), the rest to Eumenes, who had assisted at Magnesia (Livy XXXVII.55–56; Polybius XXI.24.4–9). Appian (XI.7.39) is responsible for the view that the senate moderated the terms of the armistice before ratifying them, but since the adjustments he mentions are among those performed by the appointed commission later on, according to Livy

(XXXVIII.38) and Polybius (XXI.42), Appian must be compressing events for summarization. Many moderns favor Appian over Polybius and Livy (Scullard, pp. 131–33; Holleaux, *CAH* VIII, pp. 229, 231–33), a preference that is inexplicable.

Several important considerations emerge from all this. First, the senate agreed with the ideal of policy set in the armistice: strengthening Pergamum and Rhodes so as to balance the Seleucids. But the terms were much too severe. Fifteen thousand talents were a staggering sum. Far more crucial, however, was the geographic provision excluding the Seleucids from the sources of manpower, both military and colonial, in Anatolia and Greece. Even at Magnesia, only one-third of the kings's muster was Greek; now there was no hope of rectifying that disparity. Second, Livy and Polybius show the peace to be that of the army council and Lucius Scipio, not of Africanus. Livy quotes a Seleucid request that the senate ratify, " . . . The peace proposed by Lucius Scipio the commander on the terms which he had stated. . . ." In a debate of 187 B.C., commissioners speak of the treaty "initiated by Lucius Scipio," according to Livy, or Polybius' "(treaty) agreement with Lucius Scipio."[4]

The final treaty of peace was drawn up at Apamea in 188 by the senatorial commission, presided over by Cn. Manlius Vulso. Scullard says (p. 137, n. 1) it was dominated by the Scipionic bloc; seven of the ten were friends of Scipio.

Livy (XXXVIII.38) credits the final draft of the treaty to this commission, giving Vulso, Asiatic commander in 188, small part. Polybius (XXI.41–42) differs, saying that Vulso, Eumenes, and the commissioners together discussed its provisions. Appian (XI.38–39) gives the authority to Africanus and the senate, the former being impossible as he was not in the East then. Dio (Zonaras 9.20) makes Vulso definitive, saying he was displeased with the earlier terms. Though Vulso in Livy (XXXVIII.48.1) shows expert understanding of Asiatic affairs, the evidence of Dio cannot be preferred to a consensus of Polybius and Livy on the instrumentality of the senatorial commission. Three provisions, added at Apamea, would seem to represent the controlling Scipionic faction: (1) the king must not possess more than ten decked ships of war—none for purposes of aggression—nor any ships propelled by more than thirty oars; (2) no ships must sail beyond the Calycadnus and Sarpedonian promontories, except for official bearing of tribute or envoys and hostages;

and (3) Antiochus must surrender all his war elephants and acquire no more.

These stipulations are the logical alternative to a policy of military presence such as some authorities say Scipio urged in Asia, as well as Greece: If Asia could not be occupied, the Seleucids had to be weakened so they posed no threat to Roman interests. Assuming the Scipionic partisans on the peace commission maintained their bloc's foreign policy, they must have been responsible for the disarmament clauses. It is said that these assurances were no more than Roman security required. But since the legacy of this eastern settlement was Seleucid disintegration, the disarmament clauses with the indemnity and partition were ruinous. They corroded the internal solidarity of the kingdom, causing it to fall rather than balance the East. The immediate consequence was the costly Galatian War, then the Parthian and Pontine engagements, and so on. The naïvete of Scipionic foreign policy is bared for all to see. True, it probably visualized a vastly increased and strengthened Pergamum as a counterbalance, but that only means the Scipionic politicians, like some modern authorities, vastly overestimated the leadership and potential of the Attalids.

The chief task of the commission, actually, was to interpret the terms of the armistic ratified by the senate as they affected individual cities and states in Asia Minor. All cities that had been independent before the war had their freedom confirmed unless they had aided Antiochus. Those that had been subject to Antiochus before, but had not opposed Rome in war and were not former tributaries to Pergamum, received the "free and nontributary" status. All the rest became tributary either to Pergamum or to Rhodes. A few exceptions were made: Colophon and Cyme, once tributary to Pergamum, became free; Ilium, Chios, Miletus, and other historically favored towns received territory in addition to their free status; Phocaea, which had fought Rome, was nevertheless pardoned and freed; Mylasa was expressly declared free (Livy XXXVIII. 39. 9–17; Appian XI. 44).

Rhodes inherited a bitter dispute with the cities of Lycia because the commission neglected to specify whether these cities were allies of Rhodes or tributary to her. King Eumenes of Pergamum also demanded a later clarification of the eastern boundary of the settlement—"the Taurus mountains" approached the sea in various spurs, both east and west of Pamphylia; hence the actual borderline must be defined. Eumenes wanted a port in the south on the Mediterranean and so the borderline was drawn in his favor to include Pamphylia.[5]

It is worthy of note that the differentiating principle of Greek autonomy, used as a cause for Roman opposition to Antiochus, was now sacrificed by Rome herself. Eumenes demonstrated his perfidy by demanding that the same states that had testified to the despotic tyranny of Seleucid rule now be tributary to Pergamum. The "principles" for which the war was fought became, as "war principles" usually do, a mere rhetorical exercise once the war had been won. They were useful for purposes of psychological propaganda, rousing the troops to a sense of moral indignation so they would fight zealously—but they were not to be taken seriously as criteria for the peace settlement.

IV   *Political Campaigns: The Rise of the Middle Bloc and Cato's Legal Confrontations*

The consular elections in 190 B.C. herald the appearance of the "middle bloc" (Scullard, pp. 135–36, 165 ff., 120). It rose as an alternative to Africanus and Cato and their parties and was composed of moderates from the old Claudio-Fulvian and Fabian groups. Its popularity is to be seen in the selection of both consuls from this new coalition: Cnaeus Manlius Vulso and M. Fulvius Nobilior. Scipio's group should have triumphed: C. Laelius of that faction presided over the elections, and just before the polling date news (delayed by the lag in communications) came of the naval victory over Antiochus and Hannibal, as well as the landing of Lucius' army in Asia (Livy XXXVII.47). Everything favored Scipio, but as there were three patrician candidates, none received the necessary majority of centuries in the *comitia*. At that point Laelius, the "faithful subordinate" of Scipio, probably defected. He should have been able to secure the election of Lepidus, choice of the "imperialists." Yet Laelius allowed the plebeian consul-elect, M. Fulvius Nobilior, of an old conservative alignment, to decide among the three hopefuls with the result that Vulso was named. Doubtless Laelius was disaffected because of the way Scipio had muscled into the eastern command for 190. His resentment took the form of party treason.

The charismatic leader of the moderates must have been T. Quinctius Flamininus. He was elected censor that year and the

policies one ascribes to the "middle bloc" are those championed by
him during his command in Greece, that is, strategic, negotiated
evacuation of a conquered foe's territory as opposed to either heedless, exploitative withdrawal or continuing military presence. There
is little reason to suppose this new political alignment was generi-
cally different from that mentioned before as "liberal Fabian" (pp.
94, 125). However, the gap between these moderates and the
conservative Fabians widened because of Cato's political activities
during this period of his marriage and fatherhood (Livy
XXXVII.57.9–58.2).

A follower of Scipio, Q. Minucius Thermus, sought a second
triumph in 190 B.C. for his campaign against the Ligurians (Livy
XXXVII.46.1). Cato rallied to the attack (Meyer, p. 72), saying that
Minucius had not slain the required number of enemies. Minucius
(Livy XXXIV.10.5) obtained an earlier triumph on an even more
blatant falsehood. Cato went on to charge the man with a "nefarious
deed" and a whole range of other offenses, some dealing with treatment of allied communities and deportment in war. The "deed" is
probably set forth in Cato's speech quoted by Gellius in which
Thermus was accused of flogging local officials because they did not
fully obey (X.3.17). Minucius was denied a triumph; the allegations
must have been true. Yet such was the stature of Scipio that certain
followers could later heroize even Thermus, and Livy memorialized
him as a man of "courage and energy" for no apparent reason (Livy
XXXVIII.41.3; cp. Gellius XIII.25.12).

The Scipionic faction counterattacked by bringing Cato to trial on
his conduct in Spain. Since Cato was circumspect on all matters of
corruption, the feeling among authorities is that charges must have
specified some administrative matter. Perhaps the issue is reflected
in Plutarch's eleventh chapter and Nepos' second, which are not
considered historically valid. They both speak of Cato's deliberately
prolonging his command in Spain so as to spite Africanus, who was
elected consul the year after Cato, but not to a Spanish *provincia*.
Scipio Nasica was sent as a praetor to Farther Spain instead. Yet the
tradition preserved by Plutarch may mean that Scipio tried to enforce annual commands in the senate again, so as to leave the settlement of Spanish affairs to his cousin Nasica and necessitate disa-
vowal of Cato's *acta* (public acts, ordinances, and judicial decisions)
in the province. Surely, that is implied in Plutarch's final statement
that the "Senate voted no change whatever be made in what Cato

had ordered and arranged." That interpretation would also account for Nepos' statement that "(Scipio) wished to force him to leave the province, in order himself to succeed him" (assuming Nepos' confusion of the two Scipios). However, Cato defied the desires of the clan Cornelius and even used his official escort to fight the Lacetanians, putting to death six hundred deserters whom they delivered to him after the appearance of his successor (Malcovati, pp. 20–25). It may be that this was the administrative error on which Cato was brought to book. Since the senate had ratified his *acta*, trial could hardly be based on malfeasance in that area. There would be some justification for charges of severity against the Lacetani after official termination of the provincial *imperium* unless he could prove the action was defensive. Execution of deserters certainly does not come within that category, however. What might have been an embarrassing trial was successfully diverted by Cato into a test of comparative morality and patriotic deeds, a rhetorical tactic he deplored in others. He never did refute the indictment, resorting instead to an assertion of his integrity as contrasted with the lives and careers of his attackers. He dealt with his Spanish command in detail and with no hint of a becoming modesty. Cato was able to urge that his concern for his country had become a danger to him, since he was brought into the courts for military zeal. (One might cynically interpose that Cato himself had created the same difficulty for Africanus and that trials for overzealous patriotism were becoming so common that it was an occupational hazard.)

It is almost irrepressibly ironic that Cato was able to politicize the trial against him. He concluded his remarks in defense by slurring the censors for that year, calling them fearful, timid, and slow in the extreme. Since Cato at that time contemplated a candidacy for the censorship and now drew an irrelevant parallel with the kind of censor he would be, it is obvious that something was drastically wrong with Roman judicial process. Cato even used the forensics to remind everyone of his successful performance at Thermopylae. Marcus positively throve on juristic tactics (Scullard, p. 258).

The following campaign for the censorship was a fierce struggle. Many distinguished men (Livy XXXVII.57.9–15) contended for the office. Particularly notable were T. Quinctius Flamininus, M. Cladius Marcellus, Manius Acilius Glabrio, and Cato himself. Glabrio, commander at Thermopylae, was the popular candidate because of the wine and oil *congiaria* (*congius:* a 6-pint measure) charities he distributed, apparently with great generosity, since the word "*multa*" is used. Livy says this had obliged a large part of the people to Glabrio, with the indubitable implication that the largesse had been bestowed during his candidacy, after Thermopylae. Though others were free to do likewise, the patrician senators resented the fact that this plebeian novice gained advantage by such means and inspired the tribunes of the people to bring charges of peculation against him. Testimony in the case was conflicting, some of his lieutenants and tribunes from that campaign claiming that part of the king's money and much of the booty taken in the camp of Antiochus at Thermopylae had neither been displayed by Glabrio in the triumphal procession nor turned in to the treasury.

Cato discredited himself because, although he was a candidate for the same office, wearing the *toga candida* ("white toga"), he gave testimony and people believed that he thereby improved his own chances for election. Vessels of gold and silver that were in the captured camp of Antiochus were not carried in the triumph, he testified. The assumption that Cato gave evidence for selfish reasons implies he did not realize the political consequences of testifying while a candidate. That can hardly be the case. Cato surmised the trial might cost him the election. He appeared for the prosecution knowing that it was customary for commanders to appropriate spoil for their expenses and pay troop bonuses with it. He knew that the vessels he mentioned could hardly be classified as state property rather than commander's booty. He had used such booty in Spain himself. Yet the man testified, for that was his nature (cp. Livy XXXVI.26.2).

Cato was a slave to principle. On other occasions as well, he preached the principle though his own life was testimony that it was unrealistic. He was ever one for asserting the rule, workable or no, then judging everyone else for failing to comply with it. Malcovati's fragment (p. 30) of the testimony suggests Cato also criticized Glabrio for inefficiency. That charge seems more respectable because of post-Thermopylaean operations in Greece. Yet Cato's breach of protocol mattered most to the Romans, for the incident of testimony with the *toga candida*, according to Livy, diminished his honor and so tarnished his whole career (Livy XXXVI.22–27, 34–35 on Glabrio).

Glabrio withdrew from the candidacy, denouncing the actions of Cato and his testimony. The important consideration with Glabrio seems to have been the pique of senators, for he criticized Cato who spoke out, but not the senators, the silent instigators of the entire judicial procedure. Apparently he countenanced Cato's attack but skirted an open confrontation with senators. Yet Livy (XXXVII.57.12–58.2) well comprehends the part of patricians; he says they inspired the tribunes to bring action against the "plebeian novice." The censorship was won by two moderates: T. Quinctius Flamininus and M. Claudius Marcellus.

The year 189–88 B.C. saw this first phase of the eastern wars begun by Aetolians and Antiochus brought to a close. Marcus Fulvius Nobilior finally forced the war with the Aetolians to conclusion; Cnaeus Manlius Vulso, that in Asia Minor. It was in the command of Fulvius that Cato saw further diplomatic service. He was appointed a legate to serve in Greece.

Cato's peculiar adeptness in negotiating had first been demonstrated when in the command of Glabrio and before Thermopylae he had brought Corinth, Patrae, and Aegeum over to Rome (Plutarch XII.3). As these were on the north shore of the Peloponnesus, Cato's service to Nobilior is self-explanatory. Fulvius' *provincia* ordered him to move against the island of Cephallenia (Livy XXXVII.50.4). To do so efficiently, he had to try to neutralize the considerable navy of the Achaean League. The cities with which Cato had negotiated were now in the league (Livy XXXVIII.28.5). Cato's prior acquaintance was a diplomatic asset, apparently: The Achaeans did not interfere (Malcovati, Cato's *de suis* . . . *contra L. Thermum*, p. 52).

There were also domestic political considerations in Cato's appointment as envoy. C. Manlius Vulso, consul-elect for 189, symbolizes the "middle bloc" of moderate politicians because his acts have been attacked more than those of Nobilior or the censors of 189. This is important, since moderate politics, viewed strictly as an alternative to Porcian or Scipionic extremism or as a "third party" expedient, succeeded too well. The simultaneous eclipse of the Scipionic, then the Porcian, factions caused the middle to become simply "the second party." Roman politics reverted to a barren polarity until the appearance of the Gracchi. Part of this "successful failure" can be attributed to the career of Vulso, as he represented the moderates in the field. Imperialists and conservatives unwittingly immortalized Vulso by criticizing his Asiatic campaign; notoriety enhanced political image.

The surprising consolidation of both consulships and the two censorships in the hands of the moderate Claudio-Fulvian and Fabian group in 189 B.C. was followed by overtures to compromise. This is to be seen in the gratuitous appointment of Scipio Africanus as *princeps senatus* and the gesture of making Cato envoy to the Achaeans under Nobilior. Those friendly advances died aborning; they were repaid with hostility (Livy XXXVIII.28.1–2). Scipio's friends reacted by denying a moderate praetor his *provincia* on a religious technicality (XXXVII.51.1–5). Cato also bit the hand of friendship; he later attacked Fulvius on the way crowns were awarded the soldiers for valor in the Aetolian war. Yet the prominence of the moderates was not damaged (Malcovati, p. 57). They retained the senatorial balance of power in the following year. Some of this is attributable to the prestige of Flamininus, and some to the presence of Fulvius, but the focus seems to have been that of Vulso and his actions.

V *The Career of Vulso: Campaign against the Galatians and Return to Rome*

Cn. Manlius Vulso had enjoyed an auspicious aedileship and respectable praetorship. Thereafter he showed perseverance by standing for the consulship unsuccessfully twice, in 192 and 191, though opposed by glittering batteries of Scipionic candidates. Nothing daunted, he ran again in 190 and was elected consul for 189, though he owed his success to Laelius' defection (p. 158). Cn. Manlius, victor over the East and president of the peace conference at Apamea, can hardly be overestimated. The undertone of suspicion attaching to all he did because of domestic attack and historical tradition in no way diminishes that importance, whatever the verdict on Vulso's character.

When Vulso was appointed to the eastern command, the Battle of Magnesia had not yet been reported (Livy XXXVII.50–51). He was to war against Antiochus (thus signalling official reversion to the system of annual commands), superseding Lucius Scipio and so denying Lucius the grace of completing his campaign, as Scipio had tried to replace Cato in Spain (Scullard, p. 136). It meant that the grouping of political moderates held the balance of power in the senate. Manlius was allotted the eastern army of Lucius—twenty-eight thousand infantry and twenty-three hundred cavalry—and allowed to enlist reinforcements of twelve thousand additional infantrymen with six hundred cavalry. His total effective force was to be forty thousand, less the four hundred and fifty slain at Thermopylae and Magnesia, and twenty-nine hundred cavalry, less seventy-five casualties. There are discrepancies in Livy's account, one implying that the army of Lucius returned with him rather than remaining in the East, while in three other places Livy asserts that the army served under Manlius. The assumption is here made that the three references offset the one and that the army of Manlius numbered forty-three thousand (XXXVI.14.1, 19.12, XXXVII.2.2, 44.1, 50.3, 59.6, XXXVIII.12.2, 13.8, 41.10, XXXIX.6.5). Logistics support that figure.[6]

Shortly after Cnaeus Manlius left Rome, messengers and dispatches of Lucius Scipio reached Rome declaring the victory at Magnesia. But the senate decreed there should be no change in the plan to send Manlius to Asia nor any diminution in his forces, for fear that he would be compelled to fight the Gauls. In other words, the senate now officially decided that the Asiatic command included open war on the Galatians merely by a clarification of *provincia*. Forty thousand infantry and three thousand cavalry were considered necessary to deal with them. However, the reaffirmation of Cnaeus's command and the reinterpretation of his *provincia* show a remarkably immediate grasp of eastern affairs by the senate. They appreciated the fact that conquest of Antiochus would leave a power vacuum to be exploited by marauding Gauls. Apamea's later "client states" would only be possible after the systematic reduction of Galatia. Yet authorities are anxious to condemn Manlius' spoliation of Anatolia (Scullard, *A History*, p. 261; Scullard, p. 139; *CAH* VIII, p. 228).

It seems, in sum, that Vulso's mission in the East was threefold. He must fight the Galatians, oversee the peace negotiations at Apamea, and supervise the implementation of puppet states stipulated in that settlement. All three were modifications of the original *provincia*—to continue the war against Antiochus. Other duties included collecting the unpaid balance of Antiochus' armistice indemnities and, unofficially, replenishing the treasury (Appian XI.39, 42; Polybius XXI.24.9; Livy XXXVII.50, XXXVIII.37.7, 39).

The fresh troops, together with the veterans of Magnesia, were mustered at Ephesus, where Manlius harangued them against the Gauls (Livy XXXVIII.22.3). The first installment of supplies from Sicily was transferred to army transports; then started the long march inland for which Vulso is notorious in history. Writers charge that he terrified the populace, looted towns along a devious route or allowed them to "buy freedom," and let the troops run wild (Livy XXXVIII.14.12). Interesting that these indictments are heaped upon Manlius more than upon others! The circuitous route was a charge made by his enemies opposing a triumph later on, as were those of lax discipline, and so on.

"Cnaeus Manlius . . . moving by all roundabout ways, stopping at every crossroad . . . a money-seeking consul following (Attalus) with a Roman army over all the nooks and corners of Pisidia and Lycaonia and Phrygia, exacting tribute from tyrants and commanders of out-of-the-way fortresses . . . (deserves no triumph)," said his enemies (Livy XXXVIII.45.9). The route was necessary to requisition food supplies for the army. The pattern of distribution—31,818 bushels of Sicilian grain at Ephesus, 65,807 bushels brought by Seleucus to Antiochia, and then ten thousand bushel increments at approximate forty-mile intervals—makes that certain. They "snaked" through Asia Minor because it was notoriously poor in supplies at this time (Frank, pp. 142, 158–59); the army sought known sources. Also, it had to rendezvous with the freight fleet at Termessus/Attalia in Pamphylia for the Sicilian grain tithe before plunging into the unknown dangers of Galatia. Manlius had the inspiration of using this necessity to pacify the unruly natives of Pisidia, Phrygia, Lycaonia, and Pamphylia rather than merely marching through (*CAH* VIII, p. 228).[7]

The indictment of cruelty is again a repetition of Vulso's political enemies. They characterize the Gauls as "innocent" and "dumb animals" rather than worthy enemies (Livy XXXVIII.45.9–11). Modern authorities speak of the loss of life caused by the victories of Manlius. Yet only five towns were sacked by his armies in their long journey, and of those, two had been deserted before the army arrived. Three were captured by assault, two at the invitation of the natives. The route of march suggests the territory of at least forty towns was passed through; so looting occurred in just over 12 percent of them—remarkable forbearance! As to battle casualties, Manlius was merely a typical Roman.

The price for which some towns purchased immunity, or "bought freedom," is called "disgraceful bargaining" by modern authorities. Yet that exercise in itself seems to have been an adequate show of submission and recognition of Roman dominance, as the towns that so behaved themselves in Pamphylia were officially excluded from Eumenes' later "southern corridor to the sea" across the Pamphylian plain. Polybius infers that the payment of tribute was an official act of alliance. Hence it could not be construed as extortion.[9]

The "rapacious extortions" of Manlius are rhetorical charges by adversaries (Livy XXXVIII.45.9). The amounts were deposited in the treasury, and greedy imperialism had already been demonstrated in the case of Spain, so the charge of bringing too much money back to Rome cannot have been seriously pressed. State policy seems already to have been set upon acquiring as much foreign treasure as possible. Indeed, the charge of losing some of the wealth to marauding Thracians was stressed as seriously as his greed (Livy XXXVIII.46.7). There was no trial for financial corruption. Finally, much of the money carried in Vulso's triumph must have come from his veterans' battles with Antiochus under the Scipios (Livy XXXVIII.46.8–9; Appian XI.43).

Accusations of lax discipline over the troops seem to have been a later hostile annalistic convention. Surely there was no known, openly mutinous conduct by the troops in Asia—the two battles against the Gauls and the fighting in Thrace prove firm discipline and excellent physical conditioning. An indication of the falseness of the charge is that it was not brought when Manlius' triumph was contested (Livy XXXVIII.45–46). Only in the following book does Livy begin to sound the note of Manlius' permissiveness with Roman troops (XXXIX.1.4, 6.5–6, 7.3; cp. XXXVIII.19–23). Then it is rather deliberately done in order to substantiate his theory of Roman degeneration by eastern influence, a notoriously unfair way to establish prejudicial views.

The image conveyed by these counterproofs is that of Vulso's exemplary moderation in the field. His "anabasis" displays sound diplomacy, good logistics, and loyal Romanism (Livy XXXVIII.12.6, 13.4, 15.4–6; Polybius XXI.33–35). The same may be said of his battles with the Galatians—a greatly feared horde, as is shown by the forty thousand men assigned to his army and Polybius' saying (XXI.40; cp. Livy XXXVIII.37.3) that the allies enjoyed Manlius' victory over the Gauls more than that over Antiochus; the domination by the king was more endurable than lawless Gallic violence. Manlius committed the sin of brilliance. He so easily defeated the Galatians by the use of ingenious tactics that the chagrined disciples of Scipio could only bleat, "These were not 'true Gauls' but rather

Gallogrecians" (Livy XXXVIII.46.1, 17.9). Polybius (XXI.37–39) calls them Gauls. The large Roman army and the fears of the allies argue the ability of these "Gallogrecians." But no one, much less a scion of the upstart Manlii, must presume to military fame in the same epoch as Scipio Africanus!

The explanation for Vulso's victories is easily discovered. Ancestors of the Manlii had fought the Gauls previously. Cnaeus' father may have done so in 218 B.C., as had others of the clan Manlius, and their exploits were familiar in the clan through *convivia* such as those that educated Cato (Livy XXXVII.17.8). Cnaeus deduced that Gauls were defenseless against missiles and lacked perseverance, as well as hearing they fought massed and naked, with flat shields (XXXVIII.20.1, 15.15). Vulso camped many days at Abbassius on the border of Galatia. Doubtless he used the time to reconnoitre and ascertain whether Galatians were like other Gauls, so that he could apply the tactics he had devised. Livy shows that Manlius' ingenuity was indeed crucial in the Galatian victories. But the Romans soon forgot the "knowledge of Manlius" and continued to use the old methods of fighting Gauls, unsuccessfully (XXXVIII.35, 42).

The Galatians had migrated by entire families to two mountains, Olympus and Magaba, and fortified the heights, assuming that Romans would not scale them to attack. Manlius reconnoitred Mt. Olympus for three days and then attacked up the mountain. The Gauls had stationed four thousand men to hold the single route from which their position could be approached. These braved every danger, but Manlius had devised the cunning tactic of using *velites* and missiles from a distance to beset the Galatians. Great quantities of javelins, spears, arrows, bullets, and stones had been prepared. These caused havoc among the Gauls, fighting naked, tightly massed, and with narrow, flat, piercable shields and only swords as assault weapons. They were defeated from a distance with no opportunity to fight hand-to-hand. The same was true when they fell back on their fortifications, with the difference that there their families were also victimized by the merciless missile fire of Manlius' skirmishers. The barbarians broke and fled without striking a blow in their own behalf. Livy's best guess is that forty thousand Gauls were captured and killed (Livy XXXVIII.20–23).

The second and last major engagement with the Gauls was fought on Mt. Magaba, Cnaeus having his camp set at Ancyra. The same care was lavished on preparations and on explorations of the enemy position. This battle followed the pattern of the first almost exactly as to the use of *velites*, though a charge by the heavy infantry was mounted to complete the affair and that needlessly, as the Gauls fled before sustaining it. This time the greed of the Roman soldiers prevented any pursuit, the first time discipline failed. They stopped to loot the Galatian camp. Hence only eight thousand were killed. Within the space of a few days and by tactically flawless battles, Cnaeus Manlius Vulso had ended the threat of a people who had held all Anatolia in thrall since Brennus, their legendary leader, had arrived a century before (Livy XXXVIII.26–27, 16.2).

The Gauls sent ambassadors entreating for peace, as did their allies, the Cappadocians, and all were bidden to go to Ephesus, as Manlius wished to hurry to the coast before winter began (Livy XXXVIII.27.9). The first part of his commission—to fight and sub-due the Gauls—had been performed with unquestionable honor and ingenuity. Over five hundred miles inland, through strange country, Vulso had engaged one hundred thousand of the age's most feared fighters in their own land, on the ground and conditions of their own choosing, and prevailed. To Ephesus came the embassies of Greek cities in Asia, joyfully to confer golden crowns upon Manlius for their deliverance from the Galatian menace (XXXVIII.37.1–5, XXXIX.7.1). The consul received 212 golden crowns from the grateful cities west of the Taurus alone. Lucius Scipio carried just 234 in triumph from all Anatolia, Syria, Mesopotamia, and the Middle East for his defeat of Antiochus, and Flamininus, in triumph over Philip, received only 114 golden crowns from all Greece (XXXI.59.3, XXXIV.52.8). It is here Polybius says that all the inhabitants of the country on this side of the Taurus were not so much pleased at the defeat of Antiochus as at the release from the fear of the barbarians and their lawless violence (XXI.40.1–2).

Meanwhile, the other consul, Fulvius Nobilior, returned to Rome from a successful campaign against the Aetolians in Greece to hold the consular elections for 188 and secure the proconsular *im-perium* for both himself and Manlius, so that they might conclude their provincial business (Livy XXXVIII.35.1–7). Their forthcoming promagistracies must have roused the ire of the Scipios and their followers, who had been denied that privilege just the year previ-ous. It also rallied Cato and his cohorts to the attack, as the power of the middle bloc coalition was displayed. Yet one of the consuls

elected that year was a member of the Scipionic group, and the
majority of the peace commission appointed to meet at Apamea
were followers of Scipio (Scullard, pp. 137–38, 165; Livy
XXXVII.55.7). The details of the peace of Apamea have been discussed above (pp. 156–57). Implementing that peace, Manlius sent
his brother to Oroanda in Pamphylia to secure the ratification by
Antiochus and ordered his admiral, Q. Fabius Labeo, to Patara so as
to destroy the Seleucid fleet (Livy XXXVIII.39.1, 40.1–2). The final
act of Manlius in the East was that of receiving the envoys of the
Galatians at the Hellespont, where he dictated peace terms confining them to Galatia.

Once out of Asia, Vulso faced passage through dangerous Thrace.
It was this journey, perhaps as much as anything, that seemed to
irritate his political enemies. He was attacked in the course of it,
losing a number of men, a certain amount of spoil ("much of the
baggage," by some accounts), and a commissioner who was a partisan of Scipio, Q. Minucius Thermus. Criticism was later hurled at
Manlius by speakers against his triumph for having been "defeated"
by the Thracians and disgraced. The thought that he should have
been killed himself rather than lose Thermus was mentioned,
though this discredits accusers rather than accused. Thermus was an
epitome of Roman deceit at this juncture. His membership in Scipio's group serves as an indictment. Appian, seconded by Scullard,
says that Manlius failed to send word and secure the escort of Philip
of Macedonia (Scullard, p. 140; Appian XI.43). Livy credits Philip
for Scipio's easy passage through Thrace in 190 and lays the present
attack to his treachery (XXXVII.7.16). Yet Livy contradicts himself
by saying that fifteen thousand Thracians attacked Scipio
(XXXVIII.41.12). As the disastrous attack on Manlius' army costing
the life of Thermus was mounted by just ten thousand Thracians,
Manlius correctly doubted Philip's escort (Livy XXXVIII.40–42).
Further, surprisingly, Scipio was virtually unencumbered by booty.
Manlius' train was heavily laden with spoil. Paradoxically then, the
escort of Philip attracted more marauders than a rich baggage train.
The proconsul's decision to ignore Philip was the wiser course.

Appian levels the additional charge of poor tactics on this trek
through hostile territory. The substance of his accusation is that
Manlius should have divided his army into parts so that it might
move more lightly and have what was needed more handy and that
the baggage should have been stationed between files of military for

safety (XI.43). Instead, the army was in a single long column with the baggage in the center so that neither van nor rear guard could assist it quickly by reason of the length of the column and the narrowness of the road. Livy's summary of the arguments of Manlius' political enemies hints at similar thoughts when it refers to the army being scattered in three sections, the van in one place, the rear in another, and the trains in a third (XXXVIII.40.6–7).

There is little to support the contention that Vulso's marching order was bad. He took every precaution. A base camp was established at Lysimachia so that the army might rest before plunging into Thrace. Two days' march from there was the ten-mile rough, narrow wooded path where the Thracians lay in wait. Some precaution was obviously taken to conceal the most valuable part of the booty because of the staggering sums that reached Rome with the train in spite of this attack by Thracians. Perhaps bulky and showy items were conveniently situated to attract barbarian attention and draw them away from more valuable spoil. Livy says that Thracians drove off pack animals, loads and all, as well as carrying away what was in the wagons. Further, the historian says that in order to do so, the Thracians had to kill the guards that were with the baggage, certain indication the train was not split in three parts at all—the column of baggage was under guard. Manlius' defense of his request for a triumph makes it obvious that the tactic of stationing the bulk of the army before and behind the long train was necessitated by two considerations: the terrain and deliberate tactical defensive mobility. Appian's "armed groups" would have fallen in the face of determined attack by ten thousand Thracians, but two halves of the entire army would retain a strength of about twenty thousand each with a certain amount of mobility. It was deliberate, because Manlius' speech articulates the strategy of catching attackers between the two Roman forces, and Livy says Manlius was in the van because of his concern about the unfavorable terrain (XXXVIII.49.10, 40–2).

Finally, the repulse took place in stifling heat, belying a lack of discipline. It is not certain that Thermus fell of mortal wounds. Manlius' speech implies a lack of expert care (Livy XXXVIII.49.8; Appian XI.43). It is very difficult to fault Manlius' tactics. All that is put at his door by Livy later on—degradation caused by imported eastern luxuries, dancing girls, couches, and all the debilitating vice—would be difficult to bring through a devastating combat (XXXIX.1.3–4). The attacks were not as ruinous as is supposed.

Cynically, one must laud the staunch morality of Rome. She had now been "ruined" by the importation of vice from her commanders in Syracuse, Campania, Greece, Aetolia, and twice in Asia; six despoliations of virtue within fifteen years. Since each onslaught left her inviolate to be "ruined" again, Roman society must by Vulso's time have seemed like an impregnable (or professional) virgin.[10]

A second attack a few days later was repulsed with substantial Thracian casualties. This time the army formed in close array and charged with a shout. Neither of these techniques sounds like the force described by Livy as being led by "an indulgent leader seeking popularity" so that his is a "discipline slackly and indifferently enforced" that permits "every kind of license" and "ruins the military discipline" (XXXVIII.41, XXXIX.6.5, 7.3). Passing Macedonia and Epirus, Vulso wintered his army in Apollonia rather than risk crossing the hazardous Adriatic. He crossed to Brundisium in the spring and then presented himself before the senate in Rome to request a triumph. Thus began the direct confrontation between followers of Scipio, Cato, and Flamininus. Its outcome confirmed the fate of the Roman Republic (XXXVIII.44.9).

The elections for that fateful year, 187 B.C., had been postponed until the eighteenth of February, though there was no appropriate emergency necessitating a delay. Accordingly, secondary writers assume the postponement was a political tactic to allow either the Scipionic *decemvirs* with Manlius or the proconsul Nobilior to return and influence the elections in behalf of Scipio's group or that of the moderates, respectively (Scullard, p. 140). Neither arrived in time, and the elections returned one consul of each group. One of these, Aemilius Lepidus, had been denied the consulship in 189, when Fulvius chose Vulso as his patrician colleague, and lost that of 188 also, as Fulvius presided over the elections. Livy cites the feud between these two especially in the elections for 188 and 187, openly stating that Fulvius' influence caused Lepidus to attain the consulship two years late (XXXVIII.43–44).

Lepidus, faithful member of the Scipionic group, hurled two darts at his political enemies that affected the future of the Republic. First, at year's end he questioned the validity of the *imperia* held by Fulvius and Manlius, raising the constitutional issue of replacement by a successor or termination at year's end. Assuming the latter, he called Manlius and Fulvius "private citizens" with no authority and objected to himself and his colleague both being assigned Liguria unless Manlius and Fulvius were recalled. Second, fuming under Fulvius' delaying his own consulship, Aemilius induced the Ambraciots to complain of certain wrongs suffered at the hands of Fulvius in his *provincia* of Aetolia and bring charges against him in the senate. Most important was the looting and stripping of temples there. The culmination of all this was an Ambraciot peace that benefited the new middle class, exempting them from paying port duties. Aemilius and the Scipionic bloc must have been cultivating the middle class (Livy XXXVIII.42.8–13, 53–54.6).

Cn. Manlius Vulso returned to Rome to claim a triumph over the Galatians in the midst of bitter contention. The Scipionic bloc, using the peace commissioners, tried to thwart him. They denied that Manlius had an official mandate to fight the Gauls; if he did, his methods were suspect, and his deportment in Thrace was disgraceful. Manlius' defense was a vindication in all particulars, and the middle bloc carried all, approving the triumph (Livy XXXVIII.44.9–50.3).

The first charge merits further argument. Official war had not been declared on the Galatians with all the ceremonial of the *fetiales*. But the senate had foreseen war with the Gauls and expanded the *imperium* of Manlius accordingly. If the technicality were to be stressed, Glabrio would have to be tried as well, since separate war had not been declared on the Aetolians either. But the priests had interpreted the declaration of war so as to include Aetolia (Livy XXXVI.3.8–11), and the senate had interpreted the *imperium* of Manlius (pp. 163–64).

CHAPTER 7

Cato and the Trials of the Scipios: Bloc Politics and Bacchanalia

I The Prosecution of the Scipios

CATO came to the fore again in 187 B.C. Doubtless smarting from the humiliation of Glabrio's trial, he inspired two tribunes to demand a financial accounting by Scipio Africanus in the senate. At issue were five hundred talents given by Antiochus as part of his war indemnity (Livy XXXVII.45.14; Polybius XXI.17). Polybius (XXIII.14.6–8), confirmed by Gellius (IV.18.8), asserts that the request was made of Africanus, not Lucius, because Publius had been his brother's deputy (*legatus*) there. The tone of Gellius is distinctly *ipso facto*—as deputy Africanus would surely be concerned with finance (the charge of peculation did convict one of the other *legati* and the quaestor: Livy XXXVIII.55.4–5, 58.1). There can be no question that the attack from the beginning was directly at Africanus himself, not at Africanus through Lucius, who as commander would have had supreme responsibility in Asia. Lucius was not the sort of man to shirk responsibility; if he had been accused, he would have borne the attack rather than allow Africanus to intercede. The trials were to show Lucius more calm and resourceful under attack than his famous brother. From the first, then, this inquiry centered on Africanus and involved state funds.

Polybius, supplemented by Gellius, shows that Scipio made a spectacle of himself, not only refusing to give the accounting, but then, according to Polybius (XXIII.14.7), loftily asserting he was not obliged to render account to anyone. Gellius (IV.18.7–12) agrees, adding that Africanus thought this an intolerable slur on his honor. Both accounts agree that Scipio had the records ready, to be read publicly and then deposited in the treasury. But once the issue of doubt had been raised, Publius baulked, for he refused to read the accounts as a proof of his honesty—Rome was supposed to take that element on faith; it was not open to doubt. A senator, who must have been Marcus Cato—none else would dare thus to badger the *princeps senatus*—continued to insist for the accounting and the records, according to Polybius' account. After all, he was right. Africanus was accountable for the funds expended from the war indemnity paid by Antiochus. Scipio had Lucius bring all the records of the campaign and ripped them to shreds, bidding Cato look in the fragments for the account. Then he turned to the rest of the house and asked why they demanded to know about three thousand talents (only five hundred of it was his own responsibility) from the man who had brought in fifteen thousand and made them the masters of Asia, Africa, and Spain besides. Polybius says that at this deed all were abashed and he who had demanded the account kept silence.

Abashed indeed! Never before had the *princeps senatus* wantonly destroyed official records in front of the assembled house. These were not the actions of a responsible magistrate. Belatedly realizing the enormity of his deed, Africanus sought to rally the house by another tiresome recital of his mighty acts; for though the senate had not demanded his accounting, it had witnessed his tantrum and would be the ultimate judge. But even the egotistical thrust of his appeal—I won and brought home a lot of loot, so why haggle over three thousand talents—was a harsher indictment than his deed. It is not strange that Cato kept silence. This was a direct affront, putting Scipio at a great disadvantage. The latter's intemperate actions helped Cato to shape his immediate plans. Marcus saw at once the psychological and political implications of this confrontation. He would mercilessly exploit each of them in an attempt to eliminate the Scipios from Roman affairs altogether. These things were running through Cato's mind as he silently bore the insults of Africanus.

First, the question had to be brought to an open trial, a tribunician hearing before the people (Polybius XXIII.14). The tribunes were used to convene and conduct the proceedings; they sounded the initial *summons*, to which Scipio came as a defendant accompanied, says Livy (XXXVIII.50–51), by men of every rank. Then came the *inquiry*, during the course of which there must have been an investigation of whatever evidence remained as to the disposition of the five hundred talents, since Africanus had destroyed the account by ripping it to shreds in front of the senate. The result of this phase of the hearing must have been inconclusive. Therefore the accusers, probably speaking in the considerations of the *magistrates'* *verdict*, were brutal. They had been briefed by Cato, who began with a speech *De pecunia regis Antiochi* (Malcovati, p. 31) insisting that the money in question was really the property of the Roman people and must be accounted for. This ingenious prelude "legalized" the moral onslaught that followed. If the money was indeed public, Africanus had put himself in a very bad light by refusing to document its expenditure. The forensic argument would be whether, on the basis of previous behavior, it was *likely* that Scipio had misused the funds. Arguments from probability— inferred and implied malfeasance—can be more demoralizing than proper debate. Cato had learned from the bitter confrontation in the senate that Scipio was psychologically incapable of sustaining attacks on his honor. Therefore the remainder of the day was one long tirade on the integrity of Africanus. Cato was acute enough to know that the incident of the records had aroused just enough doubt so that the public and the aristocrats would listen to argument about the character of Scipio. From the affair of Pleminius at Locri to the alleged bribes from Antiochus and the arrogance of Scipio as an administrator, Africanus' past was paraded before the public eye. None but a saint lives well enough to survive such a review! Scipio's following *appeal to the people* (*provocatio*) came just at nightfall, perhaps. In it he rebuked the Roman people for listening to the slander against him. It being night, according to Livy, the hearings were then postponed. This set of circumstances led to the tradition that the people dispersed merely on Scipio's rebuke, a tradition that is judicially absurd.[1]

The trial was not yet officially over. When the *iudicium* reconvened, Africanus did not answer the summons. He had retired to Liternum in voluntary exile (Livy, *Periocha* XXXVIII). Livy says (XXXVIII.52) Scipio was accustomed to a greater fortune than that of pleading his cause. Cato's strategy had succeeded! Exile would cause Publius to lose his Roman rights, a wonderful vindication of Cato's cunning courtroom procedure. Nor could the hearings have been allowed simply to drop, as some maintain. That would have amounted to default, probably been considered a voluntary exile again, and been attended with the same loss of rights. The entire Scipionic faction must have been in a state of panic! Their charismatic leader had been forced to flee and might lose his Roman citizenship. This would seriously jeopardize the entire Scipionic bloc. In the crisis Lucius Scipio acted with cool maturity. Certain that Africanus would eventually regain his composure and remember his responsibilities, Lucius sought to suspend the hearings on grounds that would simultaneously retain his brother's rights. The only option was that of illness: Lucius answered the defendant's summons (*diei dictio*) that fateful morning with a plea of illness. Dismayed at the prospect of losing this carefully fought, crucial case, the tribunes refused to accept the plea, insisting that it was not illness but arrogance. With a similar arrogance had Scipio disrupted the affairs of the treasury by opening its doors, against the specific regulations of the institution, and interfered with the duties of tribunes.

Lucius, in this extremity, used the last resource, that of appeal to the entire college of tribunes. They justified his expectations, saying to their colleagues that it was their pleasure that the plea of illness should be accepted and the case adjourned. There is controversy over Livy's version of the dissenting opinion given by one member of the college: T. Sempronius Gracchus (XXXVIII.52.8–53.7). He decreed that flight was sufficient cause to adjourn the case and that he would not permit Africanus to be prosecuted in his absence—a rather obvious indication of resting a case on voluntary flight in lieu of due process, as argued here—and further, that he would veto any continuing prosecution at all, if he were asked to do so—this in spite of the fact that Tiberius was an enemy of Scipio because of numerous political disagreements (Gellius VI.19.6). The decree of Gracchus is accepted here because of its obviously close relationship to the events of this first series of trials of the Scipios.

It is an oversimplification to assert that Cato used the courts to achieve political aims (Scullard, p. 143). Certainly, he was a master of the political art of exploiting forensics as a supplement to personal ambitions. Surely also, since politics, inextricably bound to power, exposes the worst characteristics in men, Cato was becoming cynical. Yet there is no proof that Cato's motives were not still primarily those of conscientious conviction rather than political deviation. The trial of Glabrio, where Cato sacrificed his chances for the censorship because of principle, is a case in point. Plutarch (XV.1–2) shows that Marcus brought only malefactors to the dock and that it was the charisma of Scipio, not the veracity of the charges against him, that defeated his indictment. Livy also makes it obvious that more drastic measures might have ensued but for the high-principled intervention of Gracchus (XXXVIII.52.4–8).

Tiberius Sempronius, in spite of his mediation on behalf of Africanus, was a bitter personal enemy. That enmity could well have begun in the East, for Gracchus, like Africanus, was a lieutenant in the command of Lucius Scipio at Magnesia in 190 B.C. Gracchus' impeccable integrity makes his opposition to Publius' politics a sufficient indictment. When that is coupled with Cato's public activities, the legal proceedings against the Scipios become more than mere political animosity (Livy XXXVII.7.11–14).

The agreement of two such circumspect, though disparate, men as Cato and Gracchus on the political behavior of Scipio is eloquent. First, there is the matter of private negotiations with Antiochus by Africanus following the capture of his son. These attempted to regulate the time of the Battle of Magnesia until Scipio himself should be present. They seemed to imply that this would be beneficial to Antiochus. Then there is the surprising intermediary function of Africanus between the army council of his brother and King Antiochus. The conviction of other lieutenants from the eastern staff on a charge of accepting bribes to work for lenient peace terms and, later, that of Lucius Scipio himself is not to be taken lightly. However one argues against actual treason by Africanus, there is a definite aura of giving illegal aid and comfort to the enemy. Nor can it be asserted that Africanus acted as a private citizen; he was a lieutenant in the command of his brother, conducting secret negotiations with the enemy, negotiations unknown to his general or the army council. Similar action by any but "Africanus the Great" would occasion instant trial for treason. Indeed, the agents of the king at one juncture had instructions to negotiate with Africanus when they did not receive their wishes from the army council.

The attitude of Scipio deserves close analysis. His assumption that, because he had risked his life and reputation to lead the state against Hannibal and triumphed, he was above the law, is important to consider. This is the primary inference to be drawn from his haughty retort to legitimate questions: He was not accountable to *anyone*. His subsequent destruction of *all* the economic records, including those kept as a duty to the state, shows that he denied even the state's right to question him. Similar arrogance attended other acts of Scipio. He illegally opened the treasury when the quaestors did not dare, declaring that he had filled it and now he would open it. Later, with a cavalier disregard for the orderly workings of the law, he attacked tribunes who were trying to arrest

178   CATO THE CENSOR

Lucius. This seems to have precipitated another intervention by Gracchus, accompanied now by a denunciation of Scipio's conduct (Livy XXXVIII.56.8–10, XXXVII.55.11–13; Polybius XXIII.14.7; Gellius IV.18.7).

None of this exonerates or vindicates Cato with regard to modern charges. However deserving of trial and criticism Africanus was, Cato's pillory of him is a damning revelation of the remorseless man of principle. His impersonal evaluation of Africanus' psychological problems and inhuman destruction of the man's character bit by unrelenting bit—the impervious objectivity with which Cato forced Publius to flee lest his very personality be shattered—show the result of Marcus' education. Born among upright folk and self-educated in rules and discipline, Cato was a man of principle. International politics had taught him that Rome was "right" in all she did because of a rationale: The goal of Roman security justified any means. He seems to have ignored the fact that legalistic ideals had to be moderated in personal relationships: He compromised when dealing with soldiers and with his own wife. Apparently, men of principle who can maintain impersonal attitudes may be completely amoral. They have no obligation to reconcile their acts in terms of acquaintance, needing only to consider whether the mechanistic goals are served; one simply ignores bothersome human obstacles. So for Cato here, the question was not one of mercy but rather the good of the state, as he personally interpreted it, and the expediency of humiliating Scipio—a frightening vignette, but not unlike Plato's "philosopher kings." Cato may well have visualized himself in that way.

The second phase in the trials of the Scipios, the prosecution and indictment of Lucius for misplacing the money, followed naturally from the conclusion of the first. Africanus had failed to account for the five hundred talents received from Antiochus; therefore Lucius must. A tribune named G. Minucius Augurinus again brought a tribunician action, pressing the demand first put by Cato that disclosure be made (Gellius VI.19). When Lucius persistently refused, the tribune imposed a fine and demanded surety for payment (Livy XXXVIII.54.11–55). Lucius failed to account for the lost money, of course, because Africanus had torn up the books. Hence the intemperate action of the one brother had destroyed the defense of the other. Lucius also refused to give surety for the fine. The reason given by Livy is that he was too poor to do so. Obviously, then,

Lucius was not guilty of corruption, only of failing to record the expenditure of five hundred talents. The tribune was about to imprison Lucius when Africanus intervened. Livy says that the latter was serving on a commission in Etruria and when he heard of the arrest, he hastened to Rome (Livy XXXVII.56.8–11). Tribunes tried to stop his interference, but he attacked them, "With more affection for his brother than respect for the laws." Failing in this, Scipio appealed to the college of tribunes once again. They also rejected his plea, but Gracchus again saved the day. He vetoed the action of Minucius while rebuking Africanus for his defiance of the laws. This nullified both fine and surety; the charge was now dropped.[3]

Though the issue is not worth a lot of space, Africanus' commission in Etruria is contentious. Since he had voluntarily exiled himself from Rome, he must have returned to public life for the purpose of this commission. It is likely that Publius had incurred an obligation to people in Etruria because of his urgent building of a fleet in their territory on the occasion of his appointment to a North African command in 205. It may be that Etrurian communities needed help, and Scipio felt honor bound to give it. He came out of retirement for that purpose. On the other hand, he was loath to return to the scene of his embarrassment in Rome. He had voluntarily exiled himself from there and perhaps felt sufficiently discredited by the entire affair that he would be no help to Lucius as his tribunician trial began. Publius Scipio did keep in close touch with it, however, through messengers. Were it not for these facts, Scipio's absence from his brother's trial would be inexplicable. The same pride of name that drove him to refuse an accounting and to question the Romans' right to examine him would surely have forced him out of retirement to defend Lucius.

II   *Quarrels between Fulvius and Lepidus, Adherents of the Middle and Scipionic Blocs*

Livy's book XXXIX is the beginning of his attempt to discredit Cn. Manlius Vulso's campaign against the Galatians. Hitherto he had been citing the arguments of others. Now he seems to contend for himself. The degradation of the East and its deleterious influence on Rome was to be a continuing theme. The burden of difference seems to be that the East was too easy to conquer; it encouraged laziness, wealth, and indifference. Liguria, on the other hand, says our historian, had the tough country, terrain, and natives to put the "fighting edge" on the Roman soldiery and sharpen them for combat. He seems to agree with Polybius that the simple conditions and primitive aspect of Latium had bred the Roman fighter who conquered the world. We have already debated that concept from the pages of history. Two things might be said in further rebuttal: Attrition (war dead) was more a consideration than any other, but no ancient author deals with it comprehensively, and Livy's comparative treatment of the Ligurians and the Galatians, on the one hand, and the Galatians and Thracians, on the other, is hopelessly tendentious. Vulso's supposed relaxation of discipline in the East and in Thrace has already been discussed. The statements Livy now makes of the "Ligurians," as contrasted to Galatians, are wrong (Livy XXXIX. 1–3).

Livy's "Ligurians" are not Ligurians at all, but rather Gauls. The Friniates, whom he mentions first, lived in Cisalpine Gaul. So also, by strict interpretation, were the Apuani, living in northern Etruria between the Apennines and the sea. They were, in other words, that species of Gallic people Vulso's father had fought, from whom Cnaeus had learned precisely how to fight the Galatians. Livy's description of them in this section is similar to that accorded the Galatians in earlier times. The ideas of Livy contradict each other. He talks of fortified places, ambuscades, narrow roads, and siege points precisely as though it were in Galatia. The difference was merely the capability of Vulso as contrasted with the consuls of 187, who had a difficult time of it. There is almost an identical similarity between Mt. Olympus in Galatia and the battle terrain now described in Livy (XXXIX. 1).

Vulso's tactics would have worked equally well against the "Ligurians," but neither Flaminius nor Lepidus had the imagination to apply them. Instead they lost men and time in small skirmishes followed by battles. All the same, they neutralized the "Ligurians" in record time, but superficially; the consuls of 185 had to subdue the Apuani all over again. This hardly supports the Livian tradition that Ligurians were hardy foes. Aemilius Lepidus disengaged his army for the building of the Aemilian Way from Placentia to Ariminium, 160 miles of roadway. This was so important to him that he failed to return to Rome and supervise the elections; he also failed to intervene in Fulvius' request for a triumph. In consequence, his party lost the elections to the middle bloc, and Fulvius celebrated his triumph (Livy XXXIX.6.1). One cannot say from this that the Ligurians were a foe whose very toughness made the difference between the perseverance and the fall of the Roman Republic, as Livy does.

Opposition to Fulvius came with his return from Aetolia to request a triumph (Livy XXXIX.4). The absent Lepidus tried to oppose through a tribune, Aburius, who announced he would veto any action on the proposal of a triumph for Fulvius before the arrival of Lepidus. Fulvius then defended himself in the matter of the Ambraciot war, claiming not only that the city had been taken by force, but also that his looting of the temples there was no worse than that in Syracuse and other cities. Cato appeared on the Scipionic side, for once, urging that Fulvius' awards of crowns to his soldiers were ridiculous: "Who ever saw anyone presented with a crown, when a town had not been taken or an enemy's camp burned?"—a statement that seems to agree with the arguments of Lepidus, except that Cato was not with Fulvius before Ambracia but was negotiating with towns. He must have returned (Gellius V.6.24; chap. 9, n. 3).

Fulvius' important argument seems to have been a plea not to permit him to be made ludicrous by an insolent personal enemy. Everyone, from all sides, says Livy, then began to persuade the tribune to capitulate. If true, this fact displays the continuing influence and power of the middle bloc. The argument that mattered, once again, was vocalized by Tiberius Gracchus.

Gracchus simply pleaded with Aburius to remember the duty of a tribune: He was to represent the people of Rome, not the wishes of one consular individual. Then he contrasted his own selfless willingness to forget personal enmities for the sake of state with Aburius' carrying on a private enmity at the bidding of one individual. These considerations won the day, and the veto was withdrawn. The triumph was then approved (Livy XXXIX.5.1–6).

This third action by Gracchus is too much for modern authorities. They maintain that the contentious, sophisticated, and principled speeches of Gracchus reflect the Late Republic, when there were questions of Roman tension and loyalty that were not a part of the contemporary political scene in the second century B.C.; during the latter period a tribune would have known where his loyalty belonged. This is indeed a redundant argument! The previous section of Livy (Book 38) refers to Cato's having influenced two tribunes, the Mummii, to withdraw a veto. Gracchus, in his argument with

Aburius, unduly influenced the latter's determination of his duty. It is a moot point, really, whether the Republic was better served by vetoing Fulvius' triumph or expediting it. Gracchus simply reviewed the duty of a tribune, not whether that duty lay in veto of the matter at issue. Indeed, the following page will suggest that Fulvius' triumph ought to have been a dirge, morally speaking. It seems, then, that all sorts of people, both good and bad, influenced tribunes now and again. The argument that speeches on the duty of tribunes must have been written in the Late Republic falls of its own weight. Protagonists see nothing inconsistent in simultaneously attributing such modern European concepts as "buffer zones," "spheres of influence," and "power balances" to the brain of Scipio—a man so remarkably hot-tempered and short-sighted that he confiscated account books that were the only legal salvation for himself and his brother. There is no more reason to doubt that Gracchus could voice first-century thoughts in the third century than there is to agree that Scipio Africanus could originate modern European concepts in the third century B.C. (Scullard, p. 144).

Having failed to deter the award of a triumph, Lepidus hastened to Rome in order to interfere with the triumph itself, only to fall ill on the way. Fulvius, "lest he have more strife in the triumph than in the war," advanced its date to the twenty-second of December. It was in connection with the award of military decorations to the troops in Aetolia that Cato attacked Fulvius, even though his service with the latter had been a conciliatory gesture. The procession itself, though not as opulent as that of Manlius, which shortly followed, was important for its elevation of the middle bloc. It came immediately before the elections and that, together with the notable success of Vulso in the East and the presidency of Flamininus over the elections, favored the middle bloc. They won both consulships for the year 186: Sp. Postumius Albinus and Q. Marcius Philippus (Livy XXXIX.5, 6; Scullard, p. 166).

One dissident note: Carried in the procession were 785 bronze statues and 230 of marble. Hence Lepidus' charge that there was excessive looting of the temples in Ambracia was probably true. The systematic stripping of shrines for a prestigious display of triumphal trophies had now become a compelling factor. Cato was later to condemn that very practice in his censorship with a speech accusing the generals of greediness, if not felony. Entirely aside from allegations by the ancients that these imports enervated Rome, the sheer quantity gives one pause. Justly could Ambraciots complain that the temples throughout their city had been emptied of all images and the very gods themselves. There was a certain sociopolitical image to be gained by spoil displayed in one's house. Fulvius himself passed off guilt as the fortunes of war and turned the images over to the Roman priests—again the unction of religion to soothe conscience (Livy XXXIX.4.12)! True to his military predecessors, Fulvius freighted works of art from that prostrate land so that he might simultaneously brag of killing Greeks and, gracing his savage abode with their art, play at being civilized (cp. Livy XIII.23.6).

The middle bloc triumph at the polls in 186 should demonstrate that the Roman people were not deceived by Scipionic attacks on Manlius or Fulvius. Manlius' army was still in station before Rome, awaiting his triumph. If it were committing the vices trumpeted by Livy (XXXIX.6.5–6), the elections would reflect it. Livy shows further prejudice by asserting that Manlius' lenience as commander could be deduced from the songs that were sung by troops in the triumphal procession. Such songs were always notorious (XXXIX.7.3). The historian notes one of the most salutary domestic actions of the age, led by the middle bloc and Manlius, but dismisses it as a ploy to curry favor (XXXIX.7.5).

Manlius' triumph overshadowed that of Fulvius, discounting the theory that much wealth was lost in Thrace. Vulso donated generously to the soldiers, perhaps doubling their pay. But Livy most laments the importation of couches of bronze, valuable robes for coverlets, tapestries, tables with one pedestal and sideboards, female players, and the new culinary skills (XXXIX.6.7–7.5).

Livy's first books are a magnificent documentary of man rising above his environment to create Rome. He now seems to feel that the later Roman, presented with "environmental indolence," was incapable of overcoming it. Perhaps Livy is human, here. It is easier to instance the change of material goods and tangible daily activities than to investigate the nebulous variation in thoughts and ideals that inspired the transition in these externals. As mentioned before, the early heroes of Rome would not have bothered to cart this kind of thing back because there was no demand for it and no wish to cultivate its use. But a good deal had happened to Roman values and folkways since the foundation of the Republic to change all that.

A prime consideration in Roman affairs throughout this period had been the wish for security. International security had been achieved, but at the cost of continual war, which created a species of "security empire," with treaties, spheres of influence, and conquered territories insulating Rome from foreign aggression. The cost of these wars and ensuing "security enclaves" overseas caused economic crises and a second security problem, that of finances. The need for economic security had already inspired shocking exploitation in Spain, and the amounts of gold, silver, and precious commodities carried in the triumphs from the East were a gloomy foretaste of things to come. For the average Roman, it was but a short step from the cynicism bred by enduring hard fighting for the fiction of "home defense security"—a thousand miles from Rome— only to become disillusioned upon observing wholesale corruption among the patrician cadre who had formulated that aggressive policy, to the wish to enjoy the proceeds and wear the trappings of victory himself. If those rewards were imperial and therefore foreign, they might encourage non-Roman consumer demands. But the base of it all was not the magnetism of luxurious material to which "helpless men" succumbed, but the very real, human need for security and its adjuncts.

People have always craved security; it involves the instinct of survival. Hardly a city was without its wall; modern "walls" are made of other stuff. These have a price, which "protectionists" tend to forget; and, alas, the longer a "wall," the greater its cost. Few have ever learned when to stop: when their "wall's" extent begins to violate the right of others to an equal security, or when the sheer cost of a "wall," either material or spiritual, reaches a point of diminishing returns among their own people. They build compulsively, fanatic eyes on their international security, while behind them the mounting discord and the injustice allowed in the interest of "security" decay the state from within. Rome's "wall" encompassed the known world, but such was its cost that when completed there was nothing truly Roman left inside it to protect. War's attrition had adulterated the clans, and "security" had altered Roman rights.[4]

III *Ascendancy of the Middle Bloc:*
Monetary Reforms and Games

The signal domestic action performed by Manlius and the middle bloc, referred to above, was the retirement of the Punic War debt. Manlius used the middle bloc's voting superiority in the senate to pass resolution that the booty from the East be used to repay the outstanding extraordinary tribute that had been exacted in the emergency of the Second Punic War. This finally liquidated the debt. As it was owed the people of Rome, there can be little doubt that the middle bloc tapped a very popular vein of public opinion. Livy, in fact, accuses them of "currying favor" (XXXIX.7.4–5). This could have been done much sooner. It is known that Manlius brought 22½ million *denarii* from the East for actual deposit in the treasury, and Fulvius added 7½ million. With this, 25½ *tributa* were repaid (Frank, pp.135–36). The Scipionic faction had brought a total of about 25 million *denarii* from various sources into the treasury since the year 201 B.C. (Frank, pp. 127–32). It must have been used to finance the eastern wars. Unauthorized payments from it were forbidden, as witness Africanus' precipitately opening the doors of the treasury in spite of the quaestors (XXXVIII.55.13; Polybius XXIII.14.5)

Failure to retire the public debt with funds available in the treasury could only have benefited the state, which had embarked upon eastern wars hard on the heels of the Punic Wars (Livy XXVI.36.11). Private loans from members of the profiteering middle class were dealt with in three equal installments, 204, 200, and 196 B.C. (XXIX.16.1). The second, coming at the beginning of the Second Macedonian War, was paid in land instead of money with the option of redeeming it for cash later. The idea had been proposed by the creditors themselves. Land lying within the fiftieth milestone was assessed and paid in lieu of one-third of the debt. It was for that reason called the *trientabulum* (one-third) (XXXI.13.2–9, XXXIII.42.2; Hill, *Rom. Mid. Class,* pp. 88–89).

M. Aemilius Lepidus, it will be remembered, sponsored a measure in 189 to the effect that Romans and allies of the Latin confederacy should be exempt from paying port duties in Ambracia. This measure particularly favored the new middle class because the 218 *Lex Claudia* had limited ships owned by senators to three hundred *amphorae* (225 bu.), suitable for farm-to-market transportation but hardly for overseas (Livy XXI.63.3; Hill, pp. 50–51). The same is true of an even more revolutionary series of measures designed directly to increase the voting power of the middle class. Q. Terentius Culleo, a pro-Scipionic tribune, secured a plebiscite in 189 that would enroll freedmen or their sons with land valued at more than thirty thousand *sestertii* the rural tribes (Plutarch, *Flamininus* XVIII.1; Livy XLV.15.1). The *trientabulum* and middle class land acquisition show the whole intent of this plebiscite was to increase their voting power (Scullard, p. 183). It based the Scipionic bloc in the assembly of the people. Since the bulk of the farmers in the rural tribes were unable to present themselves in Rome for meetings of the *comitia*, it took only a handful often to sway the voting pattern in entire tribes. As all but four of the thirty-five tribes were rural and fifteen of them distant rural but well within the fiftieth milestone, the significance of Culleo's plebiscite for the vote in the *comitia tributa* is clear (cp. Marsh, *A History*, pp. 18–31, 370–74).

The same is true of the measure enrolling the sons of freedmen in the rural tribes. The Scipionic group, sponsoring the measure, was in a position to capitalize on it by wholesale enrollment of such freedmen's sons as were in its ranks of clients and so further dominate the electorate. It could easily form a permanent electoral majority in the assembly of the tribes.

The answer of the middle bloc to this attempt has already been mentioned: retire the debt and firm up the currency. It seems that this financial move enabled the government to strengthen and stabilize the *denarius*, which promptly became the standard silver issue. Simultaneously, the impression of stabilization was improved by reducing the rate of silver to bronze from about 1:100 to 1:67 per coinage unit. But that was gradually nullified by a reduction in the size of the bronze pieces issued (Scullard, p. 255; Frank, pp. 190–91). The middle bloc projected a more progressive business acumen to the new middle class than the Scipionic bloc, because aside from sporadic charismatic support, the Scipios again seemed lacking in significant political sway throughout the trials inspired by Cato. Though Livy time and again refers to the throngs attending Africanus during his trials, the urban proletariat formed but four of the thirty-five tribes and hence were without real political significance. The veto of just one tribune, and that an avowed enemy, was a poor showing of popular influence. Scipionic support in senate and *comitia* seems to have been almost nonexistent, seeing incidents of the trials.

The monetary reforms of the middle bloc were accidentally synchronized with Cato's attack on the Scipios. There is little reason to believe, even had they not been, that the followers of Africanus would have triumphed and led Rome thereafter. The attraction and resources of the Claudian-Fulvians and Fabians of the middle group had already weaned the middle class away from the Scipios and were shortly to consolidate them on their side. Games staged by Marcus Fulvius for ten days seemed to confirm the ascendancy of the middle bloc, even as they were a further measure of changing Roman appetites. Actors came from Greece to participate, a contest of athletes was made a spectacle, a hunt of lions and panthers was given, and the number and variety of games were almost like those in the Rome of Livy, says that author (XXXIX.22.2–3).

The historian does not moralize on these games and cite the degradation of the city. Apparently he thinks that luxurious materials and couches like those carried in Manlius' triumph are more debilitating than the killing and bloodlust now offered as entertaining spectacles in the games of Fulvius. He is at best tiresomely historical. Aristotle's "viviparous, rational, mammalian biped" has always considered it "manly" to kill other animals for mere sport, on terms that assure his victory but ironically show his fear. Similarly, he has thought it "civilized" to witness other animals, whether men or beasts, locked in bloody combat in colosseum, gridiron, ring, or rink—arousing the dormant urge of cave and jungle, vicariously thrilling to the purchased passions in the arena. Surely, this is worse than Livy's "evil," provided civilization is the degree of man's difference from other animals.

Lucius Scipio's following celebration of ten days of games financed by eastern kings and cities was at best anticlimactic. Livy's account of it seems to question their authenticity; he doubts the games were really vowed for the victory against Antiochus, as Lucius claimed (XXXIX.22.8–10). Modern writers accept Livy, calling them games to counteract the influence of those staged by the middle group. All discard the tale of annalist Valerius Antias that Lucius was an ambassador to the East sent to settle the dispute between Attalid and Seleucid kings and the money and artists for the games came from that journey. But unless a fund-gathering trip of that sort is supposed, it is difficult to know where Lucius got the money for games at this juncture. He had none after the trials, for he was unable to furnish surety for a fine, and the praetor had his house and estate ransacked for the money. At any rate, the games changed no minds, nor did they inspire a popular following like that which the Scipios were rapidly loosing to the middle group (Livy XXXVIII.60.8).

IV *The Bacchanalian Persecutions: Injustice and Reaction*

One affair of 186 B.C. confirmed Rome's wish for security: the so-called Bacchanalian conspiracy. It was styled a conspiracy (*con-*

iuratio) so that the senate could deal with it as a threat to public security both in Rome and Italy. Though the worship of Dionysus or Bacchus had long been familiar to Rome as that of Liber, the orgiastic rites of Dionysiac mysteries seem not to have arrived before 186. Livy says that it came first to Etruria through "A nameless Greek . . . a priest of secret rites performed by night." Later testimony of his quoted witness, the courtesan Hispala Faecenia, locates its origin with a Campanian woman, Paculla Annia. Hispala further avers that the Bacchanalia were at first only for women, no man being admitted. Three days each year were reserved for initiations into the rites, and it was the custom to choose matrons by turn for priestesses. But Paculla Annia, when priestess, changed all that by initiating her sons and holding the rites at night rather than by day, establishing five days for initiation in every month. Performed at night, with the added stimulus of wine and commingling of sexes, no form of crime, no sort of wrongdoing was left untried. There were more lustful practices among men with one another than with women. Those who were reluctant, she said, were sacrificed as victims (Scullard, *A History*, pp. 400–401; Livy XXXIX.8.3–9.7, 10.6–8, 13.8–14).

Important considerations emerge from this discussion. Hispala's account locates the origin of the orgiastic Bacchic rites in Campania, not the East. Orphism and Pythagorean beliefs had already spread to Latium from Magna Graecia in the south. Cato himself had come under the influence of the latter and accepted it as an "Italian" philosophy. Hence it is grossly misleading to attribute either orgiastic rites or mystic Greek beliefs to the eastern conquests, "Oriental influence" or mainland Greek contacts. They came through local Italian interchange and therefore were unaffected by conquest, as such. It follows that foreign policy had little to do with this aspect of Roman degradation. Archaic Roman religion no longer suited the needs of Roman "world citizens," and they sought more satisfying forms of worship. It was this broadening of outlook that inspired the hunger for different religions, not the appeal of orgiastic rites. Livy again seems to infer the latter. Recognizing the former, the senate treated the entire affair as an offense against the state—a conspiracy—rather than a perversion of religion. It was on this aspect that Cato raised his voice in rhetoric, *"De coniuratione"* (Malcovati, p. 31), showing conservatives on the side of law, not religion. The specifically orgiastic aspects of these observances were perhaps a response to the confining pietism of the old beliefs.

The exceptional mobility of these ideas is to be connected with the unusual amount of migration from Latin allied towns to Rome in this period. It had assumed the proportions of a problem. Q. Minucius Thermus first officially recognized its implications by limiting a levy of allied troops for his campaigns in proportion to the numbers of young men fit for service in each town. The migration had been such that population was apparently depleted in allied towns. But the practice was not followed consistently, with the result that in 187 the Latins demanded repatriation of their own subjects so as to meet the increasing levies upon them. Q. Terentius Culleo was instructed to expel those who had formerly been registered as citizens of Latin allied cities, and twelve thousand Latins were forced to return to their native cities (Livy XXXIV.56.5–6, XXXIX.3.4–6).

The Latin mobility demonstrated that the problem of religious cults was an all-Italian affair rather than merely Roman. The senate took steps to enforce its proscription of Bacchic beliefs on all Italians for that reason. It stripped the religion of all its orgiastic and secret aspects and then legalized the worship, a surprisingly cunning move. There was little objectionable in the veneration of Dionysus (Bacchus), only in its more sensational aspects. But the fact that the senate arbitrarily dictated to all Italy in this fashion, and that without consulting the people of Rome as legislative assembly, boded ill for the future. The inscription conveying the decree of the senate to the allies is in the form of a *Senatus Consultum* (Livy XXXIX.14.4–9; Scullard, p. 147), which has no legal authority over the magistrates; its *de facto* coercive power should have had little effect on the decision of the Latin allied towns. That the consuls were especially tactful in communicating the senate's wishes to local authorities matters little, for the intent was clear. Edicts were to be sent throughout all Italy that no one who had been initiated in the Bacchic rites should have the right to assemble for ritual purposes. Though the *Consultum* is very careful to fix upon *conspiracy* (to commit a felony or homicide) as the crux of the punishable offence, great moral pressure was asserted both on the towns and the magistrates by this senatorial decree (Livy XXXIX.18.7–9).

Not only was this a very grave constitutional matter, but it actually encouraged perfidy. The senate used the archaic, faulty method of offering rewards for informing on members of the cult. The frightful injustices perpetrated by informers throughout the balance of Roman history were thus encouraged by the senate in what can most charitably be called a fit of naïve superstition (XXXIX.14.6, 16.1). The people of all Italy, Rome included, were seized by panic, knowing no doubt that crisis and the hinged tongues of political enemies would make little distinction between "conspiracy" and guilt by association (XXXIX.17.4). "Conspiracy" actually is a nebulous affair and often impossible to disprove. Livy himself says (XXXIX.14.4) that even senators were horrified lest some relative be involved in the mischief—guilt by consanguinity! He goes on to say that the names of many were reported and certain of these, men and women, committed suicide (XXXIX.17.4–7); more than half of the estimated seven thousand people involved were executed for "conspiracy." This appalling number surely cannot reflect individuals who were planning to commit felony or homicide, for Rome would have been in dire straits if that were true. One can only surmise that many were convicted by mere circumstance because of informers, to say nothing of those who committed suicide after the disgrace of accusation. Great numbers must have been innocent of any crime (XXXIX.18.3). The arbitrary actions of the senate and consuls should have been occasion for revolution on the basis of constitutional right.

This scandal offers an opportunity to assess the position of the senate and the elected magistrates of Rome. Unfortunately, the assessment amounts to an indictment. Hispala Faecenia, a freedwoman, became so terrified at the sight of lictors and so transfixed by consular interrogation that she was speechless and swooning, a far cry from accountability (XXXIX.12–13)! While she was in that state of fear, Postumius browbeat her, making allusions to differences of class and position. Third, the senate unilaterally imposed inquiry upon the people, informing them later (XXXIX.14.9–10). Guards were set throughout the city for security, but they also prevented citizens from leaving—detention and assumption of guilt without due process (XXXIX.17.2, 5). This curtailed the right of exile. The right of free assembly at night was forbidden. The consuls executed thousands, though the senate had required only investigation, causing such an exodus that cases had to be postponed, lacking parties to continue them. The accusations by informers, naming persons who could not be found, forced officials to conduct inquiries in the villages, transgressing the rights of communities. The independence of communities in Italy and citizens' rights continued to be violated into the following year, when the praetor Postumius sought out persons who had abandoned their sureties, pronounced some guilty, presumably executing them, and sent the rest under arrest to Rome where they were imprisoned (XXXIX.51.6–7). Those who had been initiated but done no wrong were imprisoned—a most damning invasion of privacy. To climax it all, the word used as cause for incarceration in this case is "conspiracy" to commit vice and lust by the oath of initiation alone! It is obvious, in the light of all this, that the consuls were conducting a bloody vendetta that was completely arbitrary in its treatment of people and haphazard in its use of capital punishment (XXXIX.13.3, 18.1, 3).

There seems to have been, through it all, some misconception of the use and meaning of the *Senatus Consultum*. The senate, consuls, and people acted exactly as if it were a *Senatus Consultum de republica defendenda* (later, *Senatus Consultum Ultimum*), suspending the constitution and instituting martial law. It seems certain that cases of obvious injustice would otherwise have been subject to *intercessio* and the veto power of the tribunes. Such luminaries as Tiberius Gracchus sat in that college; one who was so sensitive of the constitutional rights of a political enemy could surely be presumed to have taken action in such a universal miscarriage of justice as this. Either the tribunes became completely identified with the senate—unlikely indeed, in view of Gracchus's earlier statements—or all previous ideas of the Bacchanalian "Conspiracy" are wrong, and it marks the first historical instance of the *Senatus Consultum de republica defendenda*, sixty years before its supposed first occurrence in the time of Caius Gracchus.

The consuls for 185 were friendly to the middle bloc. Postumius, with his new austerity fresh from the Bacchanalian proscriptions, presided (Livy XXXIX.23, 32). Ap. Claudius Pulcher and M. Sempronius Tuditanus had an uneventful year, though they were called upon to resubdue the so-called Ligurian Apuani, who in reality lived in Northern Etruria and behaved themselves like Gauls. Once again, as in 187, Sempronius burned villages and forts, opening passes and territories to Roman communication. As before, the Apuani retired to a mountain and were defeated, "the handicap of unfavorable ground having been overcome," whatever that phrase may mean. Appius, on the other hand, attacked the Ligurian Ingauni on the farther side of Genoa, taking six of their towns and thousands of prisoners. He beheaded forty-three of the leaders, responsible for having dared to rebel against their Roman masters.

This contentious individual, hastening to Rome, undertook to interfere unduly in the elections, canvassing for his brother Publius, who was seeking the consulship. There is nothing to recommend the brother but a questionable feat of having fined grain dealers for hoarding the grain supply in 189 when he was curule aedile. At the least, he enforced his middle bloc's policy of sound fiscal management against the manipulations of the middle class. But his praetorship was so colorless that there is some question when it took place. It was for this questionable individual that Appius hurried to Rome and then proceeded to confound all ethics by actively campaigning while he was still in office (Livy XXXVIII.35.5, XXXIX.32.5; Broughton, p. 367).

It speaks ill of the Roman electorate that Publius Claudius was elected in spite of his lack of good "references" and his brother's violation of propriety. Livy lampoons the consul Claudius, without his lictors, "flitting about" the whole forum with his brother. Even though the greater part of the senate and his adversaries kept reminding him that he was a consul of Rome rather than the brother of a candidate, he continued his zealous canvass. It caused contention between tribunes, some being for, some against, Publius. Apparently Romans could be swayed by vigorous campaigning and false "image building," no matter what their real knowledge of the candidate and his abilities. Two of the opponents were better representatives of the middle group, so one cannot say that his election was a matter of politics. Livy calls it "Claudian violence," with his characteristic inability or refusal to deal with the inner feelings of the electorate rather than with externals.

A better indicator of the feelings of the electorate was the election of one of the conservative, or Porcian, faction to the plebeian consulship. It portrayed a thirst for return to the old Roman rights and their guarantees in a sound constitution rather than the clandestine prosecutions associated with the Bacchanalian conspiracy. This same wish for assurance caused the election of Cato himself to the censorship in 184.

Cato drove Publius Cornelius Scipio Africanus from public life in the year 184, the same year he began his famous censorship. The particulars of this last legal confrontation between Scipio and Cato, associated with the tribuneship of Marcus Naevius, are preserved in Gellius (IV.18.3–6). Again it was a tribunician hearing and the accusation was that Scipio had received money from Antiochus to make peace with Rome on easy terms. During this action, Livy says, Scipio pronounced such a magnificent speech about his deeds that clearly no man had ever been better eulogized by his own rhetoric. This is the speech that Livy (XXXVIII.54.6, 50.11, 51.7) says had the name of Marcus Naevius on its *index* (tag fastened to the projecting end of the rod on which the roll was wound), and Gellius says it was still in circulation in his day. Then, perhaps in his *provocatio*, Scipio recalled that it was the anniversary of his victory at Zama and led the people out of the forum to sacrifice at the shrines of the gods in commemoration. He next retired to Liternum, exiling himself from Rome once again. Cato allowed the case to drop, perhaps remembering that a tribunician veto from Tiberius Gracchus was a distinct possibility if he continued to prosecute Africanus in his absence (XXXVII.52.10). Scipio died at Liternum the following year (XXXIX.52). Such was his bitterness that, as Livy says, he gave orders that he should be buried in the country rather than in an ungrateful homeland (XXXVIII.53.8).

CHAPTER 8

Cato as Censor

I *The Background to Cato's Election*

CATO'S election to the censorship in 184 came after a strenuous campaign. Livy and Plutarch agree that the nobility united against him (Livy XXXIX. 41.1; Plutarch XVI. 3–4). If true, it implies that the Porcian political faction had few patrician adherents and shows the extent to which the moderate middle bloc of Claudio-Fulvians had wooed the old Fabians from Cato's conservative coalition. It would seem that Cato's only adherents were the relatives and clients of the Porciuses and Flaccuses, the latter being his patronizing family and Lucius his colleague in the censorhip. It is possible that many were estranged because of Cato's fanaticism in the prosecution of Scipio Africanus. Whatever the cause, this singular lack of a broad power base in the Roman nobility was aggravated by a dearth of adherents also among the new middle class, who, as explained earlier were enfranchised in the *comitia tributa*. Cumulatively, these defects in the politics of the conservatives doomed their reform ideals to failure. Cato had been his own worst enemy in this respect. He never sought approval, thinking it sufficient to impose laws on the electorate from above. The demise of his reforms shows the futility of the shallow "law and order" approach, which neither educates nor seeks popular support. This fiasco shocked Cato sufficiently that he later compromised with moderates.

Attempts to explain Cato's election as a popular reaction against the Bacchanalian "conspirators" are, at best, inadequate. The senators who now coalesced against him represented the hard line of repression. They had even violated the constitution in their eagerness to prosecute the conspirators and the mores they represented. Therefore, the electorate's massive defection from ties of loyalty as clients or freedmen of the nobility, all of whom opposed

Cato, requires more than the facile explanation of the latter's moral conservatism. Marcius and Sp. Postumius, consuls for 186 B.C., and L. Postumius, praetor for 185 and 184, as well as L. Pupius in 183, enforced Roman order with respect to slaves and conspirators, as a conservative should. The popular reaction that elected Cato must have been against all that. It was probably Cato's *constitutional* conservatism and legal accountability that appealed to them. Livy shows that Roman citizens fled in such numbers that the city was depopulated, largely because of the indiscriminate use of informers, prosecution without due process, and the denial of the right of exile. These same abuses were applied by Roman officials in Italy wherever the fugitives took refuge but there the prosecution was cloaked by legal pretense: Livy's "lawlessness in Tarentum" and "rebellion in Apulia". It was precisely because Cato stood against the nobility and represented old-fashioned constitutional rights and guarantees that he was elected. It was the lower and middle strata of the Roman society that voted for him, not the nobility. Well has it been said that the Romans identified the problem of justice not in terms of being fair, but rather in terms of the maintenance of existing rights. The nobility had transgressed that dictum, to their peril. The middle bloc's failure to appreciate this feeling led to an otherwise inexplicable Scipionic victory at the polls in 182, as the middle bloc administrations for 184 and 183 continued to prosecute the lower classes outside Rome despite their rights as citizens.[1]

The unrest that manifested itself from 185 to 181 B.C. as far afield as Tarentum and Apulia is properly seen as a protest against the dictatorial methods used by the Roman administration to enforce order. For example, Livy shows that fugitives from the Bacchanalian persecution had taken refuge in Tarentum and in Apulia. There was in 185 and 184 a "conspiracy" of shepherds in Tarentum, which assumed such serious proportions as to constitute brigandage: the harrassing of highways and public pasturelands. This crime is directly linked to the Bacchanalia by Livy through the countermeasures taken by L. Postumius. Therefore, by the evidence of Livy, the brigandage of the shepherds is a manifestation of the Bacchanalian affair and of the discontent of the fugitives in that area. It is instructive that the "shepherds" chose to disturb only the *public* highways and the *public* pasturelands. They wished to silhouette their protest as visibly as possible. There is a common misconception that these people were slaves. But Livy says only that there was a slave insurrection in Apulia (in 185 B.C.) and then in the next sentence that L. Postumius, the praetor with Tarentum as his province, investigated a conspiracy of shepherds there and suppressed it. Because of the proximity of Tarentum to Apulia, people have assumed that the line on the slave insurrection pertains to the conspiracy of the shepherds. It does not, as in the assignments for 183 Apulia is treated as a separate *provincia* from Tarentum and what pertains to the one does not necessarily involve the other. Hence the Bacchanalian fugitives linked to the "shepherds' revolt" in Tarentum were not slaves, but Roman citizens with rights. Those rights continued to be denied them in the "shepherd conspiracy," as L. Postumius condemned about seven thousand, many of whom were executed while some escaped (n. 1).

The total viciousness of Postumius' prosecution of the Bacchanalia is plain from Livy's saying that Postumius pronounced guilty many of the fugitives in Tarentum who had not appeared when summoned or had abandoned their sureties and others he arrested and sent to Rome. Of the latter, all were imprisoned. In other words, there was no recourse to due process at all here, and all rights were denied. The right of flight, so recently exercised twice by Scipio Africanus, was completely denied to those whose only crime, before due process, was that they were not suspects of the stature of Scipio Africanus! Further, the constitutionality of enforcing such dictatorial power in the Italian provinces should be considered (Scullard, p. 147).

The so-called "poisonings" of 184 B.C. have been styled evidence of the increasing lawlessness of the people in this period. These did Q. Naevius investigate, to the tune of two thousand more condemnations and their ensuing executions. He conducted the inquiries outside of Rome, in the municipalities and rural communities, "because this method seemed more convenient" (n.1). The use of this factor to show anything but administrative incompetence is foolishness. First, there is the Roman paranoia about poisoning. Second, the number condemned; no other historical state known to man has indicted two thousand of its citizens, either directly or implicitly, in affairs like poisoning. It smacks very much of wholesale executions to be sure of killing the single one or so that might be guilty— providing, of course, that the poison scare was not a false alarm, as it so often proved to be in later Roman history. Finally, the investigations were conducted outside the city. That is again a veiled allusion to the assumption of class involvement. The people to be found out there were Italians, slaves, and the fugitives who were actually the middle and lower classes of Rome. They were not sent back to Rome or allowed to flee, and so the same statement of injustice must be levelled at the Roman administration in this case as in the Bacchanalian prosecutions.

II *The Censorial Contio, Purges, and Appointments*

Custom decreed that censors-elect hold a *contio* on the *Campus Martius* announcing the moral principles upon which they intended to base the exercise of their censorial power and the innovations they proposed to introduce in their edict as arrangements for the census. The *contio* held by Cato and Flaccus must have been a harrowing experience for those who had opposed their candidacy. The moral presuppositions could be summarized in two expressions uttered by Livy: to chastise the new vices and to revive the ancient character (XXXIX.41.4). The tolling of arrangements for the census must have thrown fear into the calmest of politicians and the most assured of capitalists. Cato intended to impose discriminatory tax assessments on luxuries in order to discourage ostentation and force a return to austerity. It was his hope also, by the use of the censor's edict, to curtail the importation of cultural items and moral behaviorisms from the East (Plutarch XVIII; Livy XXXIX.44; Scullard, p. 156).

The first of the duties to be performed was the revision of the roll of the senate *(lectio senatus)*, which included both property and moral assessments. Cato and Flaccus were exceptionally severe, expelling seven senators from the registry. Though as many as sixteen had been expelled in one year (252 B.C.) and the number of seven was not uncommon (209, 204), those expelled before had been junior senators. Cato expelled one man of consular rank and a praetorian. Accentuating all this was the fact that the ex-consul was L. Quinctius Flamininus, brother of the famous Titus Flamininus, architect of the Greek settlement (XXXIX.42–43; Plutarch XVII). Titus was highly indignant and sought an explanation in the *contio* through an appeal to the people. Cato responded by narrating in a speech, *In L. Quinctium Flamininum* (Malcovati, pp. 32–34), that Lucius killed a Boian Gaul with his own hands just to please his lover, a Carthaginian boy named Philippus. He then challenged Lucius to a formal trial with money sureties, but Lucius admitted

his guilt by remaining silent. Cato had won a great personal triumph
that seemed to confirm his ideals (Cicero, *Cato* 12.42; Plutarch,
Flamininus XIX). The tragic result was a slighting of Flamininus.
Cato was to learn from the failure of his reforms that he needed
Titus and the moderates more than they needed him; hence his
censorship was pivotal in political ideology. This, combined with
the forcible lesson being taught the nobility by their clients' defection because of rights, was an education that changed Cato's career
(cp. Fraccaro, *Stud. stor*, pp. 9 ff.).

The fact that Lucius Flamininus was returned to his place among
the senators in the theatre and the prestige of senatorial rank by
popular demand shows conclusively that Cato was not elected by
the people for his moral conservatism; they would have heeded his
condemnation of Lucius (Plutarch, *Flamininus* XIX.4). Instead,
they demanded Lucius take his place among the senators. Clearly,
Cato was elected for different reasons. But at the same time, the
people and Cato were both hypocritical. The act that Flamininus
had committed merited the most severe censure and punishment.
It says something about the Romans that popularity could obliterate
murder (Plutarch XVII.6). As for Cato, particular reference has
been made here to atrocities committed both in Sicily and in Spain,
which were *provinciae* under the command of Romans, as was Boian
Gaul under Lucius Flamininus. There seems little to be preferred
between the single act of homicide committed by Lucius and the
mass murders committed in the name of Roman repression in Sicily
while Cato was there or in Spain while Cato was commander there.
The only difference was one of circumstance.

The other noteworthy expulsion from the senate was that of a
certain Manlius (Manilius), whose offense was that he had embraced
his wife in daylight before the eyes of their daughter. This act has
been mentioned above in connection with Cato's ideas about
women's behavior and their contradictory nature. But the present
deed of excluding Manlius from the senate was, again, a hypocritical
one. Cato, according to Plutarch, was constrained to take a second
wife in his old age because his liaison with a slave girl became so
offensive to his son and daughter-in-law. And yet he did not,
because of that obvious sexuality paraded before the two, resign
from the senate as he should have done to be consistent. Cato would
have argued that what really mattered was appearances, no doubt.
The fact of physical caress or contact personally witnessed, rather

than copulation plainly inferred from other acts, was the crucial difference. But that was the Catonic tragedy! Legislated morality never goes below the surface; it does not deal with the deep-seated feelings and wishes of the people.

The other five senators expelled from that body by Cato were not as important or noteworthy. The whole censorship of Cato is credited with as many as twenty-six speeches or as few as twenty-one, and though not all are directed against individuals, certainly many of his decisions were debated and contested (Scullard, pp. 159, 261, adds Claudius Nero and twenty-one orations; Meyer, twenty-six).

After the revision of the rolls of the senate came the review of the knights (*equites*). Historically, the knights were considered a permanent class of Roman society: the equestrian order (*equester ordo*), a second rank of nobility. But they lacked specified institutionalization and drew members from both patricians and plebeians, classes with which they continued to identify politically, rather than identifying with the "knights" as a class. So it came about that the only distinction was a certain census requirement to maintain membership in the corps: a personal property valuation of four hundred thousand *sestertii* (about twenty thousand dollars). Currently, the order was composed of eighteen centuries of horsemen, or eighteen hundred cavalrymen, aged eighteen to forty-five years. They were given their first horse by the state (*equites equo publico*), and, if our previous deductions about the grandfather of Cato are right, they had to supply the replacements for mounts lost in battle in all but cases of exceptional bravery. Apparently the state allowed ten thousand *sestertii* (five hundred dollars) for the purchase of horses. Each cavalryman had to have two, in case of loss (chap. 6, n.6).

The review of the knights consisted of each man leading his horse past the censors when his name was called, answering ritualized questions, and passing a general inspection. Disqualifications show beyond doubt that the knight's career was reviewed and signs of moral weakness or disobedience were sought out as well. These, the answers to the questions, the visible physical state of either knight or horse, passing the age of retirement, or failure to meet the property qualification were cause for discharge from the corps. Such separation was either an act of censure or a formal discharge. If the former, it was in *ignominia*, a definite social and political liability, for the review took place in the forum and was public. The public horse would then be taken away, perhaps sold, or the period of service could be extended at the knight's own expense as a form of retribution. For nonsenators, expulsion from the *equites* meant reduction to the class of the commoners (*aerarii*), rather a severe punishment. Apparently senators had adopted the practice of remaining in the *equites*, in a privileged position after the age of forty-five, though not in active service. Often the sons of senators enrolled routinely in the cavalry centuries, and that was their sole mark of distinction until they became officers, magistrates, or reached the age of forty-five, (Gellius IV.20.1–11; Cicero, *de Oratore* II.260).

Cato began the review of knights by eliminating L. Scipio Asiaticus from the group (Livy XXXIX.44.1; Plutarch XVIII.1). Cato's decision was called bias and therefore prejudiced his hopes to reform the cavalry to an effective military force. It is not known whether the knights were, in actual fact, an inefficient group (Scullard, p. 160). Though the cavalry was insufficient against Hannibal, that statement held true for the entire military establishment, and it is rather pointless to speak as though the cavalry alone stood in need of reform. One does not hear of extensive army reforms because of ineffectiveness against Hannibal, or of changes in the method of electing magistrates to ensure the choice of gifted commanders in time of war. The speech of Cato in Spain, *Oratorio quam habuit Numantiae apud equites*, cannot be construed to signify cowardice among the cavalry (Malcovati, p. 158; Livy XXXIV.13.4). It was delivered to tribunes and centurions as well as cavalrymen, and certainly not at Numantia; the title of the speech is a misnomer. Knights were of the upper class, and naturally they would be convoked with their commanders, the prefects, and the tribunes and centurions of the infantry. True, the cavalry on the right fled in Cato's battle, but that on the left did not; fifty-fifty was rather a good record against the dread Celtiberian cavalry—surely this was no cause to seek reform of the cavalry over and above that of the army. The idea, therefore, that the fortitude of cavalry and army were decaying is fallacious (Livy XXXIV.14.6).

Cato may have been trying to change the senatorial habit of remaining in the cavalry after the age of forty-five. It is possible that Lucius Scipio was now over that age. Even if this were the motive, it was supposedly tactless choosing Lucius as an example because it seemed prejudiced. It was not a disqualification in *ignominia*, at any rate. It is likely that Lucius failed to meet the census qualification, as his trial had shown he lacked the money to meet a surety. If, on the other hand, Cato used this discharge of Lucius as an occasion to stress the need for more cavalry, it may be that his censorial speech, *Ut plura aera equestria fierent*, delivered in the senate, in part vindicated the discharge of Lucius, arguing for a larger corps (Malcovati, p. 178). Defeats in the field may have been caused simply by numbers; Cato now proposed twenty-two hundred men. Presumably, Cato required that they be young, vigorous troopers and thus simultaneously argued for the retirement of senators over forty-five from the corps. It would be interesting to know how many others were discharged. Only Lucius is named by the sources, because of the notoriety that attached to his case. But Livy vaguely alludes to unspecified others whose horses were taken from them.

One such case is set forth in Gellius and substantiated by Cicero. It shows Cato's continuing doctrinaire attitudes toward the cavalry. During the review, one responded to the ritualized questions asked of knights flippantly. In answer to the question, "Have you, to the best of your knowledge and belief, a wife?" the fellow replied: "I indeed have a wife, but not, by Hercules! such a one as I could desire." For this lack of reverence and obedience, Cato and Flaccus reduced him to a commoner (*in aerarios rettulit*), says Gellius (IV.20.3–6, 11), who quotes Cato in another instance (12.2–3) also. The Roman knight whose horse was skinny or ill groomed was charged with *inpolitiae*, which meant the same as negligence. But if such a one gave a disrespectful answer to censorial questions about the horse, he could be reduced to the status of a commoner. Finally, Cato aspired to make corpulence an offense to the state. He scorned fat knights, wondering aloud how a body could be of service to the state when everything between its gullet and its groins was devoted to belly (Plutarch IX.5). He used this as a reason to deprive a knight of his horse, since Gellius says that the censors used to take the horse from a man who was too fat because he was unfit to perform the duties of a knight (VI.1–3). The knight did not lose rank because of it. In the same place Gellius adds that Cato, in a speech *On Offering Sacrifice*, makes such an occurrence serious and attended with disgrace, since there was a reproach of slothfulness also implied in the proceedings. Seeing these particulars and Cato's ideals, one may imagine the resentment.

There is more behind the purge of senate and knights in 184–83 B.C. than the ire of Cato or the mores of the upper class. Livy's brief allusion to Cato's supporting speeches for his expulsions (but the survival of only one, possibly two, of them) and the surprising reference to "other bitter orations against those who were either expelled from the senate or whose horses were taken from them" show that other senators were highly emotional about some of the expulsions (Livy XXXIX.42.6). Cato was not alone in his vituperation. There are indications in this, and in the election of Scipionic consuls for 182 B.C., of a public revulsion of feeling. No doubt the acceleration of change—reflected by the new customs coming from the East, but climaxed and heightened by the constitutional crisis that elected Cato as an unintentional reactionary—had its counterpart in senatorial undercurrents Livy cannot document. After all, Cato's election represented a schism in the system of patronage, a significant revolt of the clients. It may well be that junior or plebeian senators, less removed from the people by patrician dignity, spoke out against the administrative abuse of power in the actions connected with the Bacchanalian conspiracy. That theory, at least, explains the "acerbity" with which Livy says these other orations were delivered. It further explains the anonymity of the orators and the disappearance of their speeches. Unfortunately, it leaves no proof at all, save Livy's veiled allusions. However, this kind of movement is not without parallel. It resembles the coercion of the minor nobility to be seen in the declaration of the Second Macedonian War and that associated with the African command of Scipio in 205 B.C. These recurring divisions between major and minor nobility require a sharp deductive sense, to be rescued from Livy's obscurity or aristocratic bias.

Perhaps after reviewing the knights, maybe later, Cato moved to appoint a new *princeps senatus* to replace the deceased Africanus. Originally, the *princeps* was supposed to be the senior surviving patrician ex-censor, placed at the head of the list of senators by the censors. The only functional value in the title was that of being the first asked for an opinion on whatever issue the senate was considering. There was great prestige connected with it, of course. After 209 B.C., when the rule as to seniority had been set aside in honor of Fabius Maximus, the prime factors in selection had come to be those of merit and service to the state. Ironically, seeing that Fabius was the precedent, those same criteria opened the principate to abuse through prejudicial value judgments. That allowed Cato to pass over the claims of others and place his patron and colleague,

Flaccus, at the head of the list, thereby making him effective *princeps senatus*. Flaccus did not deserve that honor over other prominent candidates, either by the consideration of seniority or by the criteria of merit and service. Particularly glaring was the omission of Titus Quinctius Flamininus, an ex-censor who was eminently more prestigious in terms of deeds. It may be that the appointment was made, together with the publishing of the revised roll of the senate, just before the closing of the *lustrum*, eighteen months after election. Even then, the selection of Flaccus was questionable—he was not technically an ex-censor. If the *lustrum* was closed, at least, his official duties were over; but the term of office continued until 179. Cato was evidently willing to wink at the law where his own convenience or the "needs of state" as he interpreted them were concerned (Livy XXXIX.52.1–7; Scullard, pp. 157, 164; *Ox. Class. Dict.*, p. 730).

Unfortunately, giving Flamininus the honor of *princeps senatus* was just the kind of gesture that would have reconciled Titus and Cato, allowing them to compromise and work together. Again, it must be reiterated that this era of Cato's censorship and the failure of his reforms were to teach the censor that his uncompromising nature was a luxury neither he nor his country could afford. Much more was accomplished when Cato had learned that lesson.

III *The Census and Tax*

A task of the censorship implied previously was that of assessing the property of individual Romans, more for the purpose of military service and taxation, originally, than for determining political status. All persons who were citizens appeared in person before the censors and declared their property. The censors could revise or refuse their declarations of value. This registration took place in a building in the *Campus Martius*. Apparently the censors were assisted in their evaluations by sworn assessors, since Cato used them to perform the details of property valuation he ordered. But there is a problem with respect to the tax situation in the censorship of Cato. He was within his rights to direct the rate of assessment, and he did so with a vengeance. Jewels, women's dresses, vehicles worth more than fifteen thousand asses (three hundred dollars), slaves under twenty years of age bought since the previous *lustrum* for more than ten thousand asses (two hundred dollars), furniture and plate (all of which Plutarch erroneously prices at fifteen thousand *drachmae*, probably assuming the *as* equivalent to the *drachma*), were to be assessed at ten times their cost. Then Cato ordered that a tax of three asses per one thousand of assessed value be added. As the usual tax was one as per one thousand, this tax on an inflated valuation would be almost confiscatory. An item worth ten thousand asses previously taxed at ten asses would now be taxed three hundred asses: three percent of its value. That seemed a prohibitive amount to Romans. The problem alluded to previously is whether it was legal (Livy XXXIX.44.2–3; Plutarch XVIII.2–3; Frank, p. 79).

The power of taxation did not vest in the censors. Therefore, any implicaton that Cato *imposed* (*attribuo*) a tax is an assertion of illegality (Plutarch: *prostimáo*). Broad as the censor's powers of edict were, the censors could not create new taxes; they could only interpret existing ones. Thus, having been defeated on the matter of the Oppian Law in 195 during his consulship, Cato now amended the property tax to discriminate heavily against luxuries, supposedly by the censor's power of edict. The success of this approach was caused by the vagueness of the right of edict. Assessments were well within a censor's jurisdiction, but the raising of the tax from one mill to three on only specific items surely violated the intent of censorial powers. The senate alone had the right to add taxes; but once Cato had set the precedent, later censors made new taxes also. Cato's marginal abuse of this right went unchallenged (Livy XL.51.8; censors of 179 impose customs payments and duties).

The point has been advanced that the slaves were taxed because Cato desired to limit the flow into Roman homes of highly trained Greeks, worth more than ten thousand asses, whose morals and views might be harmful (Scullard, p. 156). But in this case the age limitation—twenty years old or younger—must be explained (Livy XXXIX.44.3). Unless we assume that Greeks could achieve a high level of training before they were twenty, these heavily taxed slaves were not scholars. In fact, the key may be their very youth. Physically attractive, youthful menials would be a legitimately taxable luxury. This was the opulence Cato wished to limit.

IV *Public Works and the Letting of Contracts*

Marcus' days as aedile had taught him the need to enforce the regulation of water supply. He now cut off or discontinued all private piping of water from the aqueducts directly to private homes, gardens, and fields. This prevented the tapping of the aqueducts between the city wall and the fountains where everyone was supposed to get water. Cato also apparently found evidence of land speculation involving the use of public water supply, and he fined a senator for the crime. When this worthy, L. Furius Purpureo, objected and appealed to the people, Cato gave a speech *in contione: In L. Furium de aqua, qua multam ei dixit*, in which he charged Furius with buying badly irrigated fields cheaply and then using the public waters to restore them and raise their value. Much of this speech sets forth duties of water maintenance officials (Malcovati, p. 181; Livy XXXIX.44.4; Plutarch XIX.1).

Further, Cato and Flaccus policed the use of public land for private purposes. Private buildings and perhaps personal structures built up against public buildings, thus avoiding the construction of one whole wall, they tore down on thirty days' notice. This arrested the gradual encroachment by the wealthy on the lands of state, although it had to be continued and enforced by the censors of 179 before becoming effective.

Additional duties performed by the censors were those of leasing the taxes and contracts for public works. Cato and Flaccus did both amid great clamor and disturbance. As Livy cryptically notes: They farmed the revenues at the highest and let the contracts at the lowest price. It militated against the fat profits customarily enjoyed by the Roman capitalists. These promptly agitated the politicans, and with success. Flamininus seems to have taken this opportunity to lead an attack on Cato, revenge for the expulsion of his brother. The senate bowed to combined pressure, cancelling the contracts and ordering that they be relet. The attendant debate was probably the occasion of Cato's speech *Ad litis censorias*, indicating that one must do his duty, even in a state whose administration was dissipated by laxness (Malcovati, p. 182). What Cato defined as his "duty" was made abundantly plain by a simultaneous action against a man named Oppius and his like, barring disreputable contractors from state business. The fragments of Cato's speech *Contra Oppium* (ibid.) show that the man had contracted to supply wine for public sacrifices under bond. Finding that he must take a greater loss than the bond by continuing to supply the wine at the agreed price, Oppius simply forfeited the bond and discontinued the contract. Perhaps Cato banned such businessmen from bidding on state contracts by censorial edict, and that was the occasion of the speech.

Flamininus and the senate enjoyed a minor victory over the two censors, forcing the reconsideration of contracts. Yet Cato's ban against defective contractors was reasserted as he by edict cleared the place of auction of those who had evaded their original contracts and then relet contracts at only slightly below the original figures. Flamininus and his cohorts attempted to take advantage of the division between censors and senate by bringing Cato to a hearing before the people. The boldest of the tribunes was incited to fine him two talents. Cato defended himself by what seems, from the fragments, to have been an interesting rehearsal of his accomplishments and a condemnation of the Roman indolence that permitted such a man as Cato to be prosecuted. Yet it was an appraisal of the state in its action and not, as in the case of Scipio Africanus, an assumption that the state was wrong merely because it questioned Cato. The tribune, C. Cassius, may have been joined in his action by another tribune named M. Caelius, whom Cato upbraided as so garrulous that he would hire someone to listen (Malcovati, p. 200). Marcus then alleged that Caelius interferred because his veto or his silence could easily be bought. The title of this speech, *Si se M. Caelius tribunus plebis apellasset* (If Caelius, tribune of the plebs, should have summoned him), shows that Caelius merely threatened to use the tribunician hearing on this or another occasion, but doubtless in connection with the matter of the contracts (Malcovati, p. 182).

The threatened hearing by Caelius and actual trial by Cassius both came to naught. Cato was not condemned or forced to pay the fine of two talents. It may be that another tribune interfered in his favor and vetoed the proceedings, as had been the case in the hearings of the Scipios. Yet the issue was joined between Flamininus and Cato, with dire results. Flamininus now began to fall on evil days. Championing the cause of monied men against the likes of Cato was a considerable fall from grace, measured by his earlier career in Greece. On the other hand, it was salutary from the view of middle bloc solidarity, forging the bonds that enabled it to replace the Scipionic bloc.

Ironically, these contentious censorial activities were the very reason for Cato's election. The electorate, unconstitutionally belabored by the former consuls in the Bacchanalian "conspiracy," seems to have sublimated its resentment of the obvious privileges assumed by the famous and wealthy by enjoying Cato's destruction of those traditional inequities. Senators and businessmen alike were dragged into the courts and chopped down to size by Cato's censorial edicts and assessments. The commoners applauded his doings, without a doubt. After all, election was the only string to their bow, and if that did not serve to elevate the low, it might tend to lessen the amenities of the mighty. Hence Cato served a utilitarian purpose, though again unwittingly.

Perhaps as important as any other accomplishment was the building program of Cato and Flaccus. It, too, was attended by debate and difference. Censors had access to appropriations for the purpose of preservation and construction of buildings, but as Cato's career shows, they had to justify such expenses to the senate. The cancellation of Cato's earlier contracts demonstrates the approval power of the senate, while the number of speeches Cato gave in defense of his other public works depicts the contention they caused (Plutarch XIX.2).

They paved fountain basins with stone, cleaned sewers where it was necessary, and built new sewers on the Aventine hill and elsewhere, where none had been built. Dionysius Halicarnassus shows that one thousand talents were spent on the drainage system (III.67.5). Scullard thinks that a stupendous sum, remembering that the other works of the censors combined probably cost no more than 85 talents (p. 163). The project was justified by a speech defending the construction as necessary. Yet the basilica Porcia, built as covered market in which to transact business, probably cost no more than 4 1/6 talents, not including the cost of buying the shops that had occupied the area before. This, too, was resisted by the senate, and Cato duly spoke in its behalf. Surprisingly, the building was not there in 179, when the basilica Fulvia or Aemilia was built in the same place. Perhaps Cato's structure was built primarily of wood, and it burned down in the interim (Frank, p. 153; Malcovati, p. 179; Livy XL.51).

It was with consummate knowledge of engineering and an understanding of the need for cleanliness that Cato and his colleague constructed and improved the sewer system. If, indeed, some of the mains were of the open drainage sort, it was not without point that the people honored him with a statue in the temple of Health. It was on this statue, says Plutarch (XIX.3), that they inscribed the sentiment: Cato's guidance, restraints, and sound teachings restored a tottering republic—whimsical and pedestrian naïvete, yet a genuine portrayal of plebeian feeling and so significant. One may speculate that Cato's war on privilege in the name of parochial purity brought an illusion of equity that relieved the masses.

The completion of their censorship was celebrated by Flaccus and Cato with the usual purification of the people, called a *lustratio*. A pig, a sheep, and a bull were led around the object to be benefited, the people, and then sacrificed on behalf of the assembled army in the *Campus Martius*. There was a ritual burial or disposal of the materials used, and then the term of the active censorship came to an end. Thus it was probably celebrated at the end of the term of office rather than after the census had been completed (*Class. Dict.*, p. 519).

It seems that Cato departed from custom at this time and delivered a speech defending his censorship. Apparently someone had challenged the *felicitas* (good fortune) of his *lustrum* (purification ceremony). In *De lustri sui felicitate* (Malcovati, p. 185), Cato defended himself with the argument that the fruits of harvest were ample evidence of the felicity of his *lustrum*. This would seem to demonstrate that some concept of nemesis was involved in *felicitas* and *lustratio*, as well as that the two censors terminated their office after the harvest in the year following their election. A year later would have been altogether too long. Eighteen months must have been their term.

Livy's characterization of the motives—to chastise the new vices and revive the ancient character—stated at the beginning of Cato's censorial term now seems ironic. Cato's failure to compromise, his seeming lack of realization that a political power base was needed to make the reforms work, coupled with a willful failure to recognize the realities of public desire, made his programs a mockery. The principles were stated, the ideals set forth, the ancient character asserted, but to no purpose. The only public chord of real feeling Cato touched was related to his reactionary constitutional ideals—a mere by-product of his personality. In the end, the reforms served to elevate Cato—hero to future generations—but that is an arid heritage, serving to denigrate republican institutions. A democratic folk requires self-reliance and resourcefulness—an individual moral assurance and vitality that springs from inner certainty about values and personal direction. Hero-worship or hero-imitation is a poor substitute, too often an excuse, for that kind of individualism.

Cato held no further elective office. He censured his fellow citizens for choosing any man to high office over and over again, saying that either the Romans thought little of their offices or thought few men capable of holding them. He ridiculed those who ran continually, saying they were like men who knew not where to go unless they were lighted on their way by lictors. Though he himself would hold no further public position, he was still to organize a political coalition between the conservatives, the middle, and the plebeians, that would dominate foreign affairs for years and overshadow an entire century with its philosophy. This sounds peculiar because Cato's quaint, primitive morality had already estranged him. He became a figure of more political consequence but less social influence (Plutarch VIII.5–7).

V Revival of Bacchanalian Persecutions

The Bacchanalian scare revived in Apulia in 181 B.C., with the same result of arbitrary oppression. Lucius Duronius, the praetor, was ordered to cut it off and stop it (Livy XL.19.9). The same arbitrary usage is to be seen in the case of philosophical script, found by accident on the lands of L. Petilius in the supposed tomb of Numa, a mythical Latin king of Rome. His workmen, digging at the foot of the Janiculan Hill, encountered two stone sarcophagi, each with an inscription: one to the effect that Numa Pompilius was buried there, the other, that the books of Numa Pompilius were inside. Lucius, the owner of the land, opened the chests and found one empty, the other containing two bundles tied with waxed rope and holding seven books each, looking absolutely fresh. The seven Latin books dealt with pontifical law, the seven Greek, with philosophy. Certain of the sources speculate they were Pythagorean, but there is little agreement on that aspect, Livy, Pliny, and Plutarch disagreeing as to the statements of more ancient annalists on the matter. There was a tradition that Numa had been a follower of Pythagoras, but that is debated (XL.29.3–14; Plutarch, *Numa* XXII; Pliny, *NH* XIII.84–87; Augustine, *De Civ. Dei* VII.34).

There has been an attempt to link Cato to this affair, in the role of prosecutor and with the pseudonym of "foe of foreign cults," because of his tie with the Petilii in the trials of the Scipios (Scullard, p. 172). Quintus was *praetor urbanus* ("municipal" judge, originally a judicial official) at the time and something of a patron to Lucius Petilius, having made the latter a clerk (*scriba publicus*) on his quaestorial staff. Quintus, hearing of the books, borrowed them from Lucius and determined that they were subversive of Latin religion. He then told Lucius that he intended to throw them into the fire but would, as *praetor urbanus*, countenance an appeal to the tribunes if Lucius thought the books private property he had a right to. The tribunes promptly referred the matter to the senate, which accepted Quintus' word that the books were subversive, and voted that they should be burned and their owner compensated for his property in whatever sum the praetor and tribunes thought proper. The scribe, Lucius Petilius, did not accept this (Livy XL. 29.9–14).

These allegations are outrageous. First, the modern attempt to implicate Cato in the proceedings is without foundation. Its only basis is the former acquaintance between two men and an assumption that Cato led the battle on foreign cults. On the contrary, as shown before, Marcus probably had a benevolent attitude to the Pythagorean philosophy, while nevertheless despising Greek as a substitute for Latin culture in Rome (Plutarch II). Conversely, it is not certain that Pythagorean philosophy was involved at all.

Again, the proceedings demonstrate the deterioration of individual rights. Though the books were called "subversive of religion," the only people consulted were a praetor, tribunes, and the senate. Inescapably, the matter was considered a "conspiracy," to be settled in the judiciopolitical realm; priests would certainly have been consulted otherwise. As in the case of the Bacchanalia, rights were ignored as political power humbled all considerations. Lucius Petilius wished to retain the books found on his property, but such was the superstitious fear of his kinsman Quintus that concepts of private property and individualism ceased to exist. The mere word of a praetor whose views were scarcely objective in other years seems to have been sufficient for the senate to condemn the documents and ignore Lucius' pleas.

VI *Cato's Growing Political Power*

The year 181 had further implications for Cato. He resolutely supported bills that were passed limiting the privileges of nobility by defining them. Thus the *Lex Orchia*, limiting the number of guests that might be entertained at a single party, was approved (Malcovati, p. 187). It is also likely, because of his former interest in equity for allies, that Cato spoke out on the senatorial resolution limiting the amounts that might be spent on games and the lavishness of them. It seems to be the first time the senate had expressed such a concern and speaks well for that institution. Their reason, according to Livy (XL.44.11), was shock at the expenditures made for games by the aedile Tiberius Sempronius and the financial burden they implied for Rome, the Latin allies, and the provinces. There seems to have been, then, some vestige of humanity left in the senators at this point in history. Their concern for the provinces, if Livy may be trusted, was a belated refinement but a redeeming one, had it continued. Its altruism may be questioned because it bore entirely on finances. One cannot but remember the Roman imposition of her will on Apulia in the matter of the Bacchanalia in this same year. Charitable feelings did not extend to include political or religious liberty (p. 195).

The year 181 B.C. also saw the passage of a *lex de ambitu* (law on bribery) supported by Cato (Malcovati, p. 186). It must have been an omnibus bill, containing a provision that in alternate years there should be just four praetors rather than the usual six. This would allow two two-year praetorships, which may have been one reason Cato supported it; Spain would be an obvious beneficiary of two-year governorships. There was another factor involved: Less offices were available for election that way. This part of the bill was later repealed, though not, according to some, until 176. At that time, Cato opposed the repeal (Malcovati, p. 187): *Ne Lex Baebia derogaretur dissuasio*. In the latter affair, Cato's motives may have been mixed. It was in the interests of his class, the plebs, to arrest the privilege of nobility, another manifestation of that quirk which had gained him the censorship. Perhaps for the same reason, Cato must have supported the *Lex Villia annalis* in 180 (Livy XL.44.1). It limited the frequency and availability of office to the patricians while simultaneously making the same positions more obtainable to plebeians. The latter law was proposed by a tribune, L. Villius, whose family was awarded the *cognomen Annales*. Cato was still the censor but surely not more influential than he would be later. These doings of Cato seem to have begun a species of revitalization of the plebeian class. Following years were to show the people favoring them over patricians; indeed, plebeians were elected to both consulships for three continuous years before the Third Macedonian War (p. 218). The importance of this class revival in terms of foreign policy will be shown later.

The passage of such laws as the *Lex Villia annalis*, defining the minimum ages for office-holding and perhaps decreeing a two-year interval between offices, as well as prescribing the order in which they must be held, is in the nature of badly needed constitutional reform. The *lex de ambitu* demonstrates that electoral bribery was enough of a problem that a law had to be passed to control it. Whether the penalty was death or suspension of the office-holding privilege for ten years may be debated, but the implications remain the same. There was corruption in elections. Almost inevitably that indicts the people who were running for office—the patrician and political plebeian class. In addition the *Lex Villia annalis* would seem to indicate that people were violating former custom by such expedients as simultaneous office holding, running for higher office while holding another position, and the like. It will be recalled that even Cato fell afoul of Roman notions of propriety in elections— prosecuting Glabrio while he was wearing the *toga candida* for the censorship of 189 B.C. The real significance of this legislation is that the Romans could still, in this period, reform practice and assert constitutional respectability. Yet even in Cato's lifetime that was to become virtually impossible.

The truly progressive elements in these laws were those moderating outmoded custom or usage. Marcus Cato recognized the necessity for this by approving the *Lex Baebia de praetoribus*. His position would have been caused by acquaintance with the difficulties of annual commands in Spain. His ideal was defeated, as the law was repealed. This time, in other words, Cato was the progressive one, the senate majority, regressive. It took imperial administration to force Cato to seek change; then vested interests neutralized it anyway. This may well be called a touchstone of Roman history. Constitutional reform was the crucial weak point in the following century. The failure to recognize the necessity to change and moderate imperial institutions by legal means was a corrosive element in the fall of the Republic. Just as Cato remained the man of principle in moral and religious spheres, he was a political realist. Ultimately, this realism rescued an uncompromising nature and gave Cato a great part in formulating imperial policy.

CHAPTER 9

After the Censorship: Foreign Policy Dominance and Political Compromise

I Cato's Influence on Foreign Policy: Expediency and Balance by Diplomacy

THE last phase of Cato's biography must deal with his career after the censorship. During this period he did not hold electoral office but influenced the shaping of foreign policy more than anyone else at Rome. Through a compromise with the increasingly dominant middle bloc, later rearticulated to comprise primarily plebeians and young senators, Cato seems to have imposed his ideals on all Rome's relations with other nations. Primarily, this meant the East, with its juxtaposition of Macedonian, southern Greek, and eastern interests. Rome at first appears to have championed one side, then the other, before realizing that true Roman interests lay in a balance and stability. An example is to be found in the action of Metellus, commissioned to conciliate the Achaean League and the Peloponnesians. He was rebuffed by Philip, insulted by Aetolia, and the policy failed (Livy XXXIX.24–29, 34–38; Polybius XXXIII.4–5). Another commissioner represented the middle bloc with a harder line, threatening the league. In 183 a commission headed by Flamininus was sent to draft a compromise with Achaeans and Peloponnesians, but when Philip became friendly, Rome inclined to him, leaving Flamininus to be jeered by his former Greek adherents, insults he bore in the name of policy.

King Prusias and Bithynia became the next objective; Flamininus persuaded the king to surrender Hannibal, who promptly committed suicide. Flamininus is much criticized for this, but only by a "double standard." It is considered right, by modern sanguine "codes of honor," for a Scipio Africanus arbitrarily to incite aggression against a whole nation because of his personal fear of Hannibal, plunging weary Rome against the Seleucids and killing thousands yet grotesquely failing to capture Hannibal; "Scipionic ethics," then, would deal with a one-man enemy by eliminating the entire nation he chose to reside in. Flamininus, on the other hand, who actually did capture Hannibal by diplomacy, at the cost of only one life, is called "dishonorable." It is instructive that modern authorities value human life so cheaply. "Principles" and "codes of honor" are ever talismans of the irrational—elaborate labels for conditioned reflex calculated, by emotional appeals to ancient tradition, to rouse the instinctive killer beast in man to triumph by force of violence.[1]

Finally, Flamininus visited Macedonia and contributed to the misunderstanding between Philip and his son Demetrius. This may have been instrumental in undermining their mutual faith and exacerbating the tragedy that ended in the murder of Demetrius. True, the murder was a tragic and unforeseen result of using the son as a foil to check the father. Yet Flamininus was the agent on the scene and so is responsible. All of these later deeds of the senator are "un-Flamininian," so unlike the earlier stern ethics of Titus that the man must have deliberately changed his ideals. The thing that would most readily account for such a transition is a reconciliation with Cato and the conservatives. Indicated above (p. 198) in connection with the return of Lucius Flamininus to the senate is the likelihood of an understanding between Cato and Titus. As they both started as Fabians, their ideological difference could not have been very great. The three acts of Flamininus mentioned above were highly salutary for Roman ascendancy and stability in the East, aside from their personal overtones. Rome could never relax vigilance there while Hannibal was alive, and Demetrius gave every indication of being a more formidable foe in succession to his father than Perseus proved to be. Vacillation with the Achaeans was masterful, if it brought Philip around to the side of Rome. Negotiation with Demetrius to weaken Philip was good partisan foreign politics. Flamininus' final acts were beneficial to Rome.

Cato's ideals in foreign policy were those of exploitation with noninvolvement. They seem followed to perfection by Flamininus here, and they did work effectively for Rome. A new era of completely impersonal internationalism characterized by systematic pacification of troublesome areas in the Roman sphere and an objective levelling diplomacy now began, and it is our contention that this policy did not merely evolve, or just happen. It was guided by the ideals of Cato backed by a revitalized Fabian bloc united in the persons of Flamininus and Cato. Their political clout was not realized in personal or familial political office but in working through the middle bloc and moulding the increasingly young and plebeian magistrates of that group to practice the politics of pure expediency: weakening the strong either militarily or diplomatically, then strengthening the weak to create a balance. The impartial, often inhuman, application of this policy worked so well that Rome virtually had to create a diversion for military intervention so the army would not lose its fighting readiness.

II *Plague and Poison*

The year 180 saw once again in epidemic of some sort that became another poison scare. A number of the elected officials for the year died, including a consul and praetor as well as several highly placed priests. Implicated in the death of the consul was his wife Hostilia; evidence was brought forward that served to convict her of murder. Particularly germane was a speech of hers in which she upbraided her son, Q. Fulvius Flaccus, for having lost the election for consulship that her husband won. Those who witnessed this speech said that she bade him prepare to apply for the office again and she would bring it to pass within two months that he should become consul. In time her second husband, C. Calpurnius Piso, died, and her son was elected *consul suffectus* (substitute consul). The open declaration of this scandal and the number of deaths growing from the plague inspired the ugly suspicion that human guilt was partly to blame. The senate decreed that C. Claudius Pulcher, elected *praetor peregrinus suffectus* in place of the praetor who had died, be intrusted with investigation of poisonings within Rome to the tenth milestone, and Gaius Maenius, assigned to Sardinia, be given the task of investigating poisonings in the country: the rural settlements and communities (Livy XL.37.1, 42.6, 35.8).

Lamentably, but with a now predictable prejudice, no cases of conviction are reported in the city, the jurisdiction of Claudius, but there were three thousand persons initially condemned in the investigations of Maenius. At that point Maenius wrote the senate saying that the inquiry was becoming broader because of the evidence received, and he must either discontinue the proceedings or give up his *provincia*. The sources do not say which alternative the

senate allowed, but the fact that a praetor was regularly chosen for
Sardinia the next year and none was elected to continue the investigations of Maenius, while one was designated to carry on those of
Claudius, indicates that Maenius finished his rural inquiries. One
can only speculate about how many more defenseless Italians were
persecuted without recourse to due process; the words, "the inquiry
was becoming broader because of the evidence received," are
ominously indicative of further injustices. Livy does not link these
hearings to the Bacchanalian conspiracy, though they have been so
regarded recently. Surely, it was similar to the hysteria attending on
that persecution, and formed another severe blow to self-
determinism (XXXIX.19.3, 36.14, 43.2, 44.6; Scullard, p. 177).
There is some speculation that Cato partook in the cases of 180 and
the poison scare by championing a man, Lucius Autronius, who was
involved in such a litigation, though Cato's speech could date
elsewhere (Malcovati, p. 207).

III   Bloc Politics and Social Class

The elections of 179 seem to have signalled a cooperation between two old enemies, laying the ground for a Fulvian, or continuing middle bloc, predominance. According to F. Münzer, M. Fulvius Nobilior and M. Aemilius Lepidus reconciled their differences
for political reasons (Rom. Adels., p. 200), working so Lepidus became pontifex maximus and princeps senatus while both were
elected to the censorship and Quintus Fulvius was co-opted to the
office of pontiff. All this was done with the connivance of the Fulvian
group. It happened that two brothers of the Fulvii had been elected
to the consulship; one of them, adopted by L. Manlius Acidinus,
qualified for the patrician consulship while the other was, naturally,
the plebeian. In addition, the elections were presided over by
another Fulvius, consul in the previous year. The compromise of
Fulvii and Lepidus served to dominate the electoral picture and
make Fulvii ascendant between 180 and 175 B.C., says Scullard (p.
180).

Fulvius and Aemilius, as censors, reformed the Comitia Tributa so as to allow further representation of the new middle class
in the rural tribes. The details are obscure, but the threat to rural
representation for basically rural tribes would have been contested
by Cato. The latter had just mended his fences with Flamininus and
now began a challenge for leadership of the middle bloc. He at-

tacked Fulvius personally, as he had done in the past after the latter's consulship in Aetolia and in spite of the fact that Cato had served under Fulvius in that command, though not in the continuation of the command or proconsulship of Fulvius in the year 188 B.C. Cato took Fulvius to task over his supervision of the public waterworks; little else is known of the actual speech. This would be a notoriously picayune ground for attack; there must have been other substantive matter in the whole oration. Whatever the basis, Cato challenged the *felicitas* of Fulvius' *lustrum*, as his own had formerly been impugned. The main burden of criticism may well have been the reform of the *Comitia Tributa*, which adulterated the rural tribes.[3]

It was in 178 that a Manlius returned once again to the political arena. The Manlii had not been prominent since the consulship and triumph of Cnaeus in 189 to 187, perhaps because of the attacks by Cato and others on Cnaeus. Aulus Manlius Vulso won the consulship together with Marcus Junius Brutus, through the agency of the dominant Fulvii, according to Scullard (pp. 184–89). The influence of their coalition with Aemilii and its preemption of Roman politics carried them through the following three years as well. Vulso accomplished a victory in the field after a near disaster, and the latter was cause for a probable debate in the senate over military affairs during which Cato may have delivered a speech: *De re Histriae militari* (Malcovati, p. 188). Perhaps Marcus adopted a tone of conciliation in this speech, in line with his effort to challenge for ideological leadership of the middle bloc.

Fulvian decline was marked by the elections of 174 and 173, in part a response to the ambitions and attacks of conservatives, but also a continuing reaction to the Bacchanalian persecutions. In 173 the electorate actually began to create an ascendancy of youth and plebeianism in the administration, for obvious reasons, by electing Postumius and Popilius consuls (Livy XLI.28.4). Another plague in 174 was so severe that the goddess of funerals, taxed to the limit by the large number of funerals in 181 and 180, could not accomodate those of free men in 174 (XLI.21.5). Anticipating illegal prosecutions, people voted for Postumius and Popilius, whose opposition to the establishment was known. Accordingly, there was no poison scare. These nonconformist consuls are characterized as tyrants on their conduct of foreign affairs by the entirely aristocratic historians. But the people of Rome demonstrated their intense satisfaction by confounding the senate and electing young plebeians to both consulships in 172—the first such occurrence in Roman history (Broughton, pp. 410–20)! They again selected two plebeian consuls in 171 and 170. Plebs were also elected to all six praetorships in 172, four in 171, and five in 170.

These years mark the first rebellion of the plebs since the fabled secessions of early Rome. It was much more general, being aided by the colonies and allied cities, whose rights were even more severely curtailed by Bacchanalian persecutions and the poison investigations. Indications of attempts to conciliate this massive discontent are to be seen in the public works carried on by Q. Fulvius Flaccus, the censor, in Pisaurum, Potentia, Fundi, and Sinuessa during the years 174–169 B.C. These are all cities in Italy, representative of the communities abused by arbitrary justice (Livy XLI.27).

IV   *Foreign Policy: The Politics of Expediency and War on Macedonia*

One may imagine the consternation of the patricians during these years. The rebellion of the electorate caused such dire misgivings that all senators but those away on government business in 170 were recalled to Rome (XLIII.11.4) to unite for the cause of collegiality, though the stated reason was concern over the progress of the war against Macedonia (Scullard, p. 202; Livy XLI.22.4, XLII.2, 11, 18.6, 19.3). The senate had not acted against Macedonia before 171, supposedly because of the young, inexperienced consuls. This idea assumes that the events of Roman foreign policy during the years of youthful plebeianism were accidental.

The reverse is instead true, and what seems a blundering ineptness internationally was the emergence of a politics of total expediency, inspired by Cato's ideal—foreign exploitation without involvement. The plebeian consul for 173, M. Popilius, dealt arbitrarily with Statellae in Liguria (XLII.7.3–9.6). The Statellates, of all Liguria, alone had never warred on Rome, yet Popilius disarmed them, demolished their town, sold their property, and auctioned them into slavery. Senatorial censure was the result, its indictment ordering Popilius to restore the liberty of these people and return their property and arms. Popilius defied the senate, returning to attempt coercion by bluff, then refusing to carry out the decree. Indeed, he warred on the Statellates again and slew six thousand (XLII.21.1–6). The people did not condone these deeds. Their tribunes forced

Popilius to return to Rome or be condemned *in absentia*, then unanimously voted the Statellates be vindicated and their oppressors punished. Yet Livy shows that the decrees of the people were evaded by trickery (XLII.22.1–8). Even so, the brother of Popilius was elected consul for 172, emphasizing that the people voted according to domestic issues; the philosophy of foreign policy was quite something else (XLII.9.7).

The beginnings of the politics of expediency here feature destruction of a town merely because it was located in Liguria, a territory that had given Rome grievous trouble for years. The consul for 176 was killed fighting there, and Liguria was assigned as a consular command every year from 188 to 172 B.C. The senate, which so assigned it, knew the situation; partisan politics must have caused the pretended offense at Popilius' doings. Indeed, with an eastern crisis brewing, they had to stabilize Liguria, which for eleven of the previous sixteen years had required the military attention of both consuls, much longer than it was to take to subdue Macedonia herself. Popilius was applying the Porcian levelling policy, officially approved by the presence of Cato's son Licinianus in his army as a raw recruit. The boy stayed even when his legion was discharged. Cato was proud, but wrote Popilius to renew the legionary oath voided by discharge. The personal correspondence and the failure to dissociate his son from Popilius, now under senatorial censure, by recalling the lad with the discharged legion show Cato's support for Popilius (Cicero, *de Officiis*, I.36).

Cato had trained and educated Marcus, disdaining to use Greek pedagogues (Plutarch XX.3). Drilling in the manual of arms, swimming in the Tiber, reading, and doing sums—Cato taught as he had learned. He even went to the length of guarding his words that his son might not learn profanity from his lips and took care never to bathe with him for the shame of nakedness. Sources say that Cato became a historian, writing the history of Rome in large letters so that his son might have an aid to acquaintance with his country's ancient traditions in his own home. It was written in Latin, in seven books, and called the *Origines* (Origins). The first book, according to Nepos, set forth the age of the kings; the second and third, the origin of all the Italian states; the fourth, the First Punic War; the fifth, the Second Punic War; the sixth and seventh, the history from the Punic Wars to the year 148 B.C. (III.1).

Cato's accomplishment in Latin letters makes him the father of

Latin prose. He wrote in summary fashion, says Nepos, setting forth historical actions annalistically, but not mentioning names of individuals. Yet Plutarch also says that Cato was most lavish in his own praise, then quotes Cato's own self-assessment as though it came from a written source (XIX.5). If it was the *Origines*, then he did become personal about his own deeds. If, indeed, the work was written in large characters, it is possible either that Cato had become near-sighted or that the work was to be a textbook (Plutarch XX.5). Near-sightedness is backed by Nepos' statement that Cato was already an old man when he began to compose books. The tradition that the *Origines* was written in about 168 must be refined to a beginning in that time, since Livy's *Periocha* XLIX shows a speech of 149 was included in the *Origines*; the book must still have been in process of composition.

The senate (Livy XLII.31.5, 32.1–6), meanwhile, decided to war on Macedonia, despite the two plebeian consuls of 170, and dispatched P. Licinius Crassus, Licinia's kinsman, to the East. Selection of military tribunes was made by consuls and praetors, a policy supported by Cato in an oration: *De tribunis militum* (Malcovati, p. 189). The politics of expediency required that its practitioners be able to escape prosecution for waging war where "necessary" but without senatorial consent, by judicious appointment to commissions elsewhere in the field. Because all this was done in the name of middle and plebeian politics, Cato could plead that such freedom of appointment by the magistrates of the people gave the electorate more power through its representatives (cp. Scullard, p. 197; Janzer, p. 62).

Livy says the other consul, C. Cassius Longinus, made a vain attempt to lead his legions into Macedonia, having failed to accomplish anything in Gaul. All that is said of Cassius' action, however, shows his theatre of action to have been Venetia rather than Gaul. He was allowed a total of twenty-two thousand infantry and one thousand cavalry, demonstrating the unsettled nature of that area. On learning of Cassius' supposed violation of *provincia*, the senate's first concern was that he had left the northern frontier unprotected against "so many tribes." Cassius, like Popilius earlier, failed to heed the senate's alarmed commands to return, leaving that body embarrassed to answer indignant claims by ambassadors whose tribes were devastated in his line of march. "Such was the humiliation of a senate which had become involved in a major war while unable to control some of the leaders whom the people had put forward," says a leading authority. Once again, "The People" are to bear the blame (Livy XLIII.1.4–12, 5.1–10, XLII.31.4, 32.4; Scullard, p. 198).

The complaining ambassadors give the lie to Livy's idea that nothing was accomplished in "Gaul" and to theories of senatorial humiliation (Livy XLIII.1.5–9, 5.1–10). The acts of Cassius are to be identified, once again, with the deliberate policy of pacifying and levelling Roman domain in accord with Porcian ideal. Livy's hypothesis that Cassius' destination was Macedonia is mistaken, based on the latter's requisition of guides who knew the roads from Italy into Macedonia and his issuance of thirty days' rations. Far from embarking on a hare-brained expedition to Macedonia, Cassius commanded a foresighted campaign along the lines of "search and destroy." He sought out the routes to Macedonia, hence the guides, conducted a march of spoliation along them to midpoint, then returned to Venetia and laid waste most threatening of the natives there: the Alpine Gauls, Carnians, Histrians, and Iapydes, thus forcibly neutralizing the entire hinterland at the head of the Adriatic, which geographically flanked any expeditionary force in Greece as well as threatening a vacant central Italy. This is the only explanation that makes sense of the events in Livy. Explicitly set forth are the following facts: first, the request for guides; second, the peaceful departure with rations; third, the return from mid-journey; and fourth, the destruction of the tribes. Finally, a previous concern for advance bases protecting Roman beachheads from the hinterland in Epirus and Illyria can be shown in 172 before Cassius' consulship.[4]

Though at first the senate was outraged by an imagined defiance of its appointed *provincia*, there is every indication that it meekly recanted when members of the Porcian compromise pointed out the advantages of Cassius' action. The senate sent a curiously inexperienced embassy to find Cassius and remind him of his limitations, then lamely alibied to the irate envoys from destitute tribes that Cassius could not be prosecuted in his absence. They did not, as with Popilius earlier, force Cassius to return by threatening prosecution *in absentia*. Indeed, Cassius and his cohorts had planned in advance that he should follow his consulship with an appointment as tribune in Macedonia, just in case. That explains Cato's earlier championing of magisterial appointments of tribunes in the speech *De tribunis militum*. Concluding the drama were mollifying presents given to the envoys as tokens of Roman goodwill and escorts back home by rather distinguished senators—the first appearance of the levelling diplomacy that offered friendship as a guaranty of security, an opiate that, administered or withdrawn in judicious quantities, should keep those addicted to "Roman peace" uniformly weak and dependent (XLIII.1.12, 5: Cethegus became consul in 160).

Cato had other connections with the Macedonian campaign. Instrumental in encouraging Rome to war with Macedonia had been a visit from King Eumenes of Pergamum. Livy, Appian, and Plutarch speak of the prestige enjoyed by this king and the honors heaped upon him by the senate. Cato cautioned against such treatment, saying that the animal known as king was carnivorous by nature and not one of the kings lauded by men was comparable to a Pericles, Epaminondas, Manius Curius, or Hamilcar Barca. Yet he did admit that Eumenes was a good man and a friend of Rome, a grudging concession to policy, as Rome might need friends in the coming war with Perseus. Plutarch says (VIII.7) heads of state strove to be near Eumenes; to Scullard (p. 199) that means such action was taken by the "rash element" of new plebeian magistrates, who now began to overcome the conservative caution relative to war with Macedonia. Cato must have favored the war, if Scullard's guesses about his young plebeian compatriots are right. Macedonia would be regarded a thorn in the side of eastern policy by Cato with his utilitarian ideals (Livy XLII.11.2–13.12; Appian IX.11.1).

Meanwhile, an embassy sent to various parts of Greece in 172 by the senate and led, again, by plebeian magistrates—Quintus Marcius Philippus and Aulus Atilius Serranus—offers a perfect demonstration of Porcian levelling diplomacy (Livy XLII.37–47). Holding out a specious hope of peace, they persuaded Perseus to negotiate further with Rome, though they knew Rome had determined on war; Perseus was prepared, and Rome was not, so they lied "for the good of state." They successfully broke up the Boeotian League, attaching the communities individually to Rome and sponsoring pro-Roman parties to control each. Finally, they persuaded the council of the Achaeans to intervene militarily in Chalcis, involving that league in Roman affairs. Roman friendship thus seemed to replace international leagues in general Greek planning for security; and that elusive will-o'-the-wisp was wielded in turn by amoral politicians guided only by Roman interests. Livy now distinguishes between this kind of diplomacy and that of "old Rome," quoting from the thought of ancient senators as though he had a vision from the grave. "Not by cunning but by real bravery did our ancestors win wars," his hallucination might be paraphrased. "Final conquest of the spirit occurs when one has been overcome not by craft but by hand-to-hand force in a proper and righteous war." He concludes by saying that the majority of the senate, to whom the pursuit of advantage was more important than that of honor, approved the "new wisdom." That merely means the Porcian conservative and middle coalition now controlled the senate (XLII.47.4–9; Polybius XIII.3).

Considerations on the morality of Marcius' committee finally decide Livy to say that about the war with Macedonia's Perseus which he should have documented about all Rome's "imperial" wars before—that Rome was the aggressor, in the name of "security" so interpreted as to justify her every act. Thus it happens that modern historians are finally enlightened about Roman wars and this Third Macedonian is an acknowledged war of aggression. But since our generation of antiquarians cannot tolerate the inference that the Roman *patres* were any but the most honorable of men, they find it necessary to distinguish events of this war from those previous, carefully associating the latter with "honor" and the patricians and then styling the Third Macedonian "dishonorable" and attributing it to "the people" and the plebeian magistrates. Livy himself provides the ancient context; the graveside hallucination quoted immediately above defines bravery and a "righteous war" as real courage devoid of cunning and the hand-to-hand clash of force: physical strength, skill, and courage, in other words. He even provides us with a biased racial index, styling Roman behavior as "scrupulous," Greek as "sly," and Carthaginian as "artful" in his definition of honor and bravery.

We have taken pains in this work to show how the continual war footing of Rome, the fabrication of imperial "security," and the pursuit of gain had wrought a change in the Roman spirit that touched senators before anyone else, being evident even in the career of Cato. We are not inclined, therefore, to accept romantic idealism about the honesty of patricians from anyone at this point. It is particularly ironic to hear moral ideals attributed to the men who were themselves living from the proceeds of ill-gotten gains.

There was scandal also in the West during the year 171, a fact used by Scullard to assert that the younger officials in Spain were the creators of oppression there. Both provinces complained of the

rapacity of their magistrates, and a court was established to try
claims for redress (*quaestio repetundae*). The plaintiffs from Hither
Spain chose Cato and Scipio Nasica as patrons in this suit, and those
from Farther Spain chose Aemilius Paulus and Sulpicius Gallus.
Livy (XLIII.2) shows they would not allow charges against influential men! Chapter 5 above and the statistics gathered there list the
unbelievable booty brought from Spain in and before the time of
Cato's consulship, just for the public treasury, aside from private
and personal spoil. In Spain, at least, the young merely practiced
that enterprising vice taught them by the "exemplary" patricians of
old (Scullard, p. 201).

Lucretius, accused of rapaciousness while praetor under Licinius
in Macedonia, offers a further example of the operation of the Porcian compromise. His offense was that he arbitrarily and without
senatorial consent beseiged, reduced, and sacked the city of Haliartus in Boeotia, an ally of Rome. Though Lucretius behaved as sin-
fully as all Romans with the proceeds from his generalship and was
as heinously Roman in his treatment of Haliartus as his earlier patrician preceptors, he cannot be blamed for anything else. Haliartus
was strategically important, commanding the pass between eastern
and western Boeotia. One of the commissioners of Philippus in 172,
Lentulus, had been left in charge of Boeotia and given a squadron of
Italian soldiers by the senate to keep Boeotia under control. This
man, for reasons not stated in Livy, had begun the siege of Haliartus. He was relieved of that duty by Lucretius when he arrived.
Therefore the whole affair of Haliartus was technically launched
under senatorial auspices. Lucretius was thus unfairly prosecuted
and was fined one million asses by the suggestion of the tribunes
and unanimous vote of thirty-five tribes. Again, as with Popilius, the
people who elected Lucretius failed to identify with Porcian foreign
diplomacy. Lucretius, like Popilius and Flamininus, sacrificed himself for state policy (Livy XLII.35.3, 47.9, 48.5, 49.9, 56.1 63.3,
XLIII.4.6, 8.1).

The same was true, ultimately, of the consul Licinius. He razed
Coronea and several other cities in central Greece that had been
friendly to Philip, selling the prisoners into slavery. The Romans
thought it disgraceful, liberated the cities, repurchased and freed
the slaves, and then fined Licinius for his arbitrary action (Livy
XLII.67.11, XLIII.4, 5, 11, *Periocha*; Dio, Zonaras 9.22).

It is difficult to understand this Roman action. Licinius had made reprisals against the Greek cities after an initial setback suffered fighting Perseus. He may have felt the inconstancy of cities formerly related by treaty to Philip was a threat in those circumstances, especially since winter was approaching and he must quarter his army among them. Thebes, in Boeotia, had implored Licinius to winter in Boeotia because of harrassment by Coronea. Lentulus, earlier commissioned by the senate to maintain control of Boeotia for Rome, found it necessary to besiege Haliartus. Northern Boeotia, strategically important in this war—particularly Coronea and Haliartus, in the pass between eastern and western Boeotia— had become notorious for its intransigence. But reprisals against Greek cities, not even questioned when exercised later by Aemilius Paulus for less cause, had become a matter for partisan politics.

Elections for 169 saw a return to collegiate consulships. All senators were recalled to Rome except those absent on public business. Livy says this rallying of the patricians was because of concern over the war; Scullard infers it was to assure a patrician consul. But the consuls-elect were unable to muster the troop levy decreed for the year and the war (XLIII.11.2, 12, 14). Consuls blamed the commons for not presenting themselves even though of age, but two of the praetors-elect vowed that the consuls were favoring the commons, not enlisting any against their will. These praetors were appointed to complete the muster, amid jeers at the helplessness of the consuls. If, then, all senators had rallied to Rome in order to elect seemly consuls, it eventuated in the *faux pas* of their using praetors to supplement the incompetents they chose!

It is likely that the senators rallied because of the gravity of affairs, but as Livy hints earlier, the Porcian compromise had a majority. The patrician candidate favored the commons, which is why he was endorsed, together with the plebeian, by the Porcians. Even so, Livy's listing of the plebeian Marcius first indicates that he led the voting. Once again, the people were asserting themselves. Since many soldiers were home on leave from Macedonia, the feeling that too many leaves had been granted arose, and this, in turn, was thought due to currying political favor. The censors elected in 169 determined to enforce foreign service and relieve this situation by requiring all men to return to their province within thirty days and reviewing all cases of discharge from the army. They further requested a new general oath in the census, testing whether all under forty-six years had seen military service and asking the reasons for any deficiency. This action was successful, in that so many men gathered in the city for the census that it was burdensome to the Romans. It is noteworthy, however, that the unusual procedure necessitated here proves an unrest of the commons and their testing of the authority of state. That issue would have electrified Cato. Plebeian rights and influence were one thing; rebellion against the authority of the senate, quite another. Certainly, Cato endorsed the action of the censors on the army levy. His feelings about their subsequent deeds are more difficult to diagnose (XLIII.11.2–12, 14.5–10).

The censors, Claudius Pulcher and Tiberius Gracchus, expelled seven senators and deprived many knights of their horses. They then limited the letting of public taxes and contracts to those who had not enjoyed either in the previous censorship. This aroused the ire of the veteran capitalists who soon found a disgruntled tribune to bring a legal action against the limitation of state contracts. During the public hearing, Claudius was heckled by people, and he ordered the heralds to restore order, whereon the tribune left, effectively adjourning the meeting because, he complained, the proceedings had been taken out of his hands by Claudius' action. This the tribune construed a violation of his tribunician powers and next brought suit against the censors for abridging the power of a tribune, a far more serious charge. Claudius very narrowly averted condemnation, being saved by the mummery of leading senators, who put on dark togas of mourning and entreated the plebs, but chiefly by his colleague Gracchus, who vowed to resign and be exiled with Claudius, should he be indicted. Even then, the condemnation lacked but eight centuries. Rome nearly impeached two censors (XLIII.16.1–16).

The ridiculous spectacle of mourning, begging senators, chauvinistically haughty Claudius, and suicidally sincere Gracchus, against the backdrop of the ominously vengeful and surprisingly effective knights, gives one pause. An obvious immediate cause for this confrontation was the nature of Claudius. He already had a reputation for harsh and arbitrary action from his consulship of 177, when he flaunted custom, attempted to arrest ex-counsuls, and bathed Histria in blood. His continuing intransigence is to be seen in the expulsion of knights and the letting of contracts during the census of 169. Doubtless his election to the censorship was owing entirely to the fact that the Claudii were allied to the Fulvian conservatives and so received Porcian support. Otherwise such a man would not have mustered the votes to be elected latrine orderly. It is exceeding gauche that the accident of election now sheltered him and that such as eminent senators and respectable Gracchus felt impelled to protect him, despite his own outrageous acts, lest the entire institution of the censorship be imperilled and, so they must have thought, the government with it. The principle does Gracchus and the senate little credit. It shows the same basic distrust of people that had plagued Cato all his life—an austere loneliness that held to institutions and principles rather than individuals and now began to distinguish Tiberius from his famous sons. So, there is a requiem to republican ideals. Gracchus' Rome, like that of Cato, was swiftly becoming an empty shell of institutions (XLI.10.5–11.9; Scullard, pp. 37–38, 61 ff.).

The dichotomy is particularly notable in the matter of the army levy. Livy shows that the war was unjust, waged by men who were clever rather than brave. The people hesitated to come forward and enlist for service in Macedonia. If Gracchus were as closely identified with the people as his popularity suggests, he would have pointed out the injustices of the war, as well as its futilities, and championed the popular doubts about service in such a war. He did not, and so Rome fought the war without disclaimer and continued on the road to empire and democratic ruin.

The year 169 saw Cato himself speaking in favor of the Voconian Law, which forbade one of the highest property to make a woman his heir and limited other legacies as well. According to Cicero, Cato was then sixty-five years old, and he spoke with "loud voice and mighty lungs" (*Cato*, V.14; Livy *Periocha* XLI), trying to stop the concentration of large estates in the hands of women and thus check their increasing liberation. It can be shown that the number of marriages known as "free marriage" (*sine in manu conventione*), where wives were no longer subject to their husband's authority, was increasing. Plutarch says Marcus quoted Themistocles on the power of women (VIII.2): "All other men rule their wives; we rule all other men, and our wives rule us." Further, he said, "The woman brings a great dowry and holds back a large sum of money," when describing the women as rich. According to Gellius (XVII.6.1), he meant that women have a great dowry and then retain possession of a large sum of money. From that property they keep, they lend money to their husbands, making the latter their debtors. Then, if they become vexed, they appoint a slave of their very own to demand the money back from heir husbands. This is the situation Cato deplores, as far as Gellius is concerned.

V   Cato's Training of His Son: Military Advice and Economic Example

The Porcian involvement in affairs continued. Young Cato fought nobly in the final battle against Perseus' Macedonians in 168 (Plutarch XX.6–8). Plutarch says that the youth's sword chanced to fall or be stricken from his hand (Paulus, XXI.1–3, X.3). Distressed, he rallied his friends, and together they recovered Marcus' sword from the thick of the battle. He was at that time a lieutenant (legatus) in the army of Aemilius Paulus, consul for the Macedonian command (Broughton, p. 431). Paulus was greatly impressed with this brave deed and, whether for this or other reasons, married his daughter Tertia to young Marcus later on. Two sources say that she was a very small child at the time of Pydna, the terminal battle of the Macedonian War won by Paulus, when the death of her pet dog named Persa was considered an omen of victory over Perseus. It is likely that after this personal display at Pydna by Marcus, his father wrote a letter of congratulations, heaping praise on the young man for recovering his sword honorably. Plutarch mentions it, as does Cicero, though the latter says it was for the purpose of cautioning the youth to renew his soldierly oath before entering any other battle, since he had been discharged by the consul after the battle (de Off. I.37). One can only speculate on the reason. Perhaps Paulus knew, as did Cato, that the lad was delicate and chose to relieve him. Certain it is that the discharge was not derogatory (Cicero, de Div. I.103).

It was shortly after this, it seems, that young Marcus advanced admirably in learning. Perhaps, like his father, he began active life in the city of Rome after his military service, for Gellius says he wrote admirable works on The Science of Law (XIII.20.9). He was encouraged by his father to study the law, even as Cato the Elder had encouraged his son. There was a difference, though, which is to be seen in the kind of work done by each. Cato actively practiced law and fought litigation in the courts. He brought others to book and was himself sued. Licinianus, on the other hand, seems to have stressed legal theory in his work; he was less strenuously involved in the courts and less a figure of contention. Yet Gellius stresses the quality of Licinianus' books, and Plutarch praises the product of Cato's educational tutelage (XX.8).

It was this same son, however, whom he schooled in almost shameful economics, Plutarch says (XXI); other sources disagree. The biographer writes that Cato said it was the part of a widow woman, not a man, to lessen his economic substance. A man was godlike if the final inventory of his property showed that he had added to it more than he had inherited. Cato himself seems to have changed his monetary views as he grew older, if Plutarch is right. He came, according to the latter, to regard agriculture as more entertaining than profitable and to invest his money in business that was safe and sure. He bought ponds, hot springs, districts given over to fullers, pitch factories, land with natural pasture and forest, and the like, which could not be ruined by environmental circumstance. Plutarch implies Cato had had enough, finally, of the gamble and uncertainty of the farm. He lent money in what Plutarch correctly calls the most disreputable of all ways, namely, on ships. His method was to require the borrowers to form a company large enough so that the number of partners assured Cato a share with only a small investment while his security was protected by the size of the corporation. This meant a large profit on high-risk investment with a minimum of gamble. It was "disreputable" because it was illegal. The *Lex Claudia* of 218 B.C. limited the size of ships senators could own to two hundred *amphorae* (225 bushels or seven tons), suitable for farm-to-market transport, but hardly for overseas commerce. The intent of the law was to limit senatorial participation in commerce; as Livy says, all moneymaking was considered unseemly in a senator (XXI.63.3). Cato got around the law by using his freedman, Quintio, to represent him and accompany his clients in all their ventures: a "front-man."

Plutarch also attributes very sharp practice to Cato's dealings with his own slaves. He encouraged them to buy slave-boys with money borrowed from himself, train them for a year at his own expense, and then sell them again. Some Cato bought for himself, marking the auction price bid for them to the credit of the particular speculating slave. So as to curb the slaves' will to rebel, Cato allowed males to consort with females at a fixed price, forbidding them to approach any other women, for he believed that their sexual passions were the fuel of revolution. At the same time he became more particular about service at table, says Plutarch, flogging slaves who were remiss in their serving duties, especially if guests were present. This treatment partially curbed their ardor, and for the rest Cato encouraged feuds among them in order to keep them divided rather than allow them to unite under some grievance or other. Any convicted of capital offenses by their peers were executed.

This portrait presented by Plutarch is opposed to that painted in Cicero's *Cato Maior de Senectute* (51, *passim*). Cato is shown aging gracefully—charitable, merciful, and rejoicing in the pursuits of agriculture to a ripe old age. Though the comfortable life of rustic refinement pictured by Cicero does presuppose wealth and domestics, none of the harshness of Plutarch's image is present. On the other hand, Livy's *Periocha* XLVIII implies poverty at the death of Marcus' son Licinianus, where it says, "his father conducted his funeral at very small expense, according to his means, for he was a poor man." Cato's *de Agricultura* confirms both wealth and agricultural interests, the interests of the "gentleman farmer" whose estates exceeded two hundred *iugera* and were tended by stewards, the owner being busy with affairs (III, IX, XI). There is no accounting for Livy's summary, except possibly by means of one of Cato's orations: "They find fault with me because I lack many things; but I with them because they cannot do without them" (Gellius XIII.24.1). Cato, though he had wealth and loved to accumulate means as Plutarch implies, lived a miserly existence, forcing his family to a bare subsistence level for the vanity of a parsimonious image, except for service at table. There is the real Cato!

One so insistent upon morality in others as Cato should not himself stoop as low as this ultimate hypocrisy implies for image alone. His entire effort to achieve reform at Rome centered on legislation. But laws must convey the intent of the people, or they will be superfluous. The *Lex Claudia*, running athwart the will of senators, was ignored, violated, and flaunted at will. Cato is living proof of this legal truism. His famous statements on women and the Oppian Law, however, seem to assert the opposite. In that confrontation he inferred that laws must be legislated in spite of the will of the people. This, then, is one more instance of the censor's incapability to accomplish his own stated principles. Plutarch's account gives his blatant hypocrisy its full flavor. It is significant that the common people of Rome recognized senatorial dishonesty. Livy (XXV.7.1–5) shows how the people in 193 B.C. forced a change in the laws allowing lenders to use front-men in order to evade regulation of usury or excessive interest taking. At that time a tribune of the people, with consent of the senate, passed laws to alter the situation. The present case of commercial interests was one in which senators like Cato (and Cicero later, with Atticus) had a vested interest. Yet as the people perceived crookedness in the "front-men" of usury, they must have seen Cato's feet of clay, and his calls to reformed morality echoed hollowly among a people grown cynical even about Cato. Seen in this light, the constitutional crisis of the following century is no puzzle—strange it did not occur sooner (Livy XXXIV.3.1–6).

CHAPTER 10

Porcian Imperialism and Cato's Last Years

I *Paulus' Macedonian Victory and the Eastern Entente*

PORCIAN policy in Macedonian affairs was keynoted by Cato in a speech *De Macedonia Liberanda* (Malcovati, p. 191). It articulated the central rationale: Commitments in the Balkans would be undesirable; Macedonia should be freed, since Rome could not guard her. Cato seems genuinely to have believed that Rome could not afford to garrison or police the world because of the moral involvement and the energy drain from domestic affairs, though he did favor conquest and exploitation with no continuing cultural exchange.

The speech was delivered when the senate chose commissioners to bring its wishes on the settlement of the East to Paulus and the Illyrian commander. They emphasized freedom for Macedonia and Illyria so other nations could see the benefit of Roman conquest. Macedonia was divided into four autonomous sections, each with its own *concilium* (legislature), and was to send half the tax it paid to Perseus to Rome (Livy XLV.18). Hence the army was to be withdrawn: an almost perfect enactment of Porcian foreign policy— Cato's compromise party triumphed (Livy XLII.47.9)!

While waiting for the commission, Paulus viciously sacked three towns, the reason being mere appeasement of the army's desire for plunder (XLV.27.1). One town's offense was that it had "treated Roman soldiers as enemies"; the second had declared for Rome but then gone over to Perseus before Pydna; the third had resisted Rome more stubbornly than its neighbors. These reasons are mere pretexts, but they do display the same moral defect in the character of Paulus that we have witnessed in those of Cassius, Licinius, and Lucretius. Paulus then took a tour of Greece, revealing further

faults of personality (Plutarch, *Paulus* XXXVIII; Livy XLV.27.5–
28.11). At Delphi in the shrine of Apollo he finished columns intended as statues of Perseus in his own likeness instead. Like Fabius
Maximus and Cato, Paulus was vain. Vanity was also his weakness in
treating with Perseus (Plutarch, *Paulus* XXVI.5; Livy XLV.4.2;
Polybius XXX.10). A Roman general, he received ambassadors from
the king in dirty garb and streaming tears, and then, Livy says,
Paulus himself wept at the lot of man—the terrifying reversal of
fortune suffered by Perseus—until that same royal suppliant had the
audacity to address Paulus as though he were still a king! "King
Perseus to the consul Paulus, Greeting," Paulus read in the official
letter. Not until he struck the title "king" from his correspondence,
did the Macedonian upstart get an answer from Paulus. Plutarch
does not agree with Livy, deleting the incident of the letter and
much enlarging on the ensuing personal surrender of Perseus.

Paulus used that occasion to deliver a homily on the theme of
"Fortune and Human Affairs," to school especially the young
officers in his command to curb their pride and insolence, lest
chance deal with them as it had with Perseus. Polybius (XXIX.20–
21), unlike others, puts in a further anecdote from the sayings of
Demetrius of Phalerum on the fickleness of fate or, perhaps, historical nemesis. Plutarch and Livy precede this "tender scene" with a
criticism of the deportment of Perseus as he approached the "Great
Roman General." Paulus went to greet him with tears in his eyes,
says Livy, but both then agree that Perseus threw himself down and
clasped the knees of Aemilius, breaking out into "ignoble cries and
supplications." "This," says Plutarch, "was a most shameful sight."
Paulus derided the Macedonian, saying that such grovelling showed
Perseus deserved defeat and belittled Paulus' triumph. "Valor in
the unfortunate," said Paulus, "obtains great reverence even among
enemies, but cowardice is dishonorable." (Plutarch, *Paulus* XVI.5,
XXVII.1; Livy XLV.7.4, i.1).

One must become accustomed to the redundancies, circular arguments, and naïve anachronisms of Roman utterance. Shortly before these proud statements, Paulus had resented the lack of humility in Perseus, shown by his retention of the title of king. Along that
line, Livy talks of the folly of Perseus as one deserving no pity
because he did not realize the state of his fortunes. Perseus stubbornly insisted upon the title of king through one other embassy as
well, while Paulus urged him instead to entrust himself and all he

had to the mercy of the Romans. Then, when all other courses were futile and Perseus had to humble himself to Roman slavery, Paulus resented the fact he did not conduct himself like a king! In his own words, victory over a slave was empty indeed. Like a schoolboy, Paulus uprooted the Royal Rose from native soil to possess its beauty, then sulked as it wilted (Livy XLV.4; Plutarch, *Paulus* XXVI.6).

Finally, Aemilius allowed his army to plunder Epirus for the sake of more spoil, explaining it by saying that the senate had granted the privilege, states Livy (XLV.34.1). Plutarch also blames the senate (XXX.1, XXIX). Some modern scholars say that the pillage of Epirus, so "unlike the gentle nature of Aemilius," was a commission from the senate (Scullard, p. 213; *CAH* VIII, p. 272). These pronouncements substantiate that a Porcian policy of levelling and exploitation continued to dominate the senate, now being implemented in foreign places by men like Paulus. It was consonant with the program of systematic pacification by force begun in Illyria in 171 by Cassius and continued in Epirus in 170 by Claudius. As for the "gentle nature of Aemilius," if he were a man of so little character that he obeyed commands he considered immoral from a body he thought decadent, then his personality is a minus quantity hardly worth considering. Yet it was he who so little cared for the Macedonian command that he stated conditions under which he would accept that mandate of the people. It is impossible to make Paulus both lion and coward; the rape of Epirus was his own (Polybius XXX.15.1).

One wonders what impact all this had on the young officers whom Paulus tried to influence with his homily on "Fortune and Human Affairs." Among them, as we have seen, was Cato's son Licinianus. His baptism in fire was something like that of his father, in Sicily. Another Roman cried while thousands died. The example, including even the vanity of statues, must have been "instructive" in a negative sense. Cato's preceptors had taught him the kind of heedless expediency displayed in his Spanish consulship and his callousness toward slaves (Plutarch V.1, XXI.1, 7). Licinianus died in his praetorship, but another young officer lived to apply these lessons. Aemilius Paulus' son, adopted by the Scipios and known as Scipio the Younger, learned how to kill and cry with a like ease; he applied the "education" at Carthage in 146 B.C., where he slaughtered as lustily and wept as copiously as any Roman (Appian XIX).

The great victory in Macedonia settled problems elsewhere. Antiochus Epiphanes, King of the Seleucids, though not powerful by himself, could have been dangerous had he allied with Perseus. He was involved in a quarrel with the Ptolemies of Egypt over Coele Syria. They negotiated with Rome, which ambiguously encouraged both, at first. The ideal was to maintain the status quo balance in the East, so Rome chose no sides. But when Antiochus became too successful, the Ptolemies again appealed to the senate, and C. Popilius Laenas was sent with an ultimatum to Antiochus. Popilius also ignored his senatorial commission. He directed naval defenses from Delos, though Egypt might have fallen to Antiochus meantime, and then after Pydna intercepted the latter at Alexandria. He dramatically drew a circle about Antiochus in the sand, handed him the ultimatum, and ordered him to reply before he stepped out of the circle. The king obeyed and evacuated Egypt. This, say some moderns, signaled to the world that the "newer and older" nobility were uniting in the senate, presenting a strong front to the world. True, Popilius' diplomacy subdued the other Hellenistic powers, Egypt being patronized and Syria cowed, after Roman troops had defeated Macedonia. Rome now dominated the entire East.[1]

The final acts in the East connected with this pacification concerned Pergamum and Rhodes. With the former Rome played deceptively, attempting to excite strife between brothers of the royal house, thus weakening her, because King Eumenes had negotiated with Perseus. Failing in this, Roman senators sent an envoy to encourage the Galatians to threaten Pergamum and then conciliated Cotys, king of Thracian Odrysae, though he had actively supported Perseus in the war. The intent of this devious diplomacy was to discomfit Pergamum from north and east by approving Galatia and Thrace (n.1).

One of Cato's most famous speeches was given on the disposition of Rhodes, he thought, since he included it in book V of his *Origines*. Perhaps others agreed, since the speech also circulated as a separate publication. The issue, briefly, was that Rhodes had enjoyed good relations with Rome since 188 and the peace formulated at Apamea. These seem to have deteriorated, however, with the result that the Rhodians listened more and more to a group of pro-Macedonian statesmen. The lengthy nature of the Macedonian campaign, with its effect on trade in the eastern Mediterranean, caused them ultimately to send an embassy to Rome offering mediation. But alas! the envoys arrived at the same time as did the news of

Pydna, and their attempt to offer a congratulatory speech to the senate instead of the conciliatory one convinced no one. Some of the senators wished to war on Rhodes because of her unfriendly intent toward Rome. Cato ingeniously fixed upon the difficulty of determining intent and the injustice of being condemned for that alone (every man is an adulterer in his mind, but one does not therefore imprison all men for adultery). Rhodians were accused of arrogance, which prejudiced their case, but Cato countered by reminding the *patres* that Romans were the most arrogant of men, hardly in a position to cast the first stone. Gellius insists that Cato's speech was a brilliant piece of rhetoric, using every artful device in a clever manner, to persuade the senate almost against its will. The war was forgotten while Rhodes was allowed a grudging neutrality until 165. Then alliance was granted. This attitude kept the island completely subservient to the will of Rome without war—again, an almost perfect enactment of Porcian foreign policy.[2]

There is much cause for alarm in the doings of Roman statesmen through these pivotal years. Their blind hypocrisy was to color Roman foreign policy as unashamed exploitative conquest. Worse, these gentlemen are condemned by their avowed moral principles. That mighty vindication of the Roman folk by Livy's "vision" states the ideal: Battles and diplomacy were successful when real bravery, forthrightness, and honesty determined the outcome rather than cunning, deception, or craft; the hand-to-hand clash of force in a "righteous war" conquers the spirit of an enemy. Yet the "united senate" Scullard brags of approved settlements that were negotiated by deceit and concluded in dishonor. Polybius says the senators who tried to finesse Attalus, brother of Eumenes of Pergamum, into a fratricidal civil war were "some of the most distinguished senators." The hypothesis already proposed here is that these senators were gentlemen of the Porcian compromise between conservatives, middle bloc politicians, and plebeians. Their leader, Cato, would qualify, as would the politicians of the middle bloc. Since Livy shows that Attalus, remembering his duty, finally left Rome, at which point the "distinguished senators" spitefully broke a promise of territory and vindictively sent Crassus to rouse the Galatians against Pergamum, one can see the levelling foreign policy of the Porcian ideal once again in operation (Polybius XXX.1.6, 3, 19.1).

The cynical expediency of this posture is proven by the fact that Rhodes and Pergamum were punished, three Greek cities and seventy Epirote communities destroyed with one hundred and fifty thousand enslaved, because of their degree of enthusiasm for Rome, and not because they had aided Perseus. Yet Rome befriended Cotys of Thrace, who actively aided Perseus, and began to activate Galatia, for the same purpose (Polybius XXX.17; Livy XLV.34.10, 42.6). Pergamum had merely attempted mediation between Rome and Perseus, an act Rome thought unfriendly. In the case of Galatia, Roman policy had now come full circle. Vulso had subdued the Galatians so as to stabilize the East; now the temporizing senate was reviving that chastised nationality also to stabilize; they feared Roman power, and hence they were fitting pawns for eastern policy (Polybius XXX.6, 19.10, XXIX.5).

Deplorable though it might have been, there is no denying the effectiveness of Rome's Machiavellian international diplomacy. If one is willing to grant any validity to its justification the power of Rome and uniform suppression of all others—one must concede that that goal was achieved without war after Pydna. Instead, there was a continuation of Cato's "plebeian" politics: devilishly ingenious use of influence, innuendo, friendship, and alliance to balance foreign areas in an equal tension between powerful and weak nations so that none was a potential threat to Rome. This was an incredibly sophisticated development, featuring negotiation *à la* Flamininus or Popilius instead of military force; one man and the implicit threat of Rome replaced an army. It was necessary to the continuation of empire, for, as Cato saw earlier, Rome simply could not become the policeman of the world—no power was that strong. Polybius divined this Roman policy when he said, "Many decisions of the Romans are now of this kind: availing themselves of the mistakes of others, they effectively increase and build up their own power, at the same time doing a favor and appearing to confer a benefit on the offenders" (XXXI.10.7).

Rome was never again the same. Her extension of power was such that an envoy could draw a line in the sand at the world's end and call that careless groove the boundary of Rome, over which she assumed the right of "home defense." Another crossed it at the risk of becoming an aggressor against Rome. She now became the responsible authority for all Mediterranean affairs, on call from every quarter of the Mediterranean. The proceeds of that extension were such that Romans were relieved of paying taxes; imperial tribute assumed their burden. This gave the citizens of the city a vested interest in empire and in exploitation of other human beings. Commoners were to become very jealous of Roman citizenship, contributing to crisis in the last century of the Republic. Power seemed once again to corrupt Rome. Her internal desires and ideals were changed. The ancient ethic was far from realization (Plutarch, *Paulus* XXXVIII.38.1).

Perhaps the best indicator of this increasingly materialistic trend among the people of Rome is the donatives given soldiers during and after the Macedonian campaign in addition to the amount deposited in the public treasury. The seventy communities sacked and one hundred and fifty thousand men enslaved allowed gifts to the soldiers of two hundred *denarii* per infantryman and four hundred *denarii* per cavalryman. This did not satisfy them; Livy documents two specifics of dissatisfaction with booty among Paulus' men thereafter. Yet the general saw fit to distribute one hundred *denarii* to infantrymen, two hundred to centurions, and three hundred to cavalrymen in his triumph. Seeing that the highest amount ever given before was fifty *denarii* and that Vulso was accused of currying favor with his troops and of leniency in the Galatian campaign with his donative of forty-two *denarii*, one wonders about this alarming amount given by Paulus. Applying the same standard, Aemilius must be called twice as destructive to military discipline by reason of his distributions, though there is adequate evidence that both Vulso and Aemilius were harsh disciplinarians in the field. Of course, Vulso did not retire to his tent after victories, surrounded by adoring juveniles, and piously intone on "Fortune and Human Affairs," tearfully protesting "political necessity" before continuing his atrocities, as Aemilius did. History, hypnotized by regretful tears in the great, seems to condone the one and condemn the other (Livy XXXIX.7.2, XL.43.7, XLV.34.5, 7, 40.5).

The triumph of Paulus was further highlighted by deposit of one hundred twenty million *sestertii* in the public treasury, as well as amounts of gold and silver. It was this wealth that allowed Rome to remit taxes, but one must inquire whether that was the booty acquired by looting and killing in three countries—Greece, Epirus, and Macedonia—at the virtual cost of Paulus' soul, and measure the expense. A further interesting event associated with the triumph was an attempt by veterans of Pydna to forestall it. Galba, a military tribune under Paulus, tried to urge the massed soldiers to vote against it and very nearly won the day. Appealing to their greed—

the sensation they had not shared in the richest Macedonian spoils—and their pride—the feeling they had been exposed to excessive discipline and danger without adequate awards and honors—Galba persuaded the veterans to lead in dominating the vote against the triumph. This was an affair engineered by Paulus' army—the people of Rome had nothing to do with it; indeed, they opposed it. Livy explicitly says the soldiers filled the Capitol, where the assembly was to be held, with such a crowd that no one else could approach to cast his vote. The next sentence states that the first tribes called within the enclosure voted against triumph. That means, of course, that only the military veterans of the tribes were voting. Galba promised them that the city commons would follow their opinion. Plutarch shows the error of that statement, saying that the multitude was deeply grieved at the indignity offered Aemilius and could only cry out against this unconstitutional manipulation of the balloting. Certainly no dissent of the people or significant confrontation of classes is represented by this vote. At the same time, Galba's assumption that the city commons would support the army rather than the senate and his statement that Paulus controlled the money but the rank and file awarded the honors verify the assertive independence of the people (Livy XLV.35.5–40.1; Plutarch XXX.2–XXX.6).

The most prominent senators, shouting with outrage at all this, interrupted the voting and demanded to be heard. Represented by Marcus Servilius, they spoke to the effect that a triumph reflected as much on the soldiers and people of Rome as on the general, redounding to the credit of all. Marcus scolded the citizens by comparing Paulus with other great generals, such as Scipio Africanus, denied their just deserts by a niggardly populace and then urged them to give Paulus, at least, his due. The very gods who had been petitioned for victory would be angry were they denied their recognition by triumph. He concluded by showing his scars, all in front but for saddle callouses, and inviting comparison of his scarred skin with the smooth skin of Galba as qualification for addressing the people on military honor (Livy XLV.36.7–40; Plutarch XXXI).

Cato participated in this confrontation with a speech *To the soldiers against Ser. Galba*. All that is preserved of it is an anecdote about the cleverness of a youth in concealing senatorial affairs from his mother's prying curiosity. The purpose of this story in a speech as serious as the present one is obscure. Certain it is that Cato's influence, added to that of the senate, was more instrumental in gaining Aemilius his triumph than the emotional utterances of others (Malcovati, p. 197; Gellius I.23).

The triumphal procession of Paulus again demonstrated Roman greed. So many were the statues and colossal figures looted from Greece to be carried in procession on 250 chariots that a whole day barely sufficed for their display. Aemilius was subject to the same sort of status scramble as Fabius, Marcellus, and Fulvius had indulged in from Tarentum, Sicily, and Ambracia. At the same time, he failed miserably in trying to procure the kind of leniency and mercy for Perseus that he had promised. It is manifestly plain, therefore, that Aemilius himself had no conception of the total brutishness to which the Roman people had been reduced as a result of the very policies and campaigns he and others advised and commanded. Yet Paulus was of a metal as base as anyone; when Perseus begged to be excused from the indignity of the triumphal procession, Aemilius mocked his "cowardice" by saying that release had always been in Perseus' power, meaning that he should commit suicide rather than be disgraced. "For this," says Plutarch, "the coward had no heart, but was made weak by hope and became a part of his own spoils" (Plutarch XXXII–XXXV). Perseus, incarcerated under close arrest, either starved himself to death or else was badgered to death by his guards (Livy XLV.42.4).

Romans prided themselves on familial sensitivity. Many spectators shed tears of pity as the little children of Perseus, too young to know what had happened to them, were led in Paulus' triumph (Plutarch XXXIII). Aemilius' concern for his son adopted by the Scipios, when he was thought lost at Pydna, is a further instance, as are the affections demonstrated here between Cato, father, son, and grandson (Plutarch XXXII, XXXV–XXXVII). Most striking is Paulus' loss of his two remaining sons. One died five days before the triumph, the other three days after. One was twelve, the other fourteen years of age, and it is said that they were the heirs of Aemilius' name, his family rites, and his household. They were the minor sons who should have ridden with their father in the chariot. Speaking of this extraordinary change of fortune *in contione* (public assembly), Aemilius compared his state with that of Perseus; the latter saw his sons led prisoners before him, a prisoner, but they were at least alive; Paulus rode in triumph over Perseus though his own sons were dead. Yet Paulus, who spoke so nobly of life and death, lamenting the vicissitudes of fortune, heartlessly suggested that the father of pitiful little prisoners commit suicide so as to preserve dignity (Livy XLV.40.6). He spoke of Roman mercy to Perseus and then saw that "mercy" translated to such terms that Perseus committed suicide. One must almost conclude that Paulus' nemesis was deserved.

Affairs in the East continued to demonstrate Porcian influence after Pydna. Eumenes of Pergamum was denied a hearing, encouraging the Galatians. At the same time, Prusias of Bithynia was favored, though he conducted himself in a manner more servile than that of Perseus' surrender, making it plain that the disdain of Perseus was expedient and relative. The minor powers were encouraged, to balance the stronger. It continued; Prusias was heard again in 164, accusing Eumenes of annexing Bithynian territory, meddling in Galatia, and intriguing with Antiochus of Syria against the senatorial will. Galatia was excused for its trespass in Pergamum, provided it would not again trespass.[3]

Pergamum sent an embassy to Rome counteracting that of Prusias, but the senate dispatched two envoys to investigate. These behaved so outrageously that Polybius accuses the leader of being mentally deranged. Meantime, the Galatians, whom the senate had cautiously roused, now turned against Cappadocia. King Ariarathes of Cappadocia was officially an ally of Rome, approved by the senate through the recommendations of a commission headed by Tiberius Gracchus sent to inquire into the conduct of the eastern kings. A further mission had to be sent, under Marcus Iunius, to investigate and settle this newest rupture in the Roman international patchwork. Ariarathes also gained the goodwill of a third commission sent under Cn. Octavius to investigate affairs in the Kingdom of Syria. It would seem that Rome intervened in the Galatian wish to raid Cappadocia, to the better interests of the latter (Polybius XXXI.1.2, 3, 6.1, 7–8).

So also in Syria and Egypt. Two brothers Ptolemy quarreled over their throne. The elder had inherited, but he fled invasion by King Antiochus and was apparently captured. The Syrians made terms with him, but in the meantime Egyptians had proclaimed the younger brother king to meet the crisis. It seems that Antiochus installed his protege, the elder brother, in Memphis, while the younger ruled from Alexandria. The two reconciled their quarrel and together appealed to Rome when Antiochus threatened once again. The Romans sent Popilius, who drew his famous line in the sand and forced Antiochus out of Egypt. The brothers again fell out, the younger expelling the elder, who then sought Roman help. Before it could arrive, Egyptian reaction against the younger brother and his cruelty forced this younger man to evacuate the kingdom and give the bulk of it to his brother. The elder Ptolemy then held Egypt and Cyprus, the younger, Cyrene (Livy *Periocha* XLVI, *Periocha* XLVII).[4]

The Syrian King Antiochus succeeded in gaining the good graces of Rome, after the affair of the line in the sand, by receiving Tiberius Gracchus' inspection commission with such courtesy that he even vacated his palace so as to accomodate them in palatial surroundings. Polybius facetiously says that Antiochus almost gave up his very crown out of falsely obsequious humility, though his real feelings were just the opposite (Polybius XXIX.27, XXX.27).

Tiberius Gracchus participated in a number of senatorial commissions and directly affected eastern policy because of them. He was a middle bloc partisan and now effectively projected the Porcian policy embraced by the entire conservative-middle-plebeian coalition. The senate deferred to Tiberius because of the eastern junkets, but Polybius twice insists that the eastern kings fooled Tiberius with mock servility. He says Tiberius and his colleagues were unable to state any opinion about Eumenes and Antiochus after their missions different from that which they had formerly entertained when in Rome. Yet Gracchus' recommendations were the bases for settlements with Syria, Cappadocia, Bithynia, Pergamum, and Rhodes, and they worked so remarkably well that the East, exclusive of Greece, was held entirely by diplomacy from the time of Vulso's Peace of Apamea to that of Mithridates the Great (188 to 84 B.C.).[5]

Such achievement suggests more than the higgledy-piggledy rationale Polybius infers. If Tiberius was deceived, he chose to be and practiced the greater cunning of pretending to be taken in by a show of humility. That had the awesome effect of catching the deceivers in their own web and forcing them to live out the masquerade of friendship for Rome because this, at least, guaranteed them status quo security against each other and Roman ambition. Little did it matter whether the humility was real; international pretense achieved the same goal—the weak collectively neutralized the strong under Roman diplomatic guidance. Polybius innocently pays Roman policy a high compliment when he implies that eastern rulers hated Rome but unwittingly accepted her eastern entente. He also displays Tiberius' further application of Porcian principles in this eastern commission when he says that Gracchus simultaneously subjected people called the Cammani, probably Asiatics, to Rome, partly by force and partly by fraud (Polybius XXXI.1.1; Diodorus XXXI.17, 28).

It is montonously disillusioning to observe that Polybius, the self-styled paragon of objective excellence, partakes of Livy's bifocalism in historical casuistry. Though he deplores the earlier attempt to induce fratricidal civil war between Attalus and Eumenes of Pergamum, he calls its instigators the "most distinguished of senators," feeling little discomfort at the discrepancy between their avowed ideals and their political conduct. Similarly, he derides the international efforts of Tiberius Gracchus and accuses him of "fraud" and "violence" in taking a people hitherto unknown (what reason but sheer aggrandizement can have been the cause?) for Rome. Later, in a discussion of the character of Scipio the Younger, Polybius labels Gracchus second to none in Rome in the matter of honor! One might well ask how the historian can presume to criticize at all, since his standards of morality permit a "violent fraud" to be a man of honor.[6]

II   Roman Affairs between Macedonia and Dalmatia: Domestic and Foreign

Cato must have been enthralled at the course of foreign affairs. All his principles and ideals were being enacted. There was eastern dominance and exploitation with no territorial occupation or cultural "adulteration." According to Cato's formula then, there should be cultural domestic tranquility in the city of Rome. Affairs show the exact opposite! Polybius, in the section devoted to the younger Scipio's character, says he easily excelled others in virtue because of the growing viciousness of Roman youth after Pydna. They had learned to enjoy amours with boys as well as courtesans and to demand music, banquets, and other extravagances because they were infected with Greek laxity in such things during the war with Perseus. So great was their incontinence that many paid a talent for a male favorite and others paid three hundred drachmas for a jar of caviar. Cato condemned this tendency in a public speech, saying that it was a sure sign of state deterioration when pretty boys cost more than fields and jars of caviar more than ploughmen. Polybius attributes the deterioration to conquest, saying that the thirst for exorbitance resulted from the knowledge of world dominion and from the public display of wealth following the importation of Macedonian riches (Polybius XXXI.25.2–10; Plutarch, *Cato* VIII.1).

The ancient historian is on the mark in one sense—tracing degradation to conquest and wealth—but he is rather shallow in assuming it happened all at once, or in supposing that the young became infected with vice just during the war with Perseus. If that were so, one should have to agree that Roman ethics, mores, and folkways were so lightly taught and learned that one bout with temptation was sufficient to bury national morality. Pydna would take its place beside Syracuse, Campania, Greece, Aetolia, and Asia as another "rape" of the Roman virgin (see p. 171 above). This last attack finally sullied her fragile innocence, to stretch the metaphor, for she now turned to a career of boisterous harlotry. As in "real life," however, it was continual participation in the defilement of others, under the rubric of protectionism and the deceits that fiction required, that developed the taste for vice and capacity for self-deception. The young beheld their models—men like Africanus, Paulus, Cato, and Gracchus—continually involved in homicide, lies, and extortion "for the good of state," and defiantly sincere about it all. That is why Cato's ideal of exploitation with noninvolvement was a sophomoric delusion. One does not indulge in bloodbaths without becoming stained. Roman degradation was a foregone conclusion from the day she spilled human blood in the name of "security" far from her native shores.

Cato again became involved in litigation in 164 B.C. In this, his seventieth year, he was accused of extravagance by his enemies before the censors, L. Aemilius Paulus and Q. Marcius Philippus. Recourse was had to a defense by means of reading his achievements from an earlier speech, then protesting that no one wished to hear things like that "nowadays." From all this, Cato concluded that one may not rehearse benefits to the state because one may do evil with impunity, but not good. The entire affair smacks of an accusation that he misused public funds, but Cato had held no office for twenty years. It seems likely that the prosecution was caused by the tremendous influence of Cato and his coalition's dominance over foreign affairs. The growing power of that combination was enhanced by the marriage of Licinianus to Paulus' daughter Tertia and the addition of the conservative Aemilii to the group, an arrangement foreshadowed by Paulus' obedience to the senate during his ·Macedonian command. The consolidation of the Gracchi with the coalition is to be seen in the later marriage of Tiberius' son Gaius to Licinia, a relative of Cato's wife Licinia, as also by the Gracchan adoption of Cato's ideals.[7]

The fact that Cato in 164 stood before a tribunal of the censors— Paulus, predisposed to favor him, and Marcius Philippus, exponent of Porcian policy in the Macedonian command in 169—is perhaps eloquent of the reasons he was not convicted. Others have said that Cato had abused the *Lex Orchia* of 181, which limited the number of guests one might entertain. He had supported that law, and his enemies now took occasion to embarrass him. This supposition is based upon Plutarch's description of the manner in which Cato's personal life had changed; lavish banquets and meticulous service by slaves. It has been shown that there are contradicting versions of that life style, and Plutarch may well be exaggerating. That would eliminate the possibility of a prosecution under the *Lex Orchia*. At any rate, the prosecution failed; Pliny shows that the censor was never condemned in his life (*NH* VII.214, X. 139).

Cato's defensive speech mentioned above seems to symbolize a sweeping change in personal philosophy and belief in its conclusion. Gellius quotes: "If I have anything to use, I use it; if not, I do without. So far as I am concerned, everyone may use and enjoy what he has. They find fault with me because I lack many things; but I with them because they cannot do without them" (Gellius XIII.24.1). Cato formerly held the opinion that reform of Roman ethical standards must take place through the legislation of morals, regardless of personal ideals and desires. That was the gist of remarks given against the repeal of the Oppian Law, and he had maintained that opinion. Thus the lines, "So far as I am concerned, everyone may use and enjoy what he has," represent a true change of philosophy. Perhaps family—the realities of raising children and maintaining standards in the family unit—forced an attitude of leniency. So, too, would the necessities of compromise in politics inevitably change one's principles. Instances of hypocrisy in the matter of military life and culture have already been indicated, and they no doubt combined with those of family life and politics to moderate the harsh conservatism of Cato.

Roman affairs in the western Mediterranean seem to have continued successfully after 164. Sardinia briefly gave trouble, but it was settled with little fuss. Connected with it was a peculiar incident of religious concern: Gracchus recalled a consul from Sardinia and Corsica; he (Gracchus) had not taken proper auspices before holding the election. This leads to speculation that his piety was politically motivated: Gracchus had previously served both islands and may have been jealous of that preserve (Scullard, p. 226; Livy *Periocha* XLVI). Such pettiness is an unnecessarily low view of him (Polybius XXXI.2, 7, 11–15, 32–33).

In the East, the simultaneous deaths of Ariarathes of Cappadocia and Antiochus of Syria complicated affairs. Each was succeeded by a namesake, but they were thereafter beset with contention for the throne. Demetrius, cousin of Antiochus, petitioned for the succession at Rome, where he was hostage. He was refused, says Polybius, because the senate thought the young king would be more tractable. A commission was sent, headed by Cn. Octavius, to assure the succession and destroy some ships and elephants being held in excess of those allowed by the Peace of Apamea. But Demetrius fled Rome with the help of Polybius, who was a hostage there from Achaea. Octavius, the Roman commissioner, was murdered, and Demetrius established himself in Syria as successor, killing the young Antiochus. Then he sent envoys to Rome, together with the assassins of Octavius, to clear himself of blame (Polybius XXXI.15.1, XXXII.2–3.14).

Demetrius interfered in the affairs of Cappadocia, intriguing to dethrone Ariarathes, who was supported by the newly crowned Attalus of Pergamum, and to place Orophernes on the throne. The senate sent Tiberius Gracchus once again with a commission to supervise affairs in the interest of Rome, while envoys were sent from these eastern kingdoms to Rome as well. Tiberius conducted affairs exactly as before: the levelling effect of refusing any solid commitment anywhere and maintaining a balanced uncertainty. Everyone was forced to court Rome. The senate, dominated by the Porcian coalition, refused to recognize the embassy from Demetrius bringing the assassins of Octavius to Rome. Polybius caustically comments: "For the senate . . . scarcely gave a reception to these envoys, but kept the grievance open so as to have the power to make use of the accusations when they wished. The reply they gave to Demetrius was that he would meet with kindness from Rome if his conduct during his reign was satisfactory to the senate." Once again, Machiavellian diplomacy prevailed over forceful intervention, even though the provocation was the murder of a Roman commissioner. As in the case of Cassius, Popilius, Lucretius, and Licinius earlier, individuals were now expendable to state policy (Polybius XXXII.2–3, 10–12).

Rome did not choose sides in the affairs of Egypt, where the two brothers Ptolemy fell out again. The younger brother sought more than Cyrene (see p. 242), and Rome reacted with typical indecisiveness. The younger brother was an obnoxious tyrant, as is proved by Cyrene's refusing to accept his rule and by Polybius' testimony. But Rome, heedless of any consideration of justice, wished to keep Egyptian power divided between two men, rather than "dangerously" concentrated in the hands of one, and so supported the younger Ptolemy in his request. Though Cato later praised the elder Ptolemy, it is not likely that he did anything but guide the senate and acquiesce in this decision—again an almost perfect enactment of Porcian principle (Polybius XXXI.17–20, XXXIII.11; Livy *Periocha* XLVII).

One more incident in the East tested Roman diplomacy. When Attalus succeeded Eumenes of Pergamum, Prusias of Bithynia used the interval to attack Pergamum. Then Prusias defied the inevitable senatorial commission by besieging it in Pergamum. A second commission had to promote an eastern alliance against Bithynia, which finally brought Prusias to heel, while a final commission forced him to make restitution. The "old Rome" would never have tolerated so many slights on her honor or insults against her power without seeking active military retribution. Yet it must be said that the new method, with its deviousness, saved millions in gold and thousands of lives while accomplishing the same end. Cato would have applauded, as he did earlier in the case of Macedonia (Polybius XXXII.8, 12, 15, XXXIII.1, 7, 12–13).

This may well have been the culminating achievement of the Porcian coalition. Its power seems to come more into contention and allied clans seek other alignments increasingly in the 150's. An example is the career of Scipio Nasica. It was he whose consular command in Sardinia Gracchus had arrested by recall because of a defective taking of electoral auspices. Thus one can see that Tiberius' action was a triumph for the Porcian coalition and temporarily halted the reassertion of Scipionic influence in the senate. Nasica was too good a man to be kept out permanently, however. The tension between Cato and this man would have been largely one of policy. As Nasica was a Roman of the old-fashioned sort, Cato would approve his domestic and cultural posture, though he might deplore his foreign policies. Nasica became censor in 159 and consul for the second time in 155, though he had been denied this Sardinian command of 162 (Broughton, pp. 445, 448; Livy *Periocha* XLVII).

III   *Death and Marriage in Cato's Family*

Perhaps in 160 Cato's wife Licinia died. Cato was then seventy-four years of age. The sources do not give details; Licinia's must have been a quiet passing. She lived a simple life to the end, apparently getting along with little though Cato had become wealthy. He must have given her a pauper's funeral, as he later did her son, being now so vain that he had to preserve the appearance of little means though he had much, even in the final rites of those whose suffering had made the pretense possible. Plutarch's Licinia had a life of little refinement: walls without plaster, threadbare garments, and a grasping domestic budget. So Cato piously intoned on increase and thrift, enslaving his wife to a maxim. Her reward was an anonymous life, a miserly death with, doubtless, a nameless grave. The tragic orphan could not learn human relationships; his wife was a cipher; his marriage, a barren principle.[8]

Where was that spirited girl who in the first blush of matrimonial affection laughingly defied her husband's stodginess, impulsively invited other women in, and gossipped about Marcus' pseudo-weighty confidences? The continual housework, monotony of the same drab surroundings, slavish household budget, and growing weight of her husband's grim, conservative image with the collective familial obligation to maintain it had crushed her spirit, blighted her humor, obligated her affection, and silenced her tongue. Perhaps Licinia was not sufficiently prolific to retain Cato's respect and allow her to "nag" him for more of the comforts of life. They had only the one child, Licinianus, and he was somewhat frail, though well-trained. Sexual compatibility was not enough to enhance their affection, apparently, and force Marcus to ease the hard life. After all, he could and did use a slave girl to satisfy that appetite. "Why pay a wife more?" the old reprobate must have wondered. Licinia's spirit departed like a wraith in the night, and Cato took solace with a concubine for his nocturnal needs (Gellius XIII.20.7).

Marcus Licinianus must have married Tertia, the daughter of Aemilius Paulus, in about 158 B.C. Plutarch says the marriage took place after the death of Licinia, and he and Cicero agree that at the time of the battle of Pydna, Tertia was a little child. That may be interpreted as perhaps six years of age, and it seems that she would be sixteen years at the time of her marriage, hence the date. This young bride took residence in the same grim surroundings that had subdued Licinia. A child, Marcus Cato the Fourth, was soon born of that union. Shortly thereafter, Tertia and Licinianus took offense at Cato's concubine, who had a tendency to flaunt her liaison. This became obvious to Cato, who rather than offend his son and daughter-in-law, or perhaps because he was angry at their criticism, married the daughter of a client of his named Salonius. That match, however, angered Licinianus rather than appeasing him. Encouraged and accompanied by his friends, the latter inquired of Cato whether it was because of any complaint he had to make against his son that he now burdened him with a stepmother. Cato quoted sarcastically from Peisistratus of Athens that he wished only to bless himself and his country with more such sons as Licinianus. Plutarch effectively refutes that answer by questioning why, if that were the case, Cato had not remarried immediately after the death of Licinia rather than taking a concubine.[9]

Cato and his son Licinianus must have fallen out over this affair. The fact that the latter took the precaution of having friends with him when he questioned his father smacks of a legal air. Plutarch thinks Cato's second marriage was unworthy, unseasonable, and indecent; it was too late in life, with too low a rank of woman, and too much an act of cynicism (*Comparison* XXIV, VI). This was sensed by Licinianus; the latter's last memories of his father were thus unhappy ones. Once again, as with his deceased wife, Cato could not learn human relationships. His estrangement from his son must have been a bitter blow, but caused entirely by himself; Cato was his own worst social enemy, and his loneliness was almost compulsive.

It is difficult to put a date on Cato's second marriage, but it may well have been about in 156 B.C. It had to be before the death of Licinianus, which has in this work been dated 154 B.C. A son was born to Cato of this second wife, who was named Marcus Cato Salonianus. Cato was seventy-eight years old at the time of this second son, and it may be for this reason that Plutarch sounds the note of impropriety. The old hypocrite retained his sexual vigor, and that may be the cause for envy among the ancients, particularly

as this later son was more prolific than the first. He begot two
grandsons for the perpetuation of the name of Porcius. It was
through Salonianus that the line of descent extended to the later
famous conservative of Caesar's day: Cato the Younger, surnamed
Uticensis because of his suicide there to escape Julius Caesar
(Plutarch, *Comparison* III.6, XXIV, XXVII.5; Gellius XIII.20.7).

IV   *Cato's Renewed Focus on Foreign Affairs: Dalmatia, Spain, and Lesser Diplomacy*

The year after this marriage, Marcus' attention must once again
have refocused on foreign affairs. The issue was war with Dalmatia;
the reason, a commission sent there had been insulted, violently
threatened, and its horses taken, while the Dalmatians remained
adamant that they had nothing to do with the Romans. The Porcian
diplomacy would not function, of course, if subjects had no reason to
fear Rome. That fear was the essential basic element in the com-
pound of eastern settlements; now it had to be instilled in Dalmatia.
The latter had attacked Illyrians, who were allies of Rome, and so
threatened the entire Greek settlement. This war began under the
consulship of Gaius Marcius Figulus, who at first suffered reverses
but then captured several towns and besieged the central city of
Delminium. His lack of success must have embarrassed the Porcian
coalition, as the plebeian Marcii were identified with it (Polybius
XXXII.9–10). Worse still, it elevated the opposing Cornelii in the
person, once again, of Scipio Nasica, who was elected consul in 155
and successfully completed the siege of Delminium by the ingenious means of shooting flaming sticks covered with flax and smeared
with pitch into the town with catapults. Delminium, which was
built mostly of flammable materials, was forced to capitulate (Livy
Periocha XLVII; Appian X.11).

Though the important reason for this Dalmatian war was to inspire fear of Rome so that the people would yield to Porcian diplomacy, Polybius articulates another: The senate did not wish the
Italians to become effeminate owing to the long peace, it being now
twelve years since the war with Perseus. They therefore resolved to
rekindle the spirit and zeal of their own troops with the war. Two
things are extremely important in this event: the remarkable efficiency of the Porcian foreign diplomacy and the woeful thesis that
one must fight to retain a fighting edge. The latter is a touchstone of
imperialism. It shows, among other things, that the citizen militia

was no longer a defensive arm to be called up in time of emergency but rather an imperial one to be kept in readiness at all times. Hence the rationale of professionalism in the military ruled the senate, and it required only the later Marian incidentals of continuous service and regular salary to complete the transition to a dominant military establishment (Polybius XXXII.13–14).

The Porcian compromise mustered enough strength to elect both censors in 154. M. Valerius Messala, through the Valerii, was naturally allied to the conservative bloc, and C. Cassius Longinus was the adherent who had practised levelling politics in 171 B.C. in Venetia in behalf of the Porcian group and then taken service with Hostilius in 170 in Macedonia as a tribune to avoid prosecution (Valerius Max. II.9.1; Broughton, p. 449). His reward for sacrifice was this censorship, which otherwise would be inexplicable. Since the senate should have opposed both men, Valerius having been expelled from the senate himself by earlier censors and Cassius having opposed the senate's wishes in his consular command, their election can be understood only as another rebellion of the electorate. Perhaps, then, one may say that the Porcians still retained influence with the people at large. As for the dire predictions of moral ruin (the subversion of virtue) pronounced by Calpurnius Piso and associated with this year, perhaps specifically with the censorship, they may safely be ignored. Cassius and his defiance of the senate have been dealt with earlier, and enough of the senatorial expulsions by censors were purely political that a *nota* does not here carry the moral overtones Piso would attach to it. The causes of Roman loss of virtue have been dealt with (Pliny, *NH* XVII.245).

The lack of domestic accord in Rome is to be seen in the doings of these censors. Their attempt to build a permanent theater was thwarted by the senate; one can imagine the horror of Cato that partisans of the Porcian bloc would propose such a thing. He may well have supported Scipio Nasica, who swayed the senate to order the structure destroyed. This highlights the differences that existed between senators on domestic issues. Another manifestation of that is the general agreement that Cassius was forced by some charge to bring proceedings against Cato, as a censorial duty. Though the two had similar ideas and political liaison, their domestic goals differed as shown by the matter of the theater, and Cato was forced to defend himself, apparently, on a domestic issue. His only preserved thought in defense is that it is hard for one of an earlier generation to defend himself before the members of another. Seeing that he was now eighty years old, one can imagine the problem (Livy *Periocha* XLVIII; Gellius X.14.3; Plutarch XIV.4).

Affairs localized in Spain during the following period greatly affected Roman foreign posture and forced Cato, as well as others, to take certain stands. Spain, after submitting to twenty-five years of extortion, finally rebelled (Livy *Periochae* XLVII, XLVIII; Appian VI.44–60). Q. Fulvius Nobilior, consul for 153, proved completely unequal to the task of war in Spain and suffered insupportable losses; he then lost his base and had to spend the winter in a temporary camp. He was replaced by M. Claudius Marcellus, consul for 152, a much more experienced general (Polybius XXXV.1–5), who quickly subdued the Celtiberians by a combination of judicious punishment and diplomacy and then sent their envoys to the senate, recommending that terms be granted. The senate, however, was determined to impress its will on the Spanish Aravacae, who pretended humility but retained a good deal of pride. Senators faulted Marcellus, feeling he was afraid of the war, and plotted to send the new consul-elect, L. Licinius Lucullus, to supersede him. This probably shows the continuing importance of the Porcians, as Licinius would be affiliated with Cato through the clan of his deceased wife, Licinia, and through the earlier Licinian affinity with the Popilii. The Licinii were a plebeian clan. The group must have felt that the Aravacae were too proud to be tractable through diplomacy and therefore had to be humiliated first. This "levelling" assumed unforeseen proportions.

First, soldiers once again refused to enroll for the Spanish troop levy. Polybius, styling this a "fit of cowardice," says it was caused by stories of horror from the campaigns of Nobilior supplemented by the rumor that Marcellus was afraid to continue the war. According to Polybius, the impasse was resolved by Scipio Aemilianus, who shamed the men by volunteering for duty in Spain despite his prior assignment to Macedonia. Appian, on the other hand, says that the difficulty was settled with an enrollment by lot. Livy's *Periocha* adds the statement that the tribunes of the people actually had Licinius and his colleague thrown in prison for not exempting the people they favored. No one could be found even to accept appointment as staff officer or military tribune. Whether the Romans were enrolled by lot or because of shame in the end, it matters little to the further startling reassertion of the prerogatives of the people and their tribunes. The people refused service in a foreign theatre of war, and their tribunes went so far as to imprison the magistrates. It is highly significant, in this light, that there was another investigation of poisonings at about the same time. Evidence is lacking as to the details, but if it resembled the former investigations, one may assume a number of unjust proceedings and therefore a reciprocal bitterness from the people, which helps to account for this rebellion against the establishment in 151. It may well be that this final series of incidents allowed Cato and his political followers to accumulate power leading to the Third Punic War. The only individual to stand in the way was Scipio Nasica, with his rising authority and influence.

Once in Spain, Licinius was unable to restrain his lust. Marcellus had succeeded in making terms with the Aravacae, who put themselves under his protection. Licinius then directed his energies to another group, the Vaccaei, attacked a city in their territory, and slaughtered twenty thousand of the males after they had assented to a peace and made terms. This treacherous massacre reflected shame on Rome but alerted the other Spaniards so that this one town was all Licinius took and the whole campaign did not bring him any gold or silver. Appian says that part of the reason for his greed was that Licinius had a large personal debt. The feat of slaughtering innocents was repeated in the other Spanish province, where Licinius went to the aid of the praetor Galba, and the latter, under false promises of peace, slaughtered a large number of Lusitanians. One of the survivors was Viriathus, who lived to lead the Lusitanians in unremitting bloody warfare against Roman governors thereafter. For the present, war in Spain was halted.

It is impossible to say to what extent the consul and praetor were following Porcian political ideals in this Spanish campaign. One may assert that Appian shows Licinius' personal reasons for destruction, then triumphantly asserts that as to the gold and silver, for the sake of which Licinius had waged this war, he got none. That argues Licinius' motivations were personal, rather than the result of policy. The same may be true of Galba's action, since Cato later spoke for a measure condemning the praetor and asked that the Lusitanians be judged by their actions, not their intentions. This oration was given in 149, the last year of Cato's life, and therefore is to be considered together with the declaration of war against Carthage, which Cato was instrumental in achieving. Cato judged the Carthaginians for their intentions, rather than their actions. The only difference, by Appian's account, was that Galba had given his formal pledge to the Lusitanians, and this was not true of either the Vaccaei or of the Carthaginians. However, since Cato was making the distinction on the basis of the enemy's intention, he shows severe moral discrepancy in judging the Carthaginians and not the Vaccaei (Livy *Periocha* XLIX; Malcovati, p. 203).

Two associated matters came to demand attention in this Spanish affair: Marcellus was elected to the consulship after he had previously held it just three years before, and Galba used a cheap ploy to the emotions in his trial, which, together with his wealth, quashed the prosecution against him. With regard to the consulship, Cato spoke in favor of a bill in 151 that forbade second consulships. In the case of Galba, Cato wrote in his *Origines* that Galba saved himself from the flames by arousing the sympathy of the people for his children: Galba, rather than present a good defense, threw himself on the mercy of the people, bringing his two children by birth and an adopted one into court. Their weeping demanded sympathy, so that the court decided to acquit their father. Appian cynically adds the note that Galba, keeping the lion's share of the Lusitanian spoils for himself although he was already one of the wealthiest Romans, added to the general hatred against him but escaped punishment by means of his wealth. Adding insult to injury, Galba was elected consul five years later. Yet his gaudy career was not without remonstrance. A law was carried in 149 establishing a permanent court, empanelled from the senate and presided over by a praetor, to deal with cases of extortion in order to prevent further such incidents.[10]

One may gather from all this that while Cato favored the "levelling" policies espoused by the Porcian faction for the previous twenty years, he was opposed to the needless abuse of power and heedless slaughter that served little purpose but to irritate. Cato had previous experience of the Spaniards and could be expected to know something about them. Yet, contradictory to this attitude in Spain, Cato advocated the use of force in North Africa as he had elsewhere. It might perhaps be said that the man was incapable of nonprejudicial application of his own foreign policies. Only in Spain, however, did his policies fail. Elsewhere they worked well.

Egyptian affairs again beckoned for Rome's attention with a new quarrel between the Ptolemy brothers. The younger spoke of an attack on his person by the elder and showed knife wounds to the senate as proof. He also attempted to buy sympathy by leaving his realm to Rome in a will, should he die. When he took affairs in his own hands and tried to capture Cyprus, the elder Ptolemy captured him but generously restored him to Cyrene (Polybius XXXIII.11). This sly young man next asked for the hand of Cornelia, recent widow of Tiberius Gracchus, in marriage. Apparently Minucius Thermus acted as go-between, and for that he was roundly attacked by Cato, who simultaneously referred to the elder Ptolemy as the best of kings (Malcovati, p. 172; Scullard, p. 236). Egypt was then allowed to care for itself, seemingly, Egypt being too weak to matter as Rome was increasingly occupied with Carthage and Spain (Otto, *Zur Gesch.*, pp. 118 ff.).

Two other affairs involved Cato personally before the crisis with Carthage. Prusias of Bithynia asked for a remission of his indemnity, paid since his attempt to raid Pergamum and his siege of Roman commissioners in that city. The senate refused, partly because of Cato's speech supporting the counterclaims of Attalus of Pergamum (Polybius XXXVI.14). Attalus, making too much of a good thing, incited Prusias' son against him, forcing another appeal to Rome. The son, Nicomedes, had lived in Rome representing his father and had friends in the senate (Plutarch IX.1; Livy *Periocha* L). The senate chose a commission of ailing men: one had the gout, another recently had a roof tile fall on his head, and the third was infamous for his stupidity. Cato grumbled in the senate that Prusias would die and Nicomedes grow old before the commission got there, since it had neither feet nor head nor intelligence. In fact, Prusias was killed and Nicomedes succeeded him, but the ensuing accord between Pergamum and Bithynia worked to Rome's interests (Malcovati, p. 202).

The second affair concerned the Achaean hostages in Rome. They had asked for release in 155 and been narrowly defeated. Part of the reason was influence from a praetor presiding over the senate, A. Postumius. This man had knowledge of Greek and wrote a poem and a history in that language. The preface of the latter asked indulgence if he, a Roman, showed imperfect knowledge of the language. Cato ridiculed him for that conceit; as no one had ordered him to write either work, the apology was an empty circumlocution. The Achaeans were finally released in 151, when Polybius got Scipio Aemilianus to persuade Cato to intercede in the senate for them. To be sure, his support was ungracious; as the senate debated, he rose to complain: "Just as if we had nothing to do but sit here all day disputing whether some wretched old Greeks shall be carried to their graves by bearers from Rome or Achaea" (Malcovati, p. 201). When Polybius wished to ask also that they restore the honors the exiles had previously held, and asked Cato's advice, he smilingly answered with a paraphrase from Homer: Polybius, like Odysseus, wished to return to the cave of Cyclops because he had forgotten his cap and belt. History proved Cato was wrong in his derision of the "wretched old Greeks." With their return, the Achaean League took courage and defied Rome; Rome's retribution was the destruction of Corinth and the dissolution of the league (Polybius XXXIII.1, 3, 14, XXXV.6; Plutarch IX.2).

V *Licinianus' Death and Its Consequences*

The year 150 B.C. was Cato's eighty-fourth birthday. Yet he was active as almost never before, stating opinions on nearly every matter to come before the senate. This had become essential because of the gradual depletion of the Porcian bloc, making it necessary for Cato to exercise personal influence. His consequent willingness to compromise somewhat is exemplified by the influence Scipio the Younger exerted on him in the matter of the Achaean exiles and in Cato's endorsement of Scipio during the Third Punic War. Hence there was a change of orientation in Cato's politics in his final years. Perhaps the old man felt he must speak out because no other Cato was present to be heard. Marcus Licinianus must have died in 154. Only a date that early after Cato's second marriage, allowing five years before Cato's own funeral, could accommodate the related events (Livy *Periocha* XLIX; nn. 8, 9, chap. 10).

The son of Licinianus, according to Gellius, became an orator of some note, leaving many speeches written in the manner of his grandfather. It seems likely that Cato had something to do with this himself. Yet unless Licinianus died by 154, so that grandfather Cato became responsible for his grandson's tutelage during the child's fourth through ninth years, he could hardly have had much enduring influence on the boy's career. By that time Marcus Salonianus was born and perhaps two years old, so the octogenarian was responsible for the rearing of two children in his declining years. He left a lasting impression: One became an orator after the fashion of Cato; the other raised a son who fathered Cato the Younger, strong in the conservative tradition of the clan Porcius (Gellius XIII.20.7; nn. 8, 9, chap. 10).

The funeral of Licinianus was a solemn occasion. Livy shows that Marcus gave his son a pauper's burial: "at very little expense, according to his means, for he was a poor man." The mockery of those phrases, in light of the censor's obvious wealth, may be more than accidental. Cato did wish to preserve the image of poverty and self-denial. At the same time, Licinianus may have perished at a time when he and Cato were at odds, if Plutarch's estimates are right. Though it is not likely Cato was vindictive even in death, the unusual disappointment may have stiffened his resolve to appear poor. This personal austerity cost a bitter price, if Cicero is to be believed. The latter speaks of Cato's bereavement as a mournful sense of internal loss: "my Cato . . . than whom no better man, none more distinguished for filial duty, was ever born. His body was burned by me, whereas, on the contrary it were more fitting that mine had been burned by him; but his soul, not deserting me, but ever looking back, has surely departed for that realm where it knew that I, myself, must come." Cicero's words probably paraphrase Cato's true feelings. Perhaps out of habit, possibly from a sense of propriety, Cato would not say the words at his son's deathbed. His soul wept silently, hopeful that the dead would sense a love stern lips could never tell. Then he buried the urn as a Porcian would: cheaply and simply (Livy *Periocha* XLVIII; Cicero, *Cato* 84).

One wonders about Marcus Licinianus' widow, now barely twenty years old, living perhaps in the house of her father-in-law. Tertia's father Paulus had died in the same year as Licinia, 160 B.C. According to Polybius, Tertia's mother Papiria died shortly thereafter. Her estate was administered by Africanus the Younger, who generously divided it among the surviving sisters. Tertia's dowry, if Paulus' estate of sixty talents is used as an index, was inconsiderable, but her inheritance from Papiria was very significant. It had to be divided two ways (Plutarch says there were two daughters), but even so would have made her financially independent of Cato. Yet there was no ancestral home for Tertia to return to because her father's estate had reverted to a brother. Doubtless she lived with the Catos, and little Marcus was educated there.[11]

Cato's ensuing years of feverish activity, though he was in his eighties, were partially a compensation and a sublimation. Work is the best consolation for grief; the furious burst of energy after 154 is a testimony to Marcus' great sorrow. Everything he undertook in the schooling of little Marcus IV must have been a nostalgic reminder of happier days with his own son. Perhaps the old man was kind; the boy looked like Licinianus, and Cato might have begun to feel remorse for the first time in his life. The aging senator was just reaching emotional maturity: He could cry! That fundamental truth would open the door to revelation. Emotions could not be governed by principle or legislation. It is barely possible that the orphan's remorse over his "correct" behavior to Licinianus began to show him that rules and discipline are the mere beginning of education, not its goal. Laws are the sidelines, the boundaries set on the blind passion people display in their basic drive to identify: To know their own souls and learn what it is to be human creatures. Nothing in the censor's principled experience had forced him to face that issue. Long before, when the orphan was exposed to the Pythagoreans, he made the mistake of assuming their behavioral precepts were ends in themselves rather than just means. Had he bothered, in his long acquaintance with Greek tradition, to study the later philosophers and observe their careful balancing of the rational (systematic or lawlike) *"logos"* principle with the irrational *"eros"* principle (the tantalizing, intangible "teleology" or purpose that pervades organic existence), Cato might have glimpsed the nebulous force that now caused his unreasonable grief. Alas, it came too late (Plutarch XXV.2–3).

VI   *The Crisis of Carthage and Cato's Death*

Marcus was rescued from agonizing introspection by international crisis. Carthage again became a problem. The very name was enough to strike terror into one whose entire early awareness was branded with the name of Hannibal. He was chosen for a commission to Carthage because of this familiarity and was awed by the new vitality of the city. The occasion was a grievance between Rome's old ally, the Numidians led by Masinissa, and the Carthaginians on a matter of territory. Masinissa was obviously the aggressor, but that made little difference to a politic of expediency. Cato was not even interested in justice here. His main fear was the revival of Carthage. Hitherto, North Africa had been kept in balance by Roman favoritism of Numidia. After visiting Carthage, however, Cato came away electrified by the fear that she would soon defeat Numidia, dominate Africa, and again pose a threat to the world. All modern accounts of the confusing series of commissions and negotiations preceeding the Third Punic War seem to ignore the validity or accuracy of Cato's premonition and then attempt to find other grounds for his advocating war on Carthage. Yet given the mechanics of Porcian levelling policies, there seems to have been adequate reason to fear the city. It is particularly germane to remember that Carthage was never razed or besieged.[12]

All the sources stress the growing strength of Carthage. Polybius says that the great power of the city was evident, as the Carthaginians later gave up to the Romans two hundred thousand suits of armor and two thousand catapults—this before the city fought Rome and held her off for three years. Appian confirms those figures and shows that they applied after Carthage had already lost fifty eight thousand men in a foolhardy struggle with Masinissa that violated the conditions of peace with Rome and directly caused a declaration of war. Appian's statements of casualties throughout his account of the war seem to bear out that surprising estimate of Carthaginian strength. In addition, Carthage was building a fleet contrary to the terms of peace, and that gave her further power. A final commentary comes from Cato more personally. Plutarch, probably quoting from Cato's own work and supplemented by Appian, testifies to the vitality of the city: "teeming with vigorous fighting men, overflowing with enormous wealth, filled with arms of every sort and with military supplies." Appian adds the commission's observations on the richness of the land; Plutarch recalls Cato's symbolizing Carthaginian wealth by showing its large figs.

It seems obvious that as far as Cato and his faction were concerned, there was real reason to fear Carthage. He felt that Numidia would soon be unequal to the task of neutralizing the city and, indeed, that Rome herself, swollen with luxury and power, would soon be vulnerable to a revitalized Carthage. It is, on the face of it and considering the ensuing events of the war, very difficult to say that he was wrong. Carthage's attack and loss to Masinissa, her subsequent yielding of armor and catapults to placate an angry Rome, and then a three-year war afterward should demonstrate that she was strong. The attack was regrettable in that it gave Rome cause to declare war, after some further negotiation and with Cato incessantly demanding the destruction of Carthage. Polybius says that Rome had long since decided to destroy Carthage, but merely awaited a pretext. He adds the consideration of a "just war," one that would appeal to foreign nations. Both statements seem justified by other evidence: The many commissions of negotiation before the war and what Livy says about them seem to confirm that Rome's determination was of long standing, and the "just war" was a prime issue to Cato's opposition led by Scipio Nasica. Even after the report of Carthage's obvious preparation for war by the building of a fleet and army, Nasica insisted there was not just cause for war. Part of Nasica's motive, in turn, was a theory that Rome—already guilty of many excesses, proud of her prosperity, and handicapped by overbearing multitudes—needed Carthage to curb her wantonness, force her to act with greater moderation to her subjects, and promote her self-discipline (n. 12).

It is interesting that none of the views expressed by the ancients are altruistic. Nowhere does one find an advocate wishing to act thus-and-so to the enemy out of simple humanity. Nasica's "just war" was really a concern about the opinions of other nations rather than a wish for justice, and his desire to use the threat of a strong Carthage to discipline Rome and stop her growing sin and softness speaks for itself. All issues seem to agree that the enemy city must be used for the good of Rome, one way or another. Cato, who is usually made responsible for the ultimate decision to wage war, felt that Carthage must be destroyed in order to eliminate the imbalance in North Africa. Numidia was easier to deal with than a powerful Carthage would be. It is impossible to say whether he was right, since Carthage was destroyed. Ironically instructive, however, is Diodorus' paraphrase of Nasica's opinion: the destruction of Carthage would result in civil wars and stimulate the hatred of all subjects for the pride and covetousness of Roman magistrates: "all of which happened to the Romans after the destruction of Carthage" (XXXIV.33.4).

The view that Rome destroyed Carthage because she feared Numidia and Masinissa and therefore wanted to occupy the site of Carthage herself to be in a better position to balance Numidia directly is far more complex and unlikely than the simple fear of Carthage. In any event, Rome did not send any colonists to the site until the time of the Gracchi, preferring instead to give tribute-free land to Utica and others who had aided her, thus balancing Numidia by allying with friends as elsewhere. That hardly seems to justify the view that Carthage had to be destroyed in order to balance Numidia by occupying Carthage.[13]

Marcus Cato did not live to see Carthage destroyed. He died in 149, still in the thick of affairs and, as we have seen elsewhere, composing the final book of his *Origines*. He did live to receive word that the only one of the early commanders who showed old-fashioned Roman courage there at Carthage was the Younger Scipio, son of Aemilius Paulus. Cato cried that Aemilianus alone had wits, but the rest were fluttering shadows. This, however, was a quotation from Book X of Homer's *Odyssey*. Strange indeed that the last known statement from this famous old man, in the absence of any known details about his death, was a quotation from a Greek author in praise of an adopted Scipio—symbols he had fought all his life. Perhaps it is a sepulchral admission that he, too, could err. Possibly the most fitting epitaph for this farmer-statesman who lived by principle but discovered emotion, found all of his own maxims impossible to live by, influenced foreign affairs of the entire mid-second century with his Porcian policies, then died before he could see the disastrous results in the downfall of Republicanism is one he wrote himself: "And I could wish that all we mortals were dumb! for then dishonesty would lack its chief instrument" (Plutarch XXVII.4; Gellius XVIII.7.3).

Notes and References

Chapter One

1. Plutarch, *Marcus Cato*, LCL (all references in ancient works here are to the Loeb Classical Library unless otherwise specified) I.2, says that Cato's original cognomen was Priscus. F. V. Marmorale, *Cato Maior*, 2nd ed. (Bari Laterza, 1949), p. 26, and E. della Corte, *Catone Censore, la vita e la fortuna* (Torino, 1949), p. 152, support Plutarch. M. Gelzer and R. Helm, "M. Porcius Cato Censorius," *Paulys Real-Encyclopädie der classischen Altertumswissenschaft, XXXII, I, 1953, p. 108;* P. Fraccaro. *Atti e Memorie della Romana Accademia Virgiliana di Mantova*, 1910, p. 11 and note 3; and W. Schulze, *Lateinischer Eigennamen* (Berlin, 1933), pp. 141, 224, 233, 310, 358; by the implication Priscus was Etruscan oppose Plutarch. Cicero, *Cato Maior* . . . , 10, asserts that Fabius Maximus Cunctator held his first consulship in the year following Cato's birth (233 B.C.)—234 B.C. Plutarch, *M. Cato*, I.6 says the year of Cato's first campaign was his seventeenth; Nepos, *Cato*, I.2, agrees, but the date is uncertain, 217 B.C. would be mathematically correct, but D. Kienast, *Cato Der Zensor* . . . (Heidelberg, 1954), p. 37 and note 32, says 216 B.C. is "commonly accepted." F. Münzer, *Hermes*, 40, p. 65, asserts 217 B.C. I believe that 216 was the date and that Cato was born late in 234, so that most of 216 was his seventeenth birthday, even though strict calculation indicates eighteen.

2. Kienast, ibid , p. 33; Schulze, ibid., and M. Gelzer, *Die Nobilität der römischen Republik* (Leipzig-Berlin, 1912), p. 10, all argue origin. Kienast's assertion of knighthood, in view of the poverty shown in Plutarch, ibid., XXI.3, XXV.1; Cicero, ibid., 55, and Cato's Sabine estate, is difficult. Sabinum was not given citizenship until 290, when M'. Curius Dentatus marched through it. Cato's forbears, therefore, may not have been full citizens, as Scullard, *Roman Politics 220–150 B.C.* (Oxford, 1951), p. 111 and note 1, observes, noting the grandfather's lack of a *praenomen*. The patronage of the Flaccuses and Cato's admitted standing of *novus homo* are further arguments for humble origin.

3. Cato was a plebeian tribune in 207 and, as we shall see (Marmorale, ibid., p. 26, and della Corte, ibid., p. 152), held the plebeian aedileship and

supervised plebeian games, in Livy XXXII.7.13. This biography will show
"plebeianism."

4. Plutarch, ibid., I.1, does not say grandfather Cato received state
horses because he was an *eques*, but because of bravery and service.

5. See T. Haarhoff, "Education," *The Oxford Classical Dictionary*,
1957, p. 305.

6. His age is questionable. Plutarch, ibid., I.4 and III.1–2. The pleading was probably before his first military campaign, 216 B.C.

7. Scullard, "Coruncanius," *The Oxford Classical Dictionary*, 1957, p.
237, and see Pomponius' section of the *Digest*, 1.2.2.38.

8. References to the Dentati are in Plutarch, ibid., II.1; Salmon, "Dentatus," *The Oxford Classical Dictionary*, 1957, p. 270; A. Gellius, *Noctium
Atticarum*, II.xi; Livy, *Periochae*, XI, XIII; Polybius II.19.8; Cicero, ibid., 55.

9. Cicero, ibid., 43, 75. K. Beloch, *Römische Geschichte* . . . (Berlin,
1926), p. 440; Scullard, *A History of Rome* . . . (N.Y., 1961), pp. 97 ff;
Salmon, "Decius," *The Oxford Classical Dictionary*, 1957, p. 257.

10. Plutarch, *M. Cato*, I.4–5, III.1. Kienast, loc. cit., p. 36, believes that
as Cato was a knight, his work in rural courts was for his own tenants and
clients. In view of Plutarch III.1 and my rejection of knighthood, I demur.

11. Plutarch, *M. Cato*, III.1–4, implies there was only one Flaccus.
Kienast, ibid., p. 37, plausibly says Flaccus' father and son sponsored Cato.
Publius invited Cato to dine and exercised influence to help him before 216
B.C. Cato served in the army 216–15; Publius with the fleet 215–14, and
Cato was in Sicily 214–10. 209 would be too late for the "cultivated bud"
mentioned by Plutarch. Lucius was too young before 216 to exercise
influence. Publius was an ex-consul (Degrassi, *Inscriptiones Italiae*, XIII.i,
p. 440) and very influential in the senate (Livy XXIV.40.5).

12. For the geographic distances, I used Shepherd, *Historical Atlas*, 8th
ed., (N.Y., 1956). For the winter bases of Cato see Livy XXIII.36.9, 39.8,
46.9, 48.2, XXIV.7.10, 12.4. As Cato was with Fabius continuously, see also
Cicero *Cato Maior* . . . , IV.10; Livy, XXIV.14.1, 19.2, 20.3, 8. Nepos I.2
shows that he went to Sicily thereafter, but would pass through Lucania.

13. "*Avis + specio*," or "to examine a bird"; cp. Pease, "Auspicium,"
Oxford Classical Dictionary, and Cicero *de Divinatione* II.72. Livy V.46.6,
XXI.40.3 show the general's power of auspices as ". . . *ductu auspicioque.
. . .*" The *ius auspiciorum* accompanied the office, not the person; Cicero, *de
Legibus* III.10.

14. "*Haru + specio*," or "to examine entrails"; *haruspices* were from
Etruria (Ovid, *Metamorphoses* XV.577, and Cicero, *de Divinatione* I.72).
They prophesied by reading *exta* (entrails), *monstra* (prodigies contrary to
nature taken as signs of divine displeasure), and *fulgura* (signs by lightning
and thunder interpreted by frequency and by location in the 16 Etruscan
divisions of heaven).

15. Livy XXXIV.18.3 is further evidence from Cato's consulship. Plutarch, *Cato* III, X. The incident in Plutarch X directly contradicts Livy, as will be shown.

Chapter Two

1. The two sources are Plutarch, *Marcus Cato* II.3–4, and Cicero, *Cato Maior* 41. Moderns against them are Kienast, loc. cit., p. 12; Fraccaro, loc. cit., pp. 17 ff.; and Scullard, *Roman Politics*, loc. cit., p. 111, n. 2. Variations on the theme are in della Corte, loc. cit., p. 112; R. E. Smith, *Classical Quarterly* 34 (1940), p. 106; and E. Pais, "Quaestioni Catoniane . . ." *Historia* VI.

2. The argument of such as Scullard, ibid., p. 111, that it was between 210 and 207 that Cato did his pleading in country courts has been refuted by the above section of his early life. For settlement in Rome, see Plutarch, *Cato* III.3–4.

3. Plutarch, *Cato* I, IV, VII, VIII–IX, shows the personal characteristics mentioned here, together with Cicero, *Brutus* 16-17, if provable. The rest is my own feeling about Cato from the totality of research and is a function of exposure.

4. Enervation by luxuries is a favorite theme of Plutarch; cp. *Cato* IV.2 and *Marcellus* XXI.1. See Livy VI.35-6 for the rest of the details here.

5. Nero marched inland, as indicated by the tribes Frentani, Marrucini, and Praetututii, and the city of Larinum (Livy XXVII.43.10). A line passed through the heart of their territories to Sena shows that Sabinum was nowhere more than sixty miles from the line of march. Roads were later built along this route, making it a feasible one here. For the men of Firmum see Plutarch, *Cato* XIII.5.

Chapter Three

1. The sources: Cicero, *Cato* . . . 10, 45; Cicero, *Brutus* 15; Livy XXIX.9–11, 15, 25.10; Nepos I.3, II.2; and Plutarch, *Cato* III.4. Kienast, loc. cit., pp. 16 ff., is supplemented by F. Münzer, *Hermes* 40, pp. 68–70, and W. Drumann, *Geschichte Roms,* 2d ed. by P. Groebe (Leipzig, 1899 & 1929), p. 5.106. Opponents are: Scullard, loc. cit., pp. 111–12; P. Fraccaro, loc. cit., pp. 22 ff.; and F. Sobeck, *Die Quaestoren der römischen Republik* (Breslau, 1929), pp, 8ff. Kienast and Drumann are correct on the balance of evidence. Only Cicero, *Cato* 10 and *Brutus* 15, Livy XXIX.25.10, and Nepos I.3, II.2, give fixed chronology. Nepos alone associates the quaestorship of Cato with the consulship of Scipio in 205 B.C., Cicero with that of Tuditanus and Cethegus in 204. Livy avers Cato was quaestor in 204 but says nothing of the previous year, though he does show that Cato was the quaestor of Scipio. This is the crucial point and is supplemented even by Plutarch III.4, whose version is otherwise faulty. Consul and quaestor who

were associated functionally were invariably elected and appointed in the same year. The ties between them were extraordinarily close (Cicero, *In Caecilium Divinatio* 61; Nepos I.3). Scipio in 204 had not yet seen action that would rob him of a quaestor and necessitate replacement. Cicero stands alone on this issue against the consensus of Nepos, Plutarch, and Livy. He must therefore be discarded and the association of Cato's quaestorship with the consulship of Scipio preferred. Even Cicero, *Cato* 10, read carefully, shows a date of 205, saying that Cato became quaestor four years after Tarentum. That battle took place in 209, leading by simple arithmetic to 205 for Cato's quaestorship!

2. Family coalitions and political blocs are theories of Scullard, ibid., chaps. 4–5. Pp. 61–64 above, however, show the Fabian and Scipionic coalitions did not function properly. Fabius had to coerce the electorate, and Scipio to deal in sharp politics, to deliver majorities in the senate for their wishes. The same was true of the assembly.

3. G. De Sanctis, *Storia dei Romani* (Torrino, 1923), III.ii, p. 645, calls thè decree of the tribunes a forgery, as does Scullard, ibid., p. 76, n. 3. R. Haywood, "Studies on Scipio Africanus," *Johns Hopkins Studies in Historical and Political Science*, Series LI, No. 1 (Baltimore, 1933), p. 54, disagrees. Livy XXVIII.40.2 shows the "leading senators" disapproved of including Africa in Scipio's *provincia* but " . . . because of fear or else to curry favor, all the rest failed to speak out." Therefore Scipio commanded a "silent majority." The only way for "the leaders" to interrupt proceedings that would surely end in approval of the African amendment was precisely that used by Fulvius, appeal to the tribunician power of veto, actual or implied, over a legal technicality. "The leaders" wished at all costs to avoid a referendum, knowing Scipio's popularity and fearing the implications of popular interference in *provinciae*. Finally, tribunes were legally sophisticated: Witness Cato, Tiberius Coruncanius, Sextus Aelius Paetus, Tiberius Gracchus, and the like.

4. Compromise is implied by the events. The uncertainty of the senate was resolved in Scipio's day of conference, though that respite shows the man's own doubt of his following in the senate. Livy XXVIII.45.13 shows that Scipio received permission to take volunteers and receive gifts toward his command but was officially allotted no new forces in XXVIII.38.12–14 or 45.8–11. Appian conveys this more succinctly by showing Scipio's strenuous persuasive methods in VII.55, then in VIII.7, demonstrating the unofficial atmosphere of volunteers and gifts, but the senatorial connivance in their implementation. Certainly, this represented compromise. The meeting between consul and quaestor is speculation based on the certainty of the origin of supplies—it was a quaestor's business. The process of subscription and volunteers is in Livy XXVIII.45.14–21. Dio XVII (Zonaras 9.11) facetiously says the senate refused regular forces to Scipio out of jealously. Umbrians and Sabines substantiate Cato's participation in the canvass.

5. Scullard, loc. cit., pp. 111–12, and R. E. Smith, "Cato the Censor," *Classical Quarterly* 34 (1940), p. 106. Beyond doubt, Pleminius was the cause of complaint. The actual decree of the senate in Livy XXIX.20.4–9 shows that Scipio was to be implicated only if he could be shown to have ordered or consented to Pleminius' deeds. None of the moral or sumptuous questions were official. The habits of Marcellus are above in pp. 33, 38; those of Cato, in Plutarch X.4.

6. The numbers of volunteers are in Livy XXVIII.46.1, the number of the Cannae legions in XXIX.24.12–14, where additional troops are mentioned with cavalry. These, with the three hundred given in XXIX.1, yield the number given here. Livy in XXIX.25.1–4 gives wildly varying numerical estimates. Appian VIII.13 says there were fifty-two warships, four hundred transports and small craft, carrying sixteen thousand foot and one thousand six hundred troopers.

7. The secret treaty between Philip and Antiochus played no part in these considerations. Had Sulpicius known, he would have used it to substantiate his argument from "security" in Livy XXXI.7.

8. Aediles at first were plebeian assistants to the tribunes of the people. About in 367, patrician aediles were added, called "curule" to distinguish them. The curule aedileship became the lowest office to confer the *ius imaginis*—the distinctive badge of the patricians. Yet in the time of Cato's aedileship, there was no bar to either aedileship; patrician or plebeian could hold each.

9. It is interesting that forty million gallons is today considered adequate for a city of a million people. Yet Rome could not have been that large. Livy XXIX.37.6 numbers two hundred fourteen thousand male citizens in 204; there were 137,108 in 208 (XXVII.36.7); 143,704 in 193 (XXXV.9.2); and 258,318 in 188 (XXXVIII.36.10). If one assumes an average of two hundred thousand from this and triples the number to allow for families of single male citizens, a figure of six hundred thousand is the result. See T. Ashby, *Aqueducts of Ancient Rome* (1935), and E. Van Deman, *The Building of the Roman Aqueducts* (1934).

Chapter Four

1. My conversations with a modern Sardinian in Rome last year indicated that some parts of Sardinia have not been penetrated to this day. Natives exist in there who have never been seen, and the openings to their primitive valleys are so narrow that but one man can pass at a time. Trespassers are killed out of hand, and dogs used *à la* Dio's Pomponius (XII.48) are either castrated so they lose their scent and returned or killed if they are bitches. He said there are very ancient writings on portable stones there and promised me a sample that I have not received.

2. Livy, *Periocha* XX; Dio XII.18; Polybius I.88.8–12, for occupation. Dio XII.47 for piracy and assignment of a praetor. My argument for assert-

ing a praetor as early as 331 B.C. is debatable. The conquest of the island in Dio XII.48 would seem to require continuing governance, and it is in section XII.50 that Dio speaks of the indignation of the Sardinians at a praetor's being continually "set over them" (Dio uses the word "strategos," but the sense of continuous governance is there). That implies praetorial supervision before the complaint, and before Livy's *Periocha* speaks of electing four new praetors (227 B.C.). The war of 215 is in Livy XXIII.40–41.7; supplies to Scipio in Livy XXIX.36.1, XXX.2.4, 27.9, 41.2, 36.2.

3. On the *"Leges Porciae,"* see G. Bloch and J. Carcopino, *Histoire romaine*, II; . . . (Paris, 1935), p. 145; De Sanctis, loc. cit., IV, p. 530; Scullard, p. 112; and Scullard, *A History* . . . , loc. cit., p. 314. See Dio XII.46 (2) and Livy XXIII.34.10–14, for these cases of hardship in Sardinia.

4. Though based on Scullard, the supposition that Cato now led conservative Fabians has an inner logic of its own. For election to consulship in 196 Cato needed a power base. Conservative as he was, that had to be sought among elements of the old Fabians. They had been virtually leaderless since the death of Fabius himself.

5. Scullard, pp. 113, 257, where Fraccaro and E. Pais are cited for and against the speech. Scullard and Fraccaro agree it is not Cato's and contains anachronisms, such as a reference in Livy XXXIV.4.3 to Romans in Asia: "already we have crossed into Greece and Asia, places with all the allurements of vice, and we are handling the treasures of kings." On the one hand, Romans had indeed been in Greece, during the so-called "First" Macedonian War, before the Oppian debate; on the other, if the reference be imperial, Greece was not in the empire until after Cato died. Therefore the statement need not be anachronistic.

6. A. Schulten, *CAH* VII, pp. 769–86; A. Schulten, *Tartessos* (Hamburg, 1922); F. J. Wiseman, *Roman Spain* (London, 1956), pp. 1–16; C. Sutherland, *The Romans in Spain* . . . (London, 1939); *Pauly-Wissowa* . . . (Stuttgart, 1894–); R. Carpenter, *The Greeks in Spain* (Bryn Mawr, 1925).

7. The centrality of Turdetanians to Carthaginian rule in Spain; *CAH* VII, p. 787, where Turdetani are identified with Tartessians and Celtiberians are called their mercenaries, though that involves an assumption that Livy's *"Turduli"* (XXXIV.17.4) are Turdetani. The same article locates these people in Andalusia.

8. *CAH* VIII, pp. 311–12; Livy XXXIII.27.1–5, XXXIV.10.4–7, 18.1–5, XXXV.1.1–4, 7.8, 22.5–8, XXXVII.46.7–8, 57.1–2, XXIX.21, 30–1, 42.1, 56.1, XL.16.7–10, 30–4; Appian VI.8.42. Cato's unusual honesty is conveyed in Plutarch X.4–5.

9. Praetors governed after 197, but Livy often calls them proconsuls, as in XXXIX.56.1. Cp. Livy XXXII.28.2. Livy XXXIV.13.8 has Cato's "imperial" affirmation.

10. Appian is more acceptable here than Livy. Livy in the cited references gives the disarmament alternatives and then suddenly, at the end of

the section, speaks of the dismantling of walls with no prior warning or method of achievement.

11. Livy seems to rank prorogued praetors as proconsuls; XXXIX.56.1–2; cp. 32.14–15 & 38.2–3. T. Broughton, *The Magistrates Rom. Repub* . . . , p. 341, cites the *Act. Tr. Tol.* in support of the proconsulship of M. Helvius, who on p. 333 is shown to be a praetor originally. However, on p. 337 he calls Tuditanus a proconsul, citing only Livy XXXIII.25.8–9, which does not call him proconsul at all. Nor, as on p. 336, does Livy XXXIV.10.5–6 support proconsul for Helvius. The quotation of Degrassi, *Inscr. It.*, on p. 341 in Broughton, is the basis of the epigraphical reading in the text, as it also supports Cato and Flaccus.

Chapter Five

1. This extreme position, T. Frank, *CAH* VIII, p. 368, who bases the idea Scipio was responsible for the Greek policy on a letter to Heraclea in 190 (De Sanctis, *Atti della r. Acc. di Sci. di Torino*, 1922, p. 242) showing he had philhellene ideals. Scullard, though calling Flamininus bright, faults a certain shallowness, pretentiousness, ambition, and vanity that Scipio did not have (pp. 118–20, 131). It is hard for me to discover the special nuance in the sources that allows Scullard (pp. 119–20) to call Flamininus *more* power prone, ambitious, and pretentious than Scipio. On the other hand, Livy's narrative for the years 198–94 brings one to the inescapable conclusion that the Greeks virtually worshipped Flamininus: cp. XXXIV.48.2–50.11 and then 52.3–4 for the "eager senators" who vote "well-deserved triumph." There is no academically respectable way to support the modern prejudice that makes Scipio the greater of the two *in this period.* Scullard's claims as to the colonies are on p. 118.

2. "Important" since Scullard on p. 120 begins to foster the impression that Scipio's policy was triumphing for protectionist reasons—and that Africanus was causing the change by influence, rather than Flamininus conceiving it. Scullard and T. Frank are to be questioned here.

3. The whole tone of these negotiations of the commission give the lie to Greek foreign autonomy. Rome through Flamininus negotiates with eastern ambassadors, in Livy XXXIV.58–59, and consults with the Greeks only incidentally. But Roman concepts of political self-determination were involved with "rights" such as the *iures honor, suffragium, connubium,* and *commercium.* Foreign affairs were a matter for resolution in the senate, as with all Roman citizens. This is well brought out by the Chalcidenses, who argue against the Greeks in Livy XXXV.46.4–13.

4. Livy XXXIV.62, XXXV.13.6–14.12; Appian XI.9–11; Dio (Zonaras) 9.18; Plutarch, *Flamininus* XXI, *Pyrrhus* IX; Dittenberger, *SIG*, p. 617; Scullard, pp. 121, 131.

5. M. Holleaux, *Hermes* XLVIII, 1913, p. 75; Scullard, p. 121–23, 116.

Chapter Six

1. It is commonly assumed that Cato married between 192 and 191, and I feel, further, that a bridegroom would not volunteer for overseas duty—therefore the marriage came after Thermopylae. Cicero, *De Officiis* I.36, shows that Popilius, consul in 173, was the first commander of Cato's son Licinianus; probably Licinianus served when he was seventeen years old, as Cato did; hence the dates for Cato's marriage. Licinia is named in Gellius XIII.20 and Pliny, *NH* VII.61-62; Plutarch XX gives no name. Kienast, p. 47, feels considerations of rank were not the reason for late marriage; I do not believe Licinianus could have married Aemilius Paulus' daughter otherwise (Plutarch XX.7). Kienast's idea of an earlier marriage is untenable. The slave-girl concubine matter is in Plutarch XXIV.1.

2. Scullard, *A History* . . . , p. 256; Scullard, p. 128; Holleaux, *CAH* VIII, p. 216, all impose the view Scipio persuaded the senate to war in Asia. Livy XXXVI.1.2–6 and 2.2 have the original declaration of war with Africanus' carrying it in the assembly. The Aetolian clarification: XXXVI.3.9–12. The Asiatic clarification in 190 is in Livy XXXVII.2.3; Scipio's promise of lieutenancy, in 2.9. Livy XXXVII.50.1–3, 51.8–10 has the clarification of Vulso's command. It is emphasized, XXXVIII.48.9.

3. Scullard, *A History* . . . , pp. 256, 9; Scullard, pp. 128, 131; Holleaux, *CAH* VIII, pp. 219, 24, call Lucius incompetent and make Domitius commander. Appian alone agrees: XI.30, 31, 35, 36. Livy XXXVII.39.9 contradicts by making Lucius commander of the battle formation. Appian's facts are mixed; in XI.31, Domitius has command of the right wing and in XI.34 he says the right wing was defeated and pursued by Antiochus, yet he then says Domitius had the center, XI.35, which is denied by Livy XXXVII.53.18; XXXVII.39.5 makes Domitius an incompetent as well as insubordinate and that is borne out by Appian XI.30, making Domitius ambitious and haughty. Eumenes' credit to Lucius is in Livy XXXVII.53.18; 54.2 shows the envoys of Antiochus calling Lucius commander. "Asiaticus" is awarded in Livy XXXVII.58.7–59.6 and Dio (Zonaras) XIX.9.20. Cp. Livy XXXVIII.53.3, 58.9 for Gracchus' speech.

4. Livy XXXVII.55.2, 45.1; Polybius XXI.40.8 have the direct quotes. The view that the peace was ruinous to the Seleucids is in F. Peters, *The Harvest of Hellenism:* . . . (N.Y., 1970), pp. 249–50. Antiochus' Greek muster is in Livy XXXVII.50.

5. Livy XLI.6.8–12; Polybius XXV.4, XXII.5. For Pamphylia, see *CAH* VIII, p. 232–33, and E. Täubler, *Imperium Romanorum* I, pp. 75 ff.

6. One Sicilian tithe (Livy XXXVII.49.9) was allotted to Vulso's troops; T. Frank, *Economic Survey* . . . I, p. 68, estimates five hundred thousand bushels and on p. 142 says per capita army ration was a bushel a month (Polybius VI.39). Cavalrymen got 3 bu. a month and had two horses (1 replacement) receiving 5 bu. each per month (Frank, pp. 48, 64, n. 2), which totals seventy-nine thousand bu. per month for Vulso's army. Livy

XXXVIII.13 says the army marched to Antiochia, then received new supplies badly needed because the men quarreled over them, while 13.11 shows that it took "three marches" to cover twenty miles—an average of 6⅔ mi. per day (15.14 gives barely 5 mi. per day later on)—meaning that it took 10½ days to travel from Ephesus to Antiochia and therefore that the army began its inland trek from Ephesus with just 26,333 bu. of grain (10 days' supply). That would in turn require a pack train of 2,633 mules, as each mule carried 10 bu., its own needs, and those of the driver (25 *modii* a mo.)—a total load of 16 ¼ bu. (Frank, pp. 64, n. 2, 77). This would add 5,485 bu. to the supply. Thus only 31,818 bu. of the five hundred thousand Sicilian tithe reached the army before it left Ephesus. According to Cicero, *ad familias*, XII.14.1, 15.2, Roman freighters carried a fifty-ton average, meaning that just fifteen vessels would have carried the supply to Ephesus (figuring fifty lbs. to the bushel; ancient wheat was lighter than modern, and much of the animal supply was barley); the full tithe would take a fleet of 250 vessels to transport at one time.

7. Since most of the Sicilian tithe had not reached Vulso at Ephesus, the handiest secondary rendezvous after striking inland would be Termessus in Pamphylia, whose port city was Attalia. It was known to Rome from the Ptolemies (Livy XXXVII.56.4). After Termessus, the Romans took only one levy of grain, from Sagalassus: forty thousand bu. Apparently the tithe, or what the fleet could supply of it by that time, with the Sagalassus levy, was enough for the rest of the campaign (Livy XXXVIII.15.9). The charge of "buying freedom"—Manlius' threat against Moagetes of Cibyra to pay five hundred talents or suffer siege—is thoroughly Roman. Contra Holleaux, *CAH* VIII, p. 228, it escapes me how this threat is more "disgraceful" than Spanish extortions. If Manlius had received, for the sake of argument, the entire Sicilian tithe at Ephesus, the grain taken at Cibyra, or Tabae and Antiochia later, would be mere extra baggage. From Antiochia to Termessus was 150 mi., taking twenty-four days and requiring 76,363 bu. As Livy (n. 6) says, Antiochia's levy was needed, and the levies of Cibyra and Tabae furnished twenty thousand bu.; Seleucus must have brought 56,363 bu. to Antiochia plus the supply for the extra 1,511 mules needed to haul that much more grain: 9,444 bu. for the twenty-four days to Termessus. Seleucus brought 65,807 bu.

8. Towns sacked are in Livy XXXVIII.13.2–3, 14.1, 15.2–3, 6 & 8, perhaps 14, though this last mentions only deserted towns. Only Eriza, 14.1, was taken by direct, violent assault. Alabanda, 13.2–3, and Isiondensis, 15.6, were taken at the request of their natives. Lagum, 15.2–3, and Darsa, 15.8, were deserted and sacked. Compare Polybius XXI.36. See Scullard, *A History* . . . , p. 261, for cruelty.

9. Polybius XXI.34 implies Manlius was harsh on Moagetes' "buying freedom" but agrees with Livy in making Moagetes cruel and treacherous—was Manlius, then, unjust? Exempted Pamphylian cities

were Aspendus and Side (Holleaux, *CAH* VIII, p. 233; Täubler, *Imp. Rom.* I, pp. 75 ff). Polybius XXI.36 says that for a crown of fifty talents, twenty thousand medimni of barley, and twenty thousand of wheat, Manlius admitted Sagalassus into his "alliance" (*philian*). Polybius XXI.34 says the same about Moagetes; after a payment of one hundred talents and ten thousand medimni of wheat, he was accepted into alliance (*philian*). The same was true of Termessus and Aspendus, received in alliance for the payment of grain and money. Livy, on the other hand, uses the language "to grant peace" (*pacem dare/pacem impetrare*) or "give in surrender" (*civitatem dare*) (XXXVIII.13.13, 15.6, 9, 11). Yet Livy's term must also mean official act because of the later immunity of Aspendus from Eumenes' ambitions.

10. The reference here is to the speech of Flaminius (Livy XXXVIII.43.8), in which he points out that decadent spoil was brought to Rome from Syracuse by Marcellus, from Greece by Flamininus, Aetolia by Glabrio, Capua by Fulvius, and Asia by Scipio and now Manlius. Rome should have become decadent six times within fifteen years.

Chapter Seven

1. I have proceeded on the primary evidence of Polybius—all other accounts being supplementary—in the trials of the Scipios. The first trial was a demand for accounting in the senate; the second, a trial before the people, as Polybius asserts. His account must be supplemented with Livy, the only other source documenting a trial in 187. Polybius misunderstands Roman judicial process when he supposes that a rebuke by the defendant who had wantonly destroyed evidence caused adjournment. The order of the trial:—summons, inquiry, magistrate's verdict, and appeal—is standard for such hearings. It was not in this trial Scipio made the "magnificent speech" recorded by Livy. Evidence shows that came in 184. Instead he made the plea Polybius records—they should not listen to accusations of him. Thus is Polybius used in his entirety, supplemented by Gellius, Livy, and oratory.

2. Livy XXXVII.34.8, 36.1–2, 8–9, 37.8, and 38.1–4, where Lucius' ignorance of the negotiations of Africanus is obvious. 45.4–6 shows the intermediary. Though Scipio rebuked Cato in Sicily for reports made behind his back, he now presumed the right to do so with an enemy, himself!

3. I have preferred Gellius to Livy, who speaks of a praetor's court brought into being by a motion passed by the Petilii in order to investigate the money shortage. This, with the speech of Cato on the money of Antiochus, I have placed in the previous trial, for the reason that it comports better with Polybius' account.

4. For the adulteration of the clans, see Livy XXIII.23.3–7. On the adulteration of rights, recall the passage of the Hortensian Laws of 287, with their legal equality and one-man–one vote principle. Yet the senate ruled by decree in the heat of the Second Punic War, not to mention the First.

Unconstitutional though necessary acts in war include Scipio's Spanish *imperium* and the above creation of senators.

Chapter Eight

1. Livy XXXIX.41.1–2 shows the opposition of the nobility was actually a "combination" against him (*coeo/coierant*), though it would have to be unofficial—such combinations were illegal. Livy XXXIX.41.4 makes the assumption that Cato's morality elected him, as does Plutarch XVI.5–6, and they laud Roman high-mindedness over the "soft-line" opposition of Cato. Such moderns as Scullard, p. 154, agree, speaking in hushed tones of public conscience and the like, rising from the Bacchanalia. But none could possibly be more severe in prosecuting the Bacchanalia, and the freedmen and clients of the nobility and their middle-class followers would fail to see distinctions of opulence and luxury in the midst of the highly discriminatory law enforcement they were receiving from middle bloc officials. People wanted their rights, and that was what Cato represented. J. Jones, *The Law and Legal Theory of the Greeks* . . . , p. 37, makes the point of justice in terms of rights. The repressive measures of consuls for 186 are in Livy XXXIX.17–18; those of Postumius in 185, 20.8–10, and in 184, 41.5–7; those of Pupius in 184–3, in XL.19.9–11.

Chapter Nine

1. Livy XXXIX.51; Plutarch, *Flamininus* XX; Nepos, *Hannibal* XII; Appian, XI.11.

2. Polybius XXIII.3.4, 5.4; Livy XXXIX.35.2, 47.1, XLI.28.11.

3. Livy XL.51.9 is interpreted by Scullard, p. 182, and De Sanctis, *Storia* . . . , iv.i, p. 606, to affect the middle class and the *centuriata*. Only a tie to property consideration would make it so, but Livy specifies voting procedure and tribal membership, indicating the *tributa*. Scullard, p. 182 n. 3, himself argues against the idea that census classes were involved; none is mentioned; hence the *centuriata* was not reformed. The interpretation "possession of children" and "occupation" for *causisque* et *quaestibus* is as conjectural as the idea that involves classes.

P. 212 shows Cato made a speech against Fulvius' triumph of 187, on the awarding of crowns. Scullard, p. 266; Fraccaro, *Studia* . . . , pp. 272–80; and Malcovati, p. 59, say he could not have made it, as he was then serving in Greece under Fulvius. Livy XXXVIII.9.10, 28–29 show the Ambracian-Cephallenian encounters were in the year 189; 43.1–7 shows the debate against Fulvius by Lepidus and the Ambraciots was in 187. Walbank, *Philip V* . . . , puts the Cephallenian campaign in 188, still plenty of time for Cato to return and participate in the debate of 187.

More serious is Scullard, p. 267, showing the prizes were actually awarded during the triumph in 187, after the debate, based on Livy XXXIX.5.17. Yet Cato's speech on the misawarding of crowns logically fits in 187, during

either the Ambraciot presentation or the contest over the triumph. Cato and the soldiers knew well beforehand which crowns were to be donated. Polybius VI.39.2–11 shows such decorations were announced by the general in an assembly of the army called after the battle, lauded and extolled as inspiration. Crowns, taking time to make, could well have been announced after the battle but awarded during the triumph itself.
The Fragment 152 (critical of taking Ennius to Aetolia) could be in either speech.
    4. Livy XLII.18.2–3, 36.8–9, shows the praetor Cn. Sicinius with advance troops forging beachheads and advance bases in Epirus to guard access routes to Macedonia.

Chapter Ten

    1. Polybius XXIX.4.23; Livy XLIV.19.6, 29.1, XLV.10.2, 15, 11.1—12.8, 13.1; Scullard, p. 211. Polybius XXIX.5.1–9, 22.1, XXX.1, 17.19; Livy LXIV.13.9, 12, 24.1–25.12.
    .2. Malcovati, pp. 191–6; Gellius VI.3. Livy XLV.2.14–25.10, 10.4, 3.3, XLIV.35.4, 29.6, 23.4, 14.8; Polybius XXVIII.16–17, XXIX.10, 19, XXX.31.
    3. Polybius XXX.18–20, 28, 30, XXXI.1.3; Livy XLV.44.4, XLVI *Periocha*.
    4. Polybius XXVIII.18–23, XXIX.23.1–6, 26–7, XXXI.2.14, 10, 17–20, XXXIII.11.
    5. Polybius XXX.27.1, 30.1–8, XXXI.1, 3.4; Diodorus XXXI.17, 28.
    6. Polybius XXX.1–4 and Livy XLV.19.1 have the fratricidal war, and see pp. 236–37 above. On the deception of Gracchus, see Polybius XXXI.27.16.
    7. Malcovati, p. 197. Fraccaro, *Stud. stor* . . . , p. 378, shows the date of the speech was 264. The prosecution came by reason of Cato's power through the coalition, not because of mere opulence. Cp. Plutarch XXV.2.
    8. Plutarch XXIV.1 says Cato married his son to the daughter of Paulus after the death of his wife. The marriage must have been in about 158 B.C., since Tertia was a "little child" at Pydna—perhaps six years old. That would make her sixteen in 168, within the usual age of fourteen to sixteen for Roman brides. 158 is preferrable to 160 because Licinianus would have continued his military service to 163, from 173, and then begun his public career and attained the tribuneship, aedileship, and quaestorship before marriage, each office separated by two years, dying in 164's praetorship. Licinia died, therefore, perhaps in 160. The rest of the paragraph is deduction.
    9. Livy *Periocha* XLVIII places the death of Licinianus. It was four years after the probable marriage in 168. The lad Marcus, of this union, was probably raised by Cato himself, between 154 and 149, when he died himself. His influence on this child is ascertained by Gellius XIII.20—the

boy was an orator of power. The matter of Licinianus' resentment at Cato's second marriage is in Plutarch XXIV.4–6. Plutarch's reflection is in the *Comparison of Cato and Aristides* VI.2.

10. Broughton, pp. 448, 453, 470. Scullard, pp. 233, 235. Livy, *Periochae* XLIX, LVI. Appian VI.10, 60; *CIL* 12.2.583; Cicero, *Brutus* 106, *Verr. Or.* 2.3.195, 2.4.56, *de Off.* 2.75; Malcovati, p. 200.

11. Based on the above, Tertia must have been twenty years of age at this time. Polybius XXXI.28 has Paulus' estate. Livy *Periocha* XLVI, however, says the estate was not large, much less capable of paying dowry and games *in memoriam*. Polybius shows in XXXI.26–7 that Tertia's bequest included half the estate of Papiria, to whom Aemilianus had given the estate of Aemilia, wife of Scipio. Cp. Plutarch, *Paulus* V.1–2, 4–5, and Gellius XIII.20.7–12. The spirit of Cicero's *de Senectute*, 84, where he speculates about Cato's troubled heart over his own son, is carried here.

12. Appian VIII.10.69; Plutarch XXVII.1–3, XXVII; Livy *Periocha* XLVIII, XLIX; Polybius XXXVI.1–8.

13. Meltzer, *Geschichte* . . . , iii.615–17; *CAH* VIII, p. 476.

Selected Bibliography

APPIAN. *Roman History*, Tr. H. White, The Loeb Classical Library, 2 vols. (New York, 1912).

ASHBY, T. *The Aqueducts of Ancient Rome* (Oxford, 1935).

AUGUSTINE. *De Civitate Dei*, 2d. ed., Tr. J. Healy (New York, 1945).

BELOCH, K. *Römische Geschichte bis zum Beginn der Punischen Kriege* (Berlin, 1926).

BLOCH, G., and CARCOPINO, J, *Histoire Romaine* . . . (Paris, 1935).

BROUGHTON, T. *The Magistrates of the Roman Republic*, vol. I (New York, 1951).

CAESAR. *De Bello Gallico*, Tr. H. Edwards, The Loeb Classical Library (New York, 1916).

———. *De Bello Civilis*, Tr. A. Peskitt, The Loeb Classical Library (New York, 1916).

CARPENTER, R. *The Greeks in Spain* (Bryn Mawr, 1925).

CATO. *On Agriculture*, Tr. W. Hooper, rev. H. B. Ash, The Loeb Classical Library (Cambridge, 1934).

CICERO. *Ad Familias*, Tr. W. Williams, The Loeb Classical Library (New York, 1925).

———. *Brutus* . . . , Tr. H. Poteat (Chicago, 1950).

———. *Brutus* . . . , Tr. G. Hendrickson and H. Hubbell, The Loeb Classical Library (Cambridge, 1920).

———. *Cato Maior de Senectute*, Tr. W. Falconer, The Loeb Classical Library (New York, 1923).

———. *De Divinatione*, Tr. W. Falconer, The Loeb Classical Library (New York, 1923).

———. *De Legibus*, Tr. C. Keyes, The Loeb Classical Library (New York, 1928).

———. *De Natura Deorum*, Tr. H. Poteat (Chicago, 1950).

———. *De Natura Deorum* . . . , Tr. H. Rackham, The Loeb Classical Library (New York, 1925).

———. *De Oratore*, 2 vols., Tr. E. Sutton and H. Rackham, The Loeb Classical Library (New York, 1921).

——— *De Officiis*, Tr. W. Miller, The Loeb Classical Library (New York, 1926).

———. *Verrine Orations*, Tr. L. Greenwood, The Loeb Classical Library (New York, 1920).

CORNELIUS NEPOS. *De Historicis Latinis*, Tr. J. Rolfe, The Loeb Classical Library (New York, 1929).

Corpus Inscriptionum Latinarum.

DEGRASSI, A. *Inscriptiones Italiae*, XIII, i, (1947).

———. *Fasti Consulares et Triumphales*, in *Inscriptiones Italiae*, XIII (Rome, 1947).

DELLA CORTE, E., *Catone Censore, la vita e la fortuna* (Torino, 1949).

DE SANCTIS, G. "Una lettera degli Scipione," *Atti della r. Academia di Scienze di Torino*, 1922, p. 242.

———. *Storia dei Romani*, 4 vols., vol. 3 (Torino, 1923).

DE SELINCOURT, A., *Livy: The War with Hannibal* (Baltimore: Penguin Books (L145), 1965.

DESSAU, H., *Inscriptiones Latinae Selectae*.

DIO (Zonaras), *Roman History*, Tr. E. Cary, The Loeb Classical Library (New York, 1914).

DIODORUS SICULUS. *Library of History*, Tr. F. Walton, The Loeb Classical Library (Cambridge, 1957).

DITTENBERGER, W., *Sylloge Inscriptionum Graecarum*, 3d. ed. (1915–24).

DRUMANN, W., *Geschichte Roms*, 2d ed. by P. Broebe (Leipzig, 1899 & 1929).

FLORUS. *Epitome de Tito Livio Bellorum omnium annorum DCC Libri II*, Tr. E. Forster, The Loeb Classical Library (New York, 1929).

FRACCARO, P., "Sulla biografia di Catone Maggiore sino al consulato, e le sue fonti," *Atti e memorie della r. accademia virgiliana* (Mantova, 1910).

———. *Studia storici per l'antichita classica*, 1911, pp. 9 ff., 22, and 1910, p. 272.

FRANK, T., *An Economic Survey of Ancient Rome*, 2nd ed., 5 vols., vol. 1 (Baltimore, 1933–40).

FRONTINUS. *De Aquis Urbis Romae*, Tr. C. Bennett, The Loeb Classical Library (New York, 1926).

GELLIUS. *Noctium Atticarum*, Tr. J. Rolfe, The Loeb Classical Library (New York, 1922).

GELZER, M., *Die Nobilität der römischen Republik* (Leipzig-Berlin, 1912).

GREUBER, H., *Coins of the Roman Republic in the British Museum*, vols. I–III (London, 1910).

HARVEY, P., *The Oxford Companion to Classical Literature* (Oxford, 1955).

HAYWOOD, R., "Studies on Scipio Africanus," *Johns Hopkins Studies in Historical and Political Sciences*, Series LI, no. 1 (Baltimore, 1933).

HILL, H., *The Roman Middle Class in the Republican Period* (Oxford, 1952).

JANZER. B., *Historische untersuchungen zu den Redenfragmenten des M. Porcius Cato* (Würzburg-Aumühle, 1937).

JONES, J., *The Law and Legal Theory of the Greeks: An Introduction* (Oxford, 1956).

KIENAST, D., *Cato der Zensor: seine personlichkeit und seine Zeit* (Heidelberg, 1954).

LIVY. *Ab Urbe Condita*, 13 vols., vols. 5–13, Tr. B. Foster, F. Moore, E. Sage, and A. Schlesinger, The Loeb Classical Library (New York, 1926, and Cambridge, 1951).

––––. *Ab Urbe Condita, Periochae Librorum XXXVII–XL; Oxyrhyncheae*, Tr. A. Schlesinger, The Loeb Classical Library (Cambridge, 1959).

MALCOVATI, H., *Oratorum Romanorum Fragmenta; Collegit, Recensuit, Prolegomenis Illustravit*, 3 vols., vol 1 (Torino, 1930).

MALCOVATI, H., *Oratorum Romanorum Fragmenta: Liberae Rei Publicae Iterutls Curis Recensuit Collegit* (Torino, 1955).

MARMORALE, E., *Cato Maior*, 2d ed. (Bari Laterza, 1949).

MARSH, F., *A History of the Roman World 146–30 B.C.*, rev. H. Scullard (London, 1952).

MELTZER, O., *Geschichte der Karthager*, 3 vols., vol. 3 by U. Kahrstedt (Berlin, 1913).

MEYER, H., *Oratorum Romanorum Fragmenta . . .* , (Turici, 1842).

MUNZER, F., *Römische Adelsparteien und Adelsfamilien* (Stuttgart, 1920).

OTTO, W., *Zur Geschichte der Zeit des VIten Ptolemäers* (Munich, 1934).

PAIS, E., "Quaestioni Catoniane, Il Filosofo Pitagorico Nearco," *Historia. Revue d'histoire ancienne*, VI, (1932), pp.368 ff.

Paulys Real-Encyclopädie der classischen Altertumswissenschaft, vol. XXXII, (Stuttgart, 1846).

PETERS, F., *The Harvest of Hellenism: A History of the Near East from Alexander the Great to the Triumph of Christianity* (New York, 1970).

PLINY. *Naturalis Historiae*, vol. IX, Tr. H. Rackham, The Loeb Classical Library (Cambridge, 1952).

PLUTARCH. *Aemilius Paulus*, Tr. B. Perrin, The Loeb Classical Library (New York, 1918).

––––. *Comparison of Aristides and Cato*, Tr. B. Perrin, The Loeb Classical Library (New York, 1914).

––––. *Fabius Maximus*, Tr. B. Perrin, The Loeb Classical Library (New York, 1916).

––––. *Marcellus*, Tr. B. Perrin, The Loeb Classical Library (New York, 1917).

————. *Moralia*, Tr. B. Perrin, The Loeb Classical Library (New York, 1914).

———— *Marcus Cato*, Tr. B. Perrin, The Loeb Classical Library (New York, 1914).

———— *Numa*, Tr. B. Perrin, The Loeb Classical Library (New York, 1929).

POLYBIUS. *Universal History*, Tr. W. Paton, The Loeb Classical Library (New York, 1922–27).

SALLUST. *The Conspiracy of Catiline*, Tr. J. Rolfe, The Loeb Classical Library (New York, 1926).

SCHULTEN, A., *Tartessos* (Hamburg, 1922).

———— *Numantia*, 4 vols. (Munich, 1914–31).

SCHULZE, W., *Lateinischer Eigennamen* (Berlin, 1933).

SCULLARD, H., *A History of the Roman World 753–146* B.C. (New York, 1961).

————. *Roman Politics, 220–150* B.C. (Oxford, 1951).

SHEPHERD, W., *Historical Atlas*, 8th ed. (New York, 1956).

SMITH, R., "Cato the Censor," *Classical Quarterly*, 34 (1940), 106.

SOBECK, F., *Die Quaestoren der römischen Republik* (Breslau, 1929).

SUTHERLAND, C., *The Romans in Spain, 217* B.C.–A.D. *117* (London, 1939).

TAÜBLER, F., *Imperium Romanum*, vol. I. (Leipzig-Berlin, 1913).

The Cambridge Ancient History, vols. VII–VIII, S. Cook, F. Adcock, M. Charlesworth, eds. (Cambridge, 1930).

The Oxford Classical Dictionary, M. Cary et al., eds. (Oxford, 1957).

VAN DEMAN, E., *The Building of the Roman Aqueducts* (Washington, 1934).

VALERIUS MAXIMUS. *Factorum ac dictorum memorabilium.*

WALBANK, F., *Philip V of Macedon* (Cambridge, 1940).

WILLEMS, P., *Le Senat de la Republique Romaine . . .* , vols. 1 & 2 (Louvaine & Paris, 1878 & 1883).

WISEMAN, F., *Roman Spain* (London, 1956).

Index